On Dialect

For Arthur, Mike and Paul

On Dialect

Social and
Geographical Perspectives

PETER TRUDGILL

New York University Press
New York *and* London

First published in paperback 1984 by
New York University Press
Washington Square
New York, NY 10003

Library of Congress Cataloging in Publication Data

Trudgill, Peter.
  On dialect.

  Bibliography: p. 226
  Includes index.
  1. Sociolinguistics. 2. Dialectology.
  3. Language and languages — Variation. I. title.
  P40.T74   1982   417'.2   82 – 14364
  ISBN 0 – 8147 – 8169 – 1
  ISBN 0 – 8147 – 8172 – 1 pbk

Printed in Great Britain

Contents

Acknowledgements

The introduction is a revised and extended version of 'Where does sociolinguistics stop?', from W. Dressler (ed.), *Proceedings of the 12th International Congress of Linguistics* (Innsbruck University, 1978). *Chapter 1* is a modified version of 'On the limits of passive competence: sociolinguistics and the polylectal grammar controversy', from D. Crystal (ed.), *Linguistic Controversies* (Edward Arnold, 1982). *Chapter 2* is a modified version of 'The contribution of sociolinguistics to dialectology', first presented at the International Conference on Sociolinguistics, International Christian University, Tokyo, 1981. *Chapter 3* is a revision of 'Linguistic change and diffusion: description and explanation in sociolinguistic dialect geography', in *Language in Society*, 3, 1974. *Chapter 4* is co-authored with Tina Foxcroft and first appeared in P. Trudgill (ed.), *Sociolinguistic Patterns in British English* (Edward Arnold, 1978) as 'On the sociolinguistics of vocalic mergers: transfer and approximation in East Anglia'. I am grateful to Tina Foxcroft for permission to reprint this paper here. *Chapter 5* was first presented at the International Conference of Historical Linguistics, Stanford, 1979. *Chapter 6* was originally entitled 'Creolisation in reverse: reduction and simplification in the Albanian dialects of Greece', and appeared in *Transactions of the Philological Society*, 1976–7. *Chapter 7* is co-authored with George A. Tzavaras and first appeared in H. Giles (ed.), *Language, Ethnicity and Intergroup Relations* (Academic Press, 1977) as 'Why Albanian-Greeks are not Albanians: language shift and ethnicity in Attica and Biotia'. I am most grateful to George Tzavaras for permission to reprint this paper here. *Chapter 8* is from *York Papers in Linguistics*, **9**; M. W. de Silva (ed.), *Festschrift for R. B. Le Page* (1980), originally entitled 'Acts of conflicting identity: a sociolinguistic look at British pop songs'. *Chapter 9* is derived in part from 'Språk og kjønn i det engelske språket', in E. Ryen (ed.), *Språk og kjønn* (Novus, Oslo, 1976). *Chapter 10* is a revised version of 'Sex, covert prestige and linguistic change in the urban British English of Norwich', from *Language in Society*, **1**, 1972. *Chapter 11* is from *International Journal of the Sociology of Language*, **21**, 1979, originally entitled 'Standard and non-standard dialects of English in the United Kingdom: problems and policies'. *Chapter 12* is co-authored with Howard Giles, and is from F. Coppieters and D. Goyvaerts (eds), *Functional Studies in Language and Literature* (Story-Scientia, 1978). I am grateful to Howard Giles for permission to reprint this paper here.

Introduction

On the study of language variation

This book consists of studies of different aspects of language variation.[1] They are studies of dialect in its widest sense – of social and
regional varieties of language, together with their development,
diffusion and evaluation. Many of them are studies in what I, and
others, have come to call geolinguistics – sociolinguistic dialect
geography. The rest are studies in other aspects of sociolinguistics
– which leads me to acknowledge that there is a problem with the
term *sociolinguistics*. It has become apparent that it is a term
which means many different things to many different people. (In
particular, it appears to have different implications in Britain and
North America than those it has in Europe.) I want to suggest,
however, that this multiplicity of interpretations may be due to
the fact that, while everybody would agree that sociolinguistics
has *something* to do with language and society, it is equally clearly
not concerned with *everything* that could be considered under the
heading of 'language and society'. The problem, that is, lies in the
drawing of the line between *language and society*, on the one hand,
and *sociolinguistics*, on the other. And what confusion there is
results from the fact that different scholars draw the line in different places.

My own feeling is that whether you call something 'sociolinguistics' or not may not, in the very last analysis, matter very
much, but that the drawing of this line is nevertheless a matter
which deserves some discussion. My reason for arguing in this
way is that it seems to me important to give overt recognition to

---

[1] I am very grateful to Aaron Cicourel, Paul Fletcher and Torben Vestergaard for their helpful
comments on the earlier version of this chapter.

1

the fact that people working in the field of language and society
are often doing so with very different aims, and that failure to
acknowledge this fact, whether by restricting the scope of the term
sociolinguistics – as I would prefer to do – or not, can lead to
serious misapprehensions and misunderstandings.

If we examine objectives, in the area of study we have called
'language and society' – that is, if we look at why or to what
purpose workers are carrying out studies in this field – we can see
that it is possible to divide studies of language and society into
three groups: first, those where the objectives are purely linguistic;
second, those where they are partly linguistic and partly sociological or social scientific; and third, those where the objectives are
wholly sociological. Like most such divisions, this classification is
somewhat arbitrary and not easy to apply in practice, but it may
be helpful in dealing with the problem of what sociolinguistics is
and is not, and of clarifying exactly what is going on in this area.

The first category of study we can look at consists of studies in
the field of language and society which are purely linguistic in
intent. Studies of this type are based on empirical work on
language as it is spoken in its social context, and are intended to
answer questions and deal with topics of central interest to
linguistics. In this case the term *sociolinguistics* is uncontroversial,
but it should be clear that here it is being used principally to refer
to a methodology: sociolinguistics as a way of doing linguistics.

Much work of this type falls within the framework established
first and foremost by William Labov and consists of work which
Labov himself has sometimes referred to as *secular linguistics*.
Labov, as is well known, has addressed himself to issues such as
the relationship between language and social class. However, his
main objective in this has *not* been to learn more about a particular society, nor to examine co-variation between linguistic and
social phenomena for its own sake – this, I think, is an important
misunderstanding. Indeed, Labov has said that he actually resisted
the term *sociolinguistics* for some time, as this seemed to him to be
in danger of opening up the way to a series of correlational studies
of little theoretical interest. He would have preferred, that is, to
refer to his work simply as *linguistics*. Nor is work of this type
particularly concerned with the social conditioning of speech.
Rather, it is concerned to learn more about language, and to
investigate topics such as the mechanisms of linguistic change; the

nature of linguistic variability; and the structure of linguistic systems. All work in this category, in fact, is aimed ultimately at improving linguistic theory and at developing our understanding of the nature of language, and in recent years, for instance, has led to the development of 'variation theory' – the recognition of 'fuzziness' in linguistic systems, and the problems of incorporating variability into linguistic descriptions. Work of this sort, that is to say, is very definitely *not* 'linguistics as a social science'.

This does not mean to say, of course, that workers in this area are not interested in more sociological issues. One cannot easily work from tape-recorded interviews without being interested in the social psychology of conversational interaction; nor ignore the influence of social networks in urban dialectology; nor neglect socio-psychological factors such as social ambition and linguistic accommodation to others. The overall aim of such studies, however, remains linguistic.

The second category consists of studies of language and society which are, in varying degrees, both sociological and linguistic in intent. This, of course, is where the main problem with the term *sociolinguistics* lies. The problem is that some workers would include the whole of this category within sociolinguistics; others would exclude it totally; yet others would include some areas but not all.

Into this category come a number of fields of study, none of which is wholly distinct from all the others. The descriptive labels employed by scholars working in this area include terms such as: the sociology of language; the social psychology of language; anthropological linguistics; the ethnography of speaking; and discourse analysis. The social objectives of areas such as these are fairly clear. But they do also have linguistic benefits and objectives. For example, it is true that anthropologists who study kinship systems of linguistic taboo, through the study of a community's language, are concerned to learn more about the structure and values of that community than about the language itself. But there are also many studies, such as the componential analysis of kinship systems by semanticists, and investigations into linguistic relativity which, while they are often considered to be 'anthropological linguistics', are certainly of more interest to linguists than to anthropologists. Furthermore, the study of the structure of conversational discourse is as linguistic a concern as the study of text grammar generally. And students of syntactic change will note the explanation made by Sankoff and Brown (1976) of the development of relative clauses in New Guinea Pidgin English through conversational interaction between speakers. Similarly, the sociology of language, in its studies of bilingualism, links up with the study of interference between linguistic systems. And the notions of verbal repertoire, from the sociology of language, and communicative competence, from the ethnography of speaking, concern those who are interested in how far it is legitimate to extend grammars and to expand Chomsky's notion of competence. As far as the social psychology of language is concerned, Labov, in his Martha's Vineyard study, is one of many who have demonstrated that attitudes to language can be a powerful force in the propagation of linguistic changes. And social psychological theories of linguistic accommodation between speakers can help to explain the role of face-to-face interaction in the dissemination of change.

Most of the scholars working in those areas, moreover, would refer to their own work as falling under the heading of *sociolinguistics*, and it seems to me that, particularly if one should decide to use *objectives* as a criterion, this is perfectly legitimate.

The third category consists of studies in the field of language and society which are social rather than linguistic in intent. An example is provided by some aspects of the field of *ethnomethodology*. It is not easy for an outsider to give an informed or accurate characterization of ethnomethodology, but ethnomethodologists might not object too strongly to a statement to the effect that it can be regarded as a way of doing ethnography or sociology which studies people's practical reasoning and common sense knowledge of their society and the way it works. One way in which studies of this type can be carried out is by investigating the use of language in social interaction. But note that this is the study, not of *speech*, but of *talk*. The analysis of talk makes it possible for the ethnomethodologist to locate, for example, those things which a member of a society takes for granted – his 'knowledge of his ordinary affairs'.

Now it may be felt that ethnomethodological studies of some types have a link with linguistic studies of topics such as presupposition, pragmatics, and speech acts. Generally speaking, however, it seems clear that ethnomethodology, while it may deal with language and society, is fairly obviously not linguistics, and therefore not sociolinguistics. Language ('talk') is employed as data, but the objectives are wholly social scientific. The point is to use the linguistic data to get at the social knowledge that lies behind it, not to further our understanding about language.

Let me illustrate this in the following way. Some linguists have been concerned with an aspect of the analysis of conversational discourse which deals with what has been referred to as 'rules for discourse'. Studies of this kind are concerned with the problem of how it is possible to distinguish between meaningful, coherent conversations and those which are not coherent. Some workers resisted the inclusion of studies of this type within linguistics on the grounds that this would involve us in the impossible task of incorporating into descriptions or grammars everything that speakers know about the world. However, Labov, in his paper 'Rules for ritual insults' (1972b), has demonstrated that it is possible to develop rules of discourse which have the required explanatory power *without* doing this. In a now very well-known example, he says that we know that the following is a perfectly coherent piece of discourse:

A 'Are you going to work tomorrow?'
B 'I'm on jury duty.'

Now there is no obvious *linguistic* connection between A's question and B's answer. So what is the connection? Labov states that this kind of coherence can be handled by a discourse rule which says that, if B's reply cannot be related linguistically (by rules of ellipsis and so on) to A's question, then the reply is heard as an assertion that there exists a proposition known to both A and B, which *is* related and from which the answer can be inferred. In this case, the proposition known to both A and B, which B's reply can be heard as asserting, is that people who are on jury duty are not allowed to go to work. It is not, however, necessary for linguists to build this information into any linguistic description or grammar which attempts to account for the acceptability of this dialogue. It is necessary for linguistics only to be concerned with the *form* of the discourse rule itself and with the *fact* of the proposition. The *content* of the proposition, while we may take note of it, is not our primary concern. Ethnomethodologists, on the other hand, *are* interested in the study of the content of such propositions. It is precisely propositions of this type which are revealed as constituting shared knowledge through ethnomethodological studies of conversational interaction (although typically, of course, these propositions will be rather less obvious than the one discussed here). Ethnomethodology therefore provides us with a very good example of work in language and society which is not – I would suggest – sociolinguistics. It is clear, I think, that it is not the task of linguists to examine what members of a society know about how that society works (although this is of course useful background knowledge). And I think we can perhaps agree that when we come to the point where language data is being employed to tell us, not about language, but only about society, then this is the point where, while linguistic expertise might be useful to the sociologist, the student of language and society and the study of sociolinguistics have to recognize that they are doing different things.

Studies of an interdisciplinary nature are certainly of very considerable importance, and co-operation between scholars (such as linguistics and sociologists) is surely to be encouraged. Ultimately, moreover, the labelling of disciplines and the drawing of boundaries between them may well be unimportant, unnecessary, and unhelpful. As Dell Hymes (1974) has said: 'The parcelling out of the study of man among competing clans may serve petty interests, but not the supervening interests of mankind itself in self understanding and liberation.' In the case of sociolinguistics, however, we have to take care that a too widely extended umbrella term does not conceal differences of objectives to the point of misunderstanding: the many people working in the field of language and society are doing so for a number of different purposes.

The chapters in this book have been collected together under the title of *On Dialect*. It should therefore be clear that this book is located towards the linguistic end of the 'language in society' spectrum, and that a major emphasis is on dialect as dialect, and language as language. Sociolinguistics and geolinguistics are treated in this volume, for the most part, as methodologies for doing linguistics through the study of language variation. The chapters in the early part of the book are concerned mainly with linguistic theory and/or with theoretical and methodological problems associated with the empirical study of linguistic change. Towards the end of the book the studies become less linguistic and more social, and concern themselves not only with language as such, but also with issues such as personal, social and ethnic identity, and with the applications of the findings of sociolinguistics and dialectology to the solution of practical and educational problems.

Two of the twelve chapters are published here for the first time. Of the others, two have been radically revised, updated and edited so that the book can be read, if desired, as a coherent text.

CHAPTER 1

Sociolinguistics and Linguistic Theory

Polylectal grammars and cross-dialectal communication

As we have seen in the Introduction, one of the uses of the term *sociolinguistics* is as a label that refers to studies that are based on empirical work on language as it is spoken in its social context.[1] Sociolinguistics in this sense, we have said, is a methodology – a way of doing linguistics. It is intended to answer questions concerning linguistic theory and to deal with topics of central interest to linguists. In this chapter the theoretical issue on which we concentrate is the controversial topic of the polylectal grammar.

Following Weinreich's (1954) attempt to reconcile structural linguistics with dialectology, a number of linguists sought to incorporate more than one variety of the same language into a single description or grammar. Structural diasystems of the Weinreich type (e.g. Cochrane, 1959; Wölck, 1965) were followed by generative treatments which attempted to show that dialects may differ principally through the ordering or addition of rules (e.g. Newton, 1972). Most often, works of this type dealt with only a small number of varieties of a language; and they were justified by their authors on the grounds that they provided a good way of demonstrating and investigating the degree and nature of the relatedness of different dialects.

Subsequently, however, a rather stronger thesis was mooted – that of the *pandialectal* or *panlectal grammar*. A panlectal grammar was intended to incorporate not simply a few but all the varieties of a particular language; and it was justified, not as a descriptive device, but in terms of the model it was said to provide

---

[1] I am very grateful to the following for their comments on previous versions of this paper: F. R. Palmer, C.-J. Bailey, Jean Hannah, and William Labov.

of the adult native speaker's 'competence'. Associated particularly with the work of C.-J. Bailey (e.g. Bailey, 1972; 1973), the rationale behind work on panlectal grammars was summarized by Labov (1973) as follows:

We can and should write a single grammar to encompass all (or nearly all) of the dialects of a language, since the competence of the (fully adult) native speaker reaches far beyond the dialect he uses himself. Bailey argues for such grammars on the ground that (a) as native speakers become older, they become familiar with an increasingly large number of other dialects; (b) they have the ability to understand and interpret the productions of those other dialect speakers, analysing their rules as extensions of limitations of their own rules; and (c) they can even extrapolate from their own rules and predict the existence of dialects which they have never heard.

After some initial work in this area, however, it gradually came to be recognized that attempting to incorporate *all* the varieties of one language in a single grammar was an unreasonable endeavour. (One obvious argument against panlectal grammars is the well-known fact that languages are not discrete objects: no-one would want to compose a panlectal grammar encompassing all varieties of French, Occitan, Catalan, Spanish, Portuguese and Italian, and yet these varieties form a dialect continuum without sharp boundaries.) Early work on panlectal grammars was therefore followed by work on a more limited hypothesis – that of the *polylectal grammar*.

As the name indicates, the polylectal grammar seeks to include many, rather than all, of the varieties of a particular language. The notion of the polylectal grammar thus raises two interesting and challenging questions: (a) is it in fact legitimate to include more than one variety of language in a grammar? and (b) if it is, how many varieties may one include?

If the grammar is intended to be a model of native speakers' linguistic 'competence', then it should be possible to answer these questions by investigating empirically the extent of a native speaker's competence in another dialect. Labov's paper 'Where do grammars stop?' (1973) is an attempt of this type to answer question (b). The present chapter, on the other hand, is an attempt to answer question (a). Labov points out that while 'the competence of native English speakers ranges far beyond their own use', it is also true that 'there are limits to its reach'. In this chapter I shall argue that these limits are in some respects so severe that it may not be legitimate to attempt to model this 'competence' by means of a grammar. Drawing on empirical evidence from a number of sources, I will also argue that, while a grammar of rules may or may not be the correct way to model a native speaker's productive or active competence (cf. Matthews, 1979), speakers' receptive or passive competence rests on irregular and *ad hoc* types of procedure to such an extent that the best way of explicating this sort of ability may well not be in terms of extensions of and extrapolations from rules at all.

It is of course undoubtedly true that native speakers of a language can, in some sense, cope with varieties of their language other than the one they speak themselves. It is also well known that passive 'competence' greatly exceeds (and, in language learning, usually precedes) active 'competence'. However, if we examine the claim that this passive 'competence' ranges 'far beyond' a speaker's own dialect, it emerges that we should not exaggerate the extent of this ability nor, in particular, its regularity.

We proceed now to a comparison of the abilities speakers have with respect to their own dialects and those that they have with respect to dialects other than their own.

PRODUCTION OF OTHER DIALECTS

The strongest claim that one could logically make about the nature of passive 'competence' would be that it is *potentially* the same as productive 'competence', i.e. speakers *could* speak other dialects if they wanted to or if it became necessary for some reason – although they do not normally do so. This is, at its most extreme, an absurd view, and one that has never been advanced in support of the notion of the polylectal grammar. It is of interest, nevertheless, to look at those situations where speakers do attempt to turn passive competence into active competence – where they do attempt to speak other varieties – since this sheds valuable light on the nature of passive competence, and on its limitations.

The most obvious attempts to turn passive into active competence involve imitation. Some people, of course, are very good at imitating other accents and dialects; most others are not. It is, of course, not surprising if speakers older than adolescence have difficulties with the phonetics of a different accent. It can be no criticism of the polylectal grammar hypothesis if older speakers are less than successful at adjusting the automatic neurological and physiological habits involved in the production of speech sounds. This lack of imitative ability, however, extends also to grammar and, especially, phonology. Typically, errors in imitation reflect an inaccurate analysis of the imitated dialect and therefore, presumably, a mismatch between active and passive competence. Very many examples could be given, but the most obvious involve the extension of forms to environments where they do not belong, as in hypercorrection:

1   A well-known case of hypercorrection in British English is the 'correcting' of North of England /ʊ/ to South of England /ʌ/ not only in *cut* /kʊt/ > /kʌt/ but also in *foot* /fʊt/ > /fʌt/. (Not all examples of hypercorrection of this type, however, can be said to represent an inadequacy in passive competence. As Knowles (1978) points out, some cases of hypercorrection are due not to inaccurate knowledge but to inability to produce the correct form, as it were, in the heat of the moment, i.e. performance error.)

2   When imitating American accents, British speakers, including especially pop singers (see chapter 8) and actors, often reveal quite clearly that they have misanalysed some aspects of American English phonology. This is particularly true in the case of *hyper-American* /r/: the insertion of preconsonantal /r/ not only in words like *born* but also in words like *dawn*. Even excellent mimics such as Peter Sellers may have been guilty of this, but less skilled mimics in the world of popular music are particularly likely to produce hyper-American /r/ (see chapter 8, p. 148). Incorrect insertion of /r/ also occurs in the imitation of southwestern English accents.

3   In Trudgill (1973), I argued for a single grammar for the English spoken in the city of Norwich on the grounds that, *inter alia*, 'Norwich speakers are . . . able to imitate without error types of Norwich English other than those they normally use, for humorous or other similar purposes'. Outsiders, it was argued, could not do this accurately, tending to produce 'hyper-Norwichisms', cf. (2) above. However, I am now persuaded that this is not necessarily the case and that even members of the same speech community do not always have accurate passive competence of other varieties spoken in that community.

Older Norwich English has a distinction between *daze* /deːz/ <
ME ā and *days* /dæɪz/ < ME ai. Younger speakers have merged
these two vowels as /æɪ/. Further work (Trudgill, n.d.), has now
uncovered a number of Norwich speakers who, noting but analysing incorrectly, the older Norwich distinction, produce not only
daze as /deːz/ but also *days* as /deːz/ when attempting to imitate
older speakers or simply trying to speak in a more local manner.
We can perhaps refer to forms such as *days* /deːz/ as hyperdialectisms. Hyperdialectisms are not perpetrated by especially many
Norwich speakers, but the fact that they occur at all is significant.
(See chapter 2, p. 45, for a fuller discussion.)

4   As we noted above, misanalysis of other dialects is not confined to phonology. For example, hyper-Americanisms in the
speech of British people imitating American English occur also in
grammatical forms:

American English: *I've gotten one* (= I've acquired one)
                        I've got one   (= I have one)
British English: *I've got one*   (= both meanings)
Hyper-American English: *I've gotten one* (= both meanings)

5   The failure to imitate another variety correctly may extend
also to the level of language use and communicative competence.
Speakers not only have an incorrect analysis of the phonology
and grammar of other dialects, they also have an inadequate
appreciation of how they are employed in social interaction. As an
illustration of this, observe the following:

A Canadian visitor, after some months in Britain, walks into my
room at Reading University and says 'Cheers!'

This incorrect usage was based on the correct observation that in
certain forms of British English (see Trudgill, 1978b) *Cheers* can
function as a greeting. The error lay in the extension of this greeting to a situation where it was not appropriate. *Cheers*, it seems,
can be employed as a greeting only between people who are pass-
ing each other at some distance, say in the street, and where it
functions as 'hello and goodbye'.

Many other examples could be cited. One can, for instance,
readily observe that even after several months' residence in Britain, some speakers of American English have failed to acquire a

correct appreciation of the strength of the swear-word *bloody* and use it in social contexts where it may cause offence. None of the linguistic forms dealt with in this section is likely to cause any difficulty in comprehension or interpretation. British speakers readily understand the American pronunciation of *born* with an /r/ and the use of *gotten* as a past participle. Northerners know perfectly well that when southerners say /kʌt/ they mean *cut*. However, the behaviour of British people and of northerners when they actually attempt to imitate the other varieties shows that this comprehension is not due to accurate or rule-governed knowledge of how these varieties are structured. When passive competence is employed in speech production, it is shown to fall far short of the active competence speakers have in their own variety.

It is not only in imitation that we can observe the attempted use of passive competence in actual speech production. Speakers who at some stage in their lives change to another variety or acquire an additional dialect, as a result of social or geographical mobility, perform the same kind of operation and over a much longer period.

Casual observation of speakers who have changed dialects indicates that, while there are large differences between individuals in their ability (as well as desire) to effect a successful change, it is a very rare adult that successfully masters the speaking of a new dialect in all its details. Children, of course, as is well known, are much better at acquiring new varieties. However, there is reason to suppose that even the ability of children in this respect should not be exaggerated. Payne (1980), for example, has shown that children who have lived most of their lives in an area of Philadelphia, but who have out-of-town parents, have not acquired some of the detailed phonological constraints of the local accent in the same way as indigenous children, although this fact is apparent only after careful linguistic analysis.

As another example of this, my current research in Norwich shows that even adults who have lived all their lives in Norwich and who otherwise have perfect Norwich accents may not, if their parents were from some other dialect area, have mastered successfully the Norwich distinction between /uː/ and /ʌu/ (see chapter 4):

$$/\text{u:}/ \quad /\text{ʌu}/$$

moan	mown
nose	knows, etc.

Even after a lifetime's exposure to this distinction, they neither produce it nor imitate it correctly.[2] (This is further evidence against the single speech-community grammar discussed above, of course.)

Examples such as these indicate that while (particularly younger) speakers can be reasonably successful at acquiring a new variety of their language, the respects in which they fall short of total success suggest that any passive competence they may have had in the new variety before beginning its acquisition was inaccurate and insufficient. (See further, Trudgill forthcoming.)

GRAMMATICALITY JUDGEMENTS

One important ability that speakers have with respect to their own dialect is that they are able to make grammaticality judgements about it. Drawing upon their native linguistic competence, they are usually able to state whether particular grammatical constructions are or are not possible in their variety. The extent to which speakers' competence in their own dialect differs from their passive competence with respect to other dialects can therefore be tested by asking speakers to make grammaticality judgements about forms that occur in dialects other than their own. In doing this, we are interested in people's knowledge of other dialects, but we are particularly concerned with their ability to judge the grammaticality of forms that they are not aware of having heard before. If they are truly able to 'predict the existence of dialects which they have never heard', they should be able to do this.

In a study carried out at Reading University, a group of subjects were presented with a number of sentences, on paper, which they were asked to label as follows:

A   I use this kind of grammatical construction myself.

B   I don't use this grammatical construction, but other English speakers do.

---

[2] I am very grateful to the following for their collaboration in this research: Neil Brummage, Tom Geddes, Adrian Hannah, Douglas Howes, John Sandford, Sue Sandford, Eric Trudgill, Stephen Trudgill, and Colin Wills.

C   I've never heard anyone use a construction like this, but I
    would guess that some native speakers do use it.
D   The sort of thing only a foreigner (non-native speaker)
    would say.
E   Nobody would say this – not even a foreigner.

Answers A and B demonstrate first-hand knowledge of a particular construction by the subject; answers C, D and E demonstrate
genuine predictive ability and are thus the crucial ones for this
experiment.

The subjects fell into three groups: 20 non-native speakers,
most of them teachers of English, studying at Reading University;
80 first-year undergraduate students of linguistics (with about 40
hours of linguistics teaching; average age 19); and 11 lecturers and
research students from the Department of Linguistic Science. To
select subjects of this type, of course, is to bias results in favour of
the polylectal grammar hypothesis, since one can assume that
linguists will have more extensive passive competence and be
better able to predict the existence of forms in other dialects than
the rest of the population. The results show, however, that while
the lecturers were somewhat better in their predictive abilities
than the first-year students, both groups were very bad indeed and
were in some cases actually worse than the foreigners. The eight
sentences used in the test include constructions which are all current in British dialects, and it is a remarkable fact that some
subjects were totally unable to predict the occurrence of forms
used only a few miles from their own homes.

The first sentence to be evaluated was:

(a) *Look – is that a man stand there?*

This is an entirely normal, grammatical sentence in many East
Anglian dialects, and corresponds to the form *is that a man standing there* in most other dialects.

This was probably the most difficult sentence to handle, since at
least according to one interpretation it varies from other dialects
in two ways. First, non-continuous aspect is employed: *stands*
rather than *standing* (this is a feature of a number of conservative
English dialects – see Wakelin, 1972). Secondly, there is no third-
person -*s* marker: *stand* rather than *stands*. The results, given in

table 1·1, show that the accuracy of speakers of other dialects in predicting the grammaticality of this East Anglian construction is very low indeed. The most striking feature of these results is that around half of the native speakers could not imagine that *anyone* could possibly say such a thing, let alone other native speakers; and the overwhelming majority of subjects categorized this sentence as something that no native speaker would ever say. One academic linguist was prepared to concede that this construction might be a possibility in English – and so we have one actual prediction of grammaticality out of the 87 native speakers who responded. Otherwise, only two students recognized that it was a possibility, but both claimed to use the form themselves – so theirs was a grammaticality judgement about their own dialect and not some other. (One of these students came from East Anglia. The other may have given the answer A in error.)

TABLE 1·1　Sentence (a)

Label	Lecturers %	Lecturers (n)	Students %	Students (n)	Foreigners %	Foreigners (n)
A	0		3	(2)	0	
B	0		0		0	
C	9	(1)	0		5	(1)
D	45	(5)	45	(34)	47	(8)
E	45	(5)	52	(40)	47	(8)

These figures are very damaging to any polylectal grammar hypothesis. Even native speakers who, as linguists, supposedly know more about English than most, are for the most part totally unable to predict the grammaticality of this construction. The native speakers as a whole, moreover, are no better than the non-native speakers (who are presumably not assumed to have access to any polylectal grammar in their predictive ability).

The second sentence was the following:

(b) *My hair needs washed.*

This construction is the one normally employed in Scotland as well as in some areas immediately to the south of the border and in parts of the USA, and it corresponds to the sentence *My hair needs washing* found elsewhere. A rough guess suggests that perhaps 4 or 5 million native speakers of British English normally use this construction. Subjects' reactions to this sentence are given in table 1·2. Of the lecturers, two knew that the form was Scots and labelled the sentence accordingly; and one made a genuine prediction that the construction could occur in other dialects. The remaining eight could only predict that either foreigners or no-one at all would say this.

TABLE 1·2   Sentence (b)

Label	Lecturers %	(n)	Students %	(n)	Foreigners %	(n)
A	0		4	(3)	6	(1)
B	18	(2)	4	(3)	0	
C	9	(1)	3	(2)	6	(1)
D	45	(5)	38	(29)	28	(5)
E	27	(3)	52	(40)	61	(11)

The students fared even worse. More than half could not imagine anybody saying this, and altogether 90 per cent believed that no native speaker could say it. The three students who gave A were all Scots themselves, and one of the three who gave B labelled the sentence 'Scots'. We can therefore say that between two and four of the students made a genuine and correct prediction – a very low level of success.

The third sentence was:

(c) *I'm not sure – I might could do it.*

This double modal construction, as well as being current in a number of American dialects (see Butters, 1973), is a normal grammatical form in the north-west and north-east of England and in parts of Scotland. Reactions to this sentence were as in table 1·3. Once again, 44 of the native speakers were unable to predict that any speaker could say this, and altogether 74 out of the 85 native speakers who responded could not conceive of any other native speaker using it. Of the remaining 11, four of the lecturers gave the response B with the label 'Geordie' (north-eastern), while one student from Cumberland (in the north-west) used the form herself. There were thus five apparently genuine correct predictions amongst the students – or possibly six if we count the one (unlabelled) B response. This is somewhat better than the results for the previous two sentences, but still represents a low percentage of correct predictions.

TABLE 1·3   Sentence (c)

Label	Lecturers %	(n)	Students %	(n)	Foreigners %	(n)
A	0		1	(1)	0	
B	36	(4)	1	(1)	0	
C	0		7	(5)	5	(1)
D	36	(4)	35	(26)	21	(4)
E	27	(3)	55	(41)	74	(14)

The next sentence to be tested was:

(d) *She love him very much.*

The lack of the third-person singular *-s* is a feature of East Anglian (and other) British dialects (see Trudgill, 1974) as well as of a number of American varieties. The number of speakers of English who commonly use this grammatical form must be in the order of several millions. The reactions to this sentence were as in table 1·4. The lecturers did very well here, but once again it is clear that this was as a result of their *knowledge* of this linguistic form rather than of any predictive ability. (Interestingly enough, moreover, only two of the lecturers' B answers were labelled 'East Anglian'. The others mentioned 'Black American', 'West Indian', or something similar. British linguists, in other words, know about this form but, for the most part, only from non-British dialects.) As can be seen from table 1·4, one correct prediction occurred amongst the lecturers. As far as the students were concerned, the vast majority thought that only a foreigner would employ this grammatical pattern. Eight were familiar with this kind of verb form (although only two from British dialects), and four correct predictions took place – although even this figure must be in doubt in view of the large number of rock and pop music lyrics, which most students have undoubtedly heard, which contain verbs of this sort.

TABLE 1·4 Sentence (d)

Label	Lecturers %	Lecturers (n)	Students %	Students (n)	Foreigners %	Foreigners (n)
A	0		0		0	
B	91	(10)	14	(8)	17	(3)
C	9	(1)	5	(4)	6	(1)
D	0		83	(64)	50	(9)
E	0		1	(1)	28	(5)

We already have, so far, a certain amount of evidence to suggest that native speakers – including even linguists – either have first-hand knowledge of a particular grammatical form or can only imagine that foreigners (or even no-one at all) would use it: very few genuine correct predictions appear to take place. This picture is confirmed by the remaining four sentences. These were:

(e) *Where's my book? – Ah, here it's.*

This form – which presents perhaps as much of a phonological as a grammatical problem – is current in the West Highlands of Scotland. (It causes great difficulties, incidentally, for Labov's (1969) thesis on copula deletion and reduction in English.) Post-experimental questioning showed that A responses to this sentence were all the result of misreadings.

(f) *Wait a minute – I'm now coming.*

This form occurs in East Anglia in the sense of *I'm just coming.*

(g) *Had you a good time last night?*

This is normal in Scottish and some northern dialects.

(h) *It's dangerous to smoke at a petrol station without causing an explosion: petrol is very inflammable.*

This construction is found in parts of South Wales with the meaning *in case of* or *because you might cause an explosion*. Discussion of this sentence with the students after the test revealed that the A and B responders had all misinterpreted this sentence, ignored what to them was a semantic anomaly, or supposed it to have the meaning *even if you don't cause an explosion*. Results for sentences (e)–(h) are given in table 1·5.

TABLE 1·5   Sentences (e)–(h)

(i) Lecturers – percentages

Label	(e)	(f)	(g)	(h)
A	0	0	0	0
B	0	0	27	0
C	0	18	18	17
D	55	82	55	17
E	45	0	0	67

(ii) Students – percentages

Label	(e)	(f)	(g)	(h)
A	4	1	9	14
B	5	11	27	19
C	15	21	18	28
D	33	60	38	10
E	42	6	8	28

The conclusion to be drawn from the results of this test is that native speakers of English are not able to employ their passive competence in making grammaticality judgements about forms that they do not use themselves but that are habitually used by speakers elsewhere in the country – or, in the case of the student subjects, by members of the same class: sentence (b), for example, obtained student responses ranging from A to E. It could be claimed that these results are not conclusive, since only a small number of grammatical forms were employed, and since 'difficult' and out-of-the-way constructions were deliberately selected. Against this argument, we can say that there *are* only a small number of grammatical differences within British English; and that it is useless to select more familiar examples, since we would then obtain a large number of A and B responses. Subjects cannot exhibit their predictive prowess if they are presented with a form already known to them.

It should be noted, however, that speakers are able to extend their passive competence somewhat, *if they are given help*. Labov (1973) takes as an example of this phenomenon the grammatical construction

John's smoking a lot anymore.

This construction is employed with the meaning 'John's smoking a lot nowadays' in the 'positive *anymore* dialects' of the American Midwest. In a series of tests, Labov discovered that speakers from other American dialect areas found this construction to be totally ungrammatical and indeed incomprehensible. However, Labov also administered a further test to non-Midwesterners in which the function of positive *anymore* was explained. The test began:

> *Anymore* actually means 'nowadays' in these sentences, the way it's used in the Midwest. Would you guess that if some-one says *John smokes anymore*, meaning 'John smokes now-adays', that he would also say ...

and then subjects were asked to make predictions about a number of sentences. It emerged that, given this degree of help, speakers are rather good at acquiring the right sorts of intuitions. All sub-jects, for example, correctly rejected sentences such as

* *When would you rather live, in 1920 or anymore?*

as being ungrammatical, even in the Midwest.

This should not, however, lead us to be too optimistic about native speakers' abilities. It is not often that one is given such overt help with new dialects, and exposure of the normal type to positive *anymore* does not inevitably lead to a correct analysis: Labov notes that outsiders who had spent years in the Midwest and were familiar with positive *anymore* were inclined to interpret it incorrectly as meaning 'still' rather than 'nowadays'. And posi-tive *anymore* speakers themselves, when apprised of the fact that Easterners do not use *anymore* in the same way as themselves, 'seem to find it very difficult to know which of these forms would be used by Easterners' (Labov, 1973); i.e. they were not sure in which contexts Easterners would use *anymore*. Thus, even given overt guidance with or long-term exposure to new forms, there are severe limits to the extent to which speakers are able to extend their passive competence to include those forms.

COMPREHENSION OF OTHER DIALECTS

To what extent can speakers understand forms and constructions from other dialects? If they have internalized some form of poly-lectal grammar, one would not expect there to be many serious difficulties. And indeed it is obvious that speakers of different dialects of English can nearly always understand one another.

However, I want to suggest here that comprehension of other dialects does not take place by means of extensions of rule systems, or anything similar. Rather, comprehension occurs in a very *ad hoc* manner that relies heavily on linguistic and extra-linguistic context. Context, that is, plays a much greater role in the comprehension of other varieties than it does in the comprehension of one's own.

The importance of context is particularly obvious in the case of phonetics and phonology. If, when in the USA, I ask for a *pair of jeans* [ʤ eɪ inz], no American fails to understand me. However, if I say I am going to see *Jean* [ʤ eɪ in], many Americans want to know who *Jane* is. Similarly, when, employing my Norwich accent, I tell someone that I've bought a new *coat* /kuːt/, no one assumes I have bought a *coot*. If, on the other hand, I mention my friend *Joan* /ʤuːn/, people tend not to be sure whether her name is *Joan* or *June*. Thus, lexical predictability is of considerable importance.

To test this point of view further, however, we need also to see how difficult speakers find it to comprehend different *grammatical* forms out of context. The argument will go as follows: speakers comprehend forms from their own dialect even out of context. They comprehend forms from other dialects in context. Are they also able to comprehend forms from other dialects out of context? If not, then it can be argued that these forms have not become part of any polylectal grammar that the speaker has internalized and is therefore able to call upon in the passive interpretation of utterances.

A test that was intended to examine the extent of speakers' ability to comprehend such forms was carried out in the following way. A set of sentences containing grammatical forms known to be restricted to particular varieties of English were presented, on paper, to a group of 47 subjects. The subjects consisted of 21 students at Reading University who were native speakers of languages other than English, and 26 British students (second-year undergraduate, and MA-beginning postgraduates) of linguistics. The sentences were introduced as follows:

If you heard someone you supposed to be a native speaker of English say the following things, what would you think he meant? Please tick one of the interpretations under each sentence, or write in one of your own.

In each case, interpretation (a) was 'nonsense', and (e) was left blank for the subject to fill in if desired.

The sentences, with accompanying interpretations, were the following:

(1) *Don't jump off while the bus stops.*
    (b) ... when the bus stops
    (c) ... while the bus is stopping
    (d) ... until the bus stops

In parts of northern England, including Yorkshire, this construction is grammatical in the sense of (d). It was felt that, in the test, the bias would be towards subjects comprehending this sentence in the 'correct' *while = until* interpretation, since (b) is not particularly plausible semantically – or at least not as plausible as (d) – and (c) is fairly unlikely to be equivalent to (1) on grammatical grounds. Results, however, are as given in table 1·6. Interestingly enough, the non-native speakers were very much better than the native speakers at getting the 'right' answer. Of the natives, nearly a quarter, far from being able to understand this construction, thought it was nonsense. And only 15 per cent (four individuals) actually got it right. Of these four, two had lived in Yorkshire. In other words, it seems that only two genuine acts of comprehension of a new dialect form out of context took place – although even in these cases we cannot be certain that the people in question had not been regularly exposed to northern dialects at some time.

TABLE 1·6   Sentence (1)

Answer	Natives (%)	Non-natives (%)
(a)	23	9
(b)	8	14
(c)	46	34
√ (d)	15	44
(e)	8	0

We therefore have one piece of evidence to show that most speakers are unable to comprehend a dialect form in widespread use, in some cases as little as 25 miles from their own homes – not apparently a very good justification for positing polylectal competence. Now it could be argued that lack of comprehension of a form occurring in isolation, in an artificial testing situation, is not a fair test. However, it is precisely this sort of ability that speakers ought to have if they comprehend by means of rule extension. With this sort of ability, they should not require any context to help them – particularly when they are presented with the right answer in a multiple-choice test. It is the thesis of this paper that when speakers from elsewhere in the English-speaking world hear a Yorkshireman use *while* in this way, they generally understand what he means; but as the above results show, they are not able to do this by drawing on the resources of any polylectal grammar they have internalized. Rather, they depend on the context to make it clear what is meant. Bailey (cf. 1972) might have wished to argue that it is precisely this kind of process – the use of context – which speakers use in the *development* of their polylectal grammars. But we have cited evidence above (see the discussion of sentence (d), *She love him very much*) that even where speakers have certainly been exposed to forms from different dialects, and have presumably employed context to help in comprehending them, they are still unable to 'predict' their occurrence. We prefer to argue here that it is possible for *ad hoc* contextual comprehension processes to be employed many times without any 'internalization' of the rule in question taking place.[3]

It could also perhaps be claimed that alternatives (b) and (c) to sentence (1) are too plausible and gave subjects too much encouragement to select them instead of the 'right' answer. This argument cannot legitimately be employed in connection with the next example:

(2) *Whenever it was born I felt ill.*
   (b) Each time it was born I felt ill.
   (c) When it was born I felt ill.
   (d) As soon as it was born I felt ill.

This sentence is grammatical in many Northern Irish dialects, including those used by educated speakers, in sense (c). Results in this case should have been biased towards (c), since this is the only interpretation that really makes sense: there is no particular reason for selecting (d) and, while an interpretation for (b) can of

---

[3] It could be argued that in this, and subsequent sentences, it is lexical rather than grammatical differences which cause comprehension difficulties, i.e. it is simply the meaning of the word *while* that differs. It is, however, clear that differences in the function of grammatical words such as *while* are not the same order of phenomenon as differences in lexical meaning between, say, American and British *pants*.

course be contextualized, it is much less probable semantically than (c). (We do have to concede, however, that, unlike sentence (1), which is ungrammatical in all except the particular northern dialects, sentence (2) is actually grammatically, if not semantically, acceptable in all English dialects. Only in the Northern Irish dialects in question, however, is the sentence both grammatically and semantically acceptable.)

Results show, however, that the grammatical constraints of their own dialects forced a majority of subjects to select the anti-common-sense interpretation (b). Even with the semantic dice heavily loaded in its favour, interpretation (c) did not emerge from most speakers' supposed polylectal grammars as the right answer. The results are given in table 1·7.

TABLE 1·7   Sentence (2)

Answer	Natives (%)	Non-natives (%)
(a)	23	19
(b)	58	64
√ (c)	12	4
(d)	0	14
(e)	8	0

Once again, nearly a quarter of the natives can do no better than to regard this as nonsense – out of context. And only 12 per cent of the natives understood this form in the correct Northern Irish sense – and one of them comes from the West of Scotland, where this form is possibly also grammatical. (Interpretations given under (e) included 'whenever I saw a birth . . .' and 'each time they were born . . .'.) The conclusion once again is that, without any context to help them, most native speakers are unable to draw on the rule systems of their own dialect in order to understand a grammatical form new to them – even when the right answer is the semantically obvious one.

(3) *I don't want it but.*
   (b) I really don't want it.
   (c) but I don't want it
   (d) I don't want it but I'll take it.

This form is grammatical, with 'normal' intonation and primary stress on *want*, in many dialects in Scotland, Northern Ireland,

and the north-east of England, where it has the meaning (c). We have to recognize that lack of intonation may have caused difficulties here, but the full stop at the end of the sentence was clearly visible on the paper, and the subjects were explicitly told that there were no misprints of any kind on the test sheet. Results for sentence 3 are given in table 1·8.

TABLE 1·8   Sentence (3)

Answer	Natives (%)	Non-natives (%)
(a)	23	19
(b)	0	4
√ (c)	15	4
(d)	62	69
(e)	0	4

The majority of native speakers, like the non-native speakers, were not able to give it the correct interpretation. Of the 15 per cent (four) subjects who gave the right answer, one was from Scotland and one from the north-east. The success rate was thus very low indeed, in spite of the fact that some of the subjects must have heard the form, if nowhere else, either from a BBC TV comedy series current at the time and set in the north-east (in which one of the characters frequently had lines such as *I don't want it though but*), or from a well-known Scottish football club manager who appears frequently on TV and radio.

(4) *Come here till I punch you on the nose.*
    (b) so that I can punch you
    (c) while I can punch you
    (d) until I can punch you

Constructions of this type are usual in many varieties spoken in Scotland, Ireland and Liverpool in the sense of (b). The results for this sentence are given in table 1·9. Here the native speakers fared better than on the previous sentences – although no better than the non-natives – and of the 50 per cent (13) giving the right answer, five were from Scotland, Ireland or Liverpool. It is also worthy of note that more than a quarter of the native speakers could only interpret this as 'nonsense'. Interpretations written in under (e) included '*or* I'll punch you on the nose' and 'keep coming here until I punch you on the nose'.

TABLE 1·9   Sentence (4)

Answer	Natives (%)	Non-natives (%)
(a)	27	34
√ (b)	50	49
(c)	4	4
(d)	12	14
(e)	8	0

Finally, for the sake of comparison, a sentence discussed in Labov (1973; see above) was tested in the same way:

John's smoking a lot anymore.

which is grammatical in some American varieties with the meaning 'John's smoking a lot nowadays'. The British subjects did very badly here, 81 per cent regarding it as nonsense, and none getting the right 'nowadays' answer.

COMPREHENSION IN CONTEXT

Native speakers, then, are not especially successful at comprehending forms from other dialects out of context – an indication of the limitations of passive competence. As noted above, however, comprehension does take place readily in context. There are, nevertheless, limitations even to this ability – limitations which also cast doubt on the extent of passive competence.

(a)   There are a number of examples available in the literature which show that, even given context, failure to comprehend can occur in dialogue between speakers of different dialects.

For example, Labov (1973) reports the following exchange between a white American psychologist and a 5-year-old black child, Samuel, who had known each other for 6 months. The psychologist introduces Samuel to Labov, whereupon Samuel turns to the psychologist and says:

Samuel: I been know your name.
Psych.:   What?
Samuel: I been know your name.
Psych.:   You better know my name?
Samuel: I *been* know your name.

'Even after this exchange', Labov writes, 'the white adult did not know that he had failed to understand something.' The problem was that in some forms of American Black English Vernacular (BEV), stressed *been* functions as a 'remote perfect' marker. Thus, in this variety, *I been know your name* corresponds to *I've known your name for a long time* in other dialects. The psychologist's ability to comprehend other dialects, even in context, did not extend to the comprehension of this particular form.

Lesley Milroy (forthcoming) similarly reports an exchange in Donegal, Ireland, involving herself and her husband, who are both British, and Sean, a native of the area:

> Sean: How long are youse here?
> J.M.: Till after Easter.
> [Sean looks puzzled]
> L.M.: We came on Sunday.
> Sean: Ah. Youse're here a while then.

Here the failure to comprehend is recognized and repaired, but it is real enough while it lasts.

(b)   Lack of comprehension can take place, even given context, at the pragmatic as well as at the grammatical level. Students of the ethnography of speaking have noted that differences in communication norms between language communities can lead to hostile stereotyping and misinterpretation (see, for example, Scollon and Scollon, 1979, on the mutual stereotyping, in interethnic communication in Canada, of English and Athabaskan speakers as 'arrogant'). The same sort of problem may also occur in dialogue between speakers of different varieties of the same language. Again, many examples could be noted. One may suffice.

The following is an interchange between myself and an American shop assistant:

> Asst.: Would you like these things in a bag?
> P.T.: Would you mind?
> Asst.: No sir, I wouldn't mind at all. We have plenty of bags and it's really no trouble at all, sir.

Here my British use of *would you mind?*, which was intended to function as 'yes, please', was interpreted as a genuine request for information.

CONCLUSION

Controversy and argument over panlectal and polylectal grammars has continued for several years. One early dispute arose out of Chomsky and Halle's (1968) suggestion that all accents of English could be regarded as having the same underlying phonological forms. It is now clear that, while that might be a possibility for American English, it is not feasible at all for other varieties of the language: on this issue, see Becker (1967); Trudgill (1973); Chambers and Trudgill (1980, chapter 3).

Next, there was discussion of the problem of the limits of polylectal grammars. Labov's important (1973) paper is the most thorough attempt to investigate this issue. He argues that, while some forms are clearly outside a panlectal grammar, e.g. (a) *He smokes a lot anymore* and (b) BEV *It ain't no cat can't get in no coop*, there are other forms which should be included, such as negative concord (other than that of the purely BEV type, as in (b)), because they are readily comprehended. Then, Berdan (1977), in another important data-based study argues that 'grammars of polylectal comprehension may well exist' but 'documented cases of comprehension across lects fail to provide sufficient evidence for the polylectal grammar'.

Now, in this chapter, we have noted that it is a rare speaker who acquires or imitates a dialect other than his own vernacular perfectly. We have also seen that native speakers have difficulty comprehending varieties that are phonetically, phonologically or grammatically different from their own if context is unhelpful or absent. And, even given context, grammatical and pragmatic difficulties can cause severe, if often temporary, difficulties. It is my thesis that such difficulties indicate that the case for handling the polylectal passive competence of a native speaker by means of a grammar is not an especially strong one. The problems that native speakers may from time to time have, at all linguistic levels, with dialects other than their own, and the important role context plays in solving these problems, suggest rather the following.

The more different the productive competence of speaker B is from that of speaker A, the more difficulty speaker A will have in understanding speaker B. At those points where their grammars differ, A will use all the cues he can find, both linguistic and non-linguistic, in helping himself to understand B. He will, given time and practice, get better at understanding B (as Bailey suggests). But there are some forms which he may never come to comprehend fully or analyse correctly. And the fact that even those forms which are understood in context may not be understood out of context suggests that these forms never become part of any internalized, regular, passive polylectal competence.

Where forms from other dialects are comprehended, two factors can be used to explain the phenomenon. The first is familiarity. Familiarity with a form, as we have seen, does not inevitably lead to the ability to predict that it is grammatical. Neither does it necessarily lead to an ability to comprehend; but it obviously helps. All native speakers of Standard English have had considerable exposure, for example, to non-standard negative concord (other than the purely BEV type) and it is therefore not surprising if forms containing negative concord are comprehended.

The second and more important factor is *degree of linguistic difference* between the dialects. We do not, as yet, have an accurate measure of this, but there is no reason to suppose that the comprehension of grammatical forms from other dialects proceeds any differently from that of phonetic forms. If A says *face* as [feɪs] and B says [fɛɪs], it is not surprising if they understand one another. If, on the other hand, A says [faɪs] and B says [fɪəs], it would be equally unsurprising if they had some comprehension difficulties (especially in view of the similarity of B's pronunciation to A's way of saying *fierce*).

The same is surely true of grammatical forms also. If A says *I go* and B says *I goes*, the linguistic difference is so slight that we do not need to postulate a polylectal grammar to explain how they understand one another (any more than we need to postulate a polylectal grammar to explain why I understand what Dutch speakers mean when they say *Wat is het?* [vat ɪz ət]). On the other hand, the degree of difference between Standard English *There's no cat that can get in a coop* and the BEV equivalent *It ain't no cat can't get in no coop* (combined with the degree of similarity there is between the latter and Standard English *There's no cat that can't get in a coop*), explains the comprehension problem that undoubtedly exists without recourse, again, to the notion of a polylectal grammar.

CHAPTER 2

Sociolinguistics and Dialectology
Geolinguistics and English rural dialects

Dialectology is a very respectable discipline with a long and impressive history, and with a well-established methodology and literature.[1] Sociolinguistics, on the other hand, whatever this term is taken to mean, is a relatively new discipline that is still finding its feet, and still has many areas of disagreement within its ranks about methods and, more crucially, objectives (see Introduction). There are also many obvious respects in which it is very clear to all that dialectology has been, and doubtless will continue to be, of very considerable assistance to sociolinguistics. I cite a very few examples to make this point clear:

1   In my own sociolinguistic work on the English spoken in the English city of Norwich (Trudgill, 1974), I found invaluable and made frequent reference to the excellent dialectological work carried out in the area in the 1930s by the American Guy S. Lowman and kindly made available to me by Professor Raven McDavid. This work was particularly helpful in my work on linguistic change, and in pointing to problematical areas for investigation.

2   William Labov's pioneering work on Martha's Vineyard and New York City made considerable use of the work of dialectologists in connection with the *Linguistic Atlas of the United States and Canada*. Indeed, Labov has made the point a number of times that the study of linguistic change in 'apparent time' can only proceed with confidence if there are earlier records, usually dialectological, for the area or at least for neighbouring areas. Comparing the speech of older

[1] I am very grateful to J. K. Chambers for originating and developing a number of the concepts used in this chapter.

31

and younger speakers at a given time may *suggest* that certain linguistic changes are taking place, but one cannot be sure that age-grading is not taking place instead, unless older records are available for checking.

3   The Tyneside Linguistic Survey of the Newcastle area of north-eastern England started with the working assumption that very little or nothing was known about the area's English, and that they would therefore take as little for granted as possible. This seems to me to be a naive assumption in view of the large amount of dialectological data available – and one that cost the sociolinguistic survey a lot of time (and money).

One of the things that dialectology does very well is to supply data, and it is regrettable that sociolinguists often ignore this data, or discover it themselves, with surprise, decades after dialectologists knew all about it. In this connection one thinks in particular of American sociolinguists whose ignorance of the facts of English spoken outside the USA is often quite striking. Without, for example, wanting to get into the controversy about the origins of American Black Vernacular English, it must be said that discussions about the relative merits of creole and British-dialect origins ought, at the very least, to include all the relevant facts. One such fact, well-known to dialectologists and amply illustrated in the *Linguistic Atlas of England* (Orton *et al.*, 1978), is that there is a large area of northern England where possessives of the BEV-type *father boots = father's boots* are found. (It is not, of course, only American *socio*linguists who are at fault here. Many American statements about English syntactic structure falter on perfectly normal British English constructions such as *I'll give it him*, and *I'll give the book John*.)

Sociolinguistics, then, owes a considerable debt to dialectology, and it is my contention that it could benefit from dialectology even more than it has done. However, it is also clear that the reverse also applies. Dialectology has already benefited from sociolinguistic concepts and methods, but it could, I would maintain, benefit even more. I want to illustrate this general point by reference to the Survey of English Dialects and, in particular, the *Linguistic Atlas of England*. This may seem to be a narrowly ethnocentric thing to do, but one of the tenets of this chapter is the Labovian point that 'the more we know, the more we can find out', and I know more about English English than any other language variety.

THE HISTORICAL BIAS IN DIALECTOLOGY

The *Linguistic Atlas of England*, like many other dialectological projects, has an avowedly 'strong historical bias', and, as is usual in such studies, the field-workers were looking for the 'oldest kind of traditional vernacular' which is 'best found in rural areas amongst the farming community' (Orton *et al.*, 1978). This is because the aim of the work is to 'demonstrate the continuity and historical development of the language' and to 'serve as a historical baseline against which future studies [can] be measured'. This is all very acceptable in itself, and the selection of this type of informant is obviously exactly the right thing to do given these kinds of objectives. One must remember, too, that dialectologists have also typically been concerned to record and preserve older dialect forms before they become extinct.

This narrowly historical emphasis found in some (but, it must be stressed, not all) dialectological studies turns out, however, to have unfortunate consequences for those with an interest in the synchronic state of the language under investigation, in this case English, and will, one suspects, come to be a source of regret for historians of twentieth-century English. A contribution from sociolinguistics would not have removed this historical bias, ideally. Rather it would have supplemented it with an additional focus on more recent trends and developments. One of the central concerns of sociolinguistics has been the study of linguistic changes in progress – as opposed to the dialectologist's interest in changes that have already taken place. Sociolinguists thus appreciate the vast amount of material available in the *Linguistic Atlas of England*, but cannot help observing also that there is a marked lack of information about the origins of features of current interest. One of these is the development of intrusive /r/ in environments such as *saw it, India and*, etc. Mention of this particular feature in the Atlas is relegated to one footnote to the map for the word *thawing*. A map showing the presence of this form would have been both useful and striking: as far as one can ascertain from the Survey of English Dialects' Basic Materials volumes, intrusive /r/ in rural dialects seems to be confined to a single area which includes the south Midlands, East Anglia and the Home Counties. One would be more confident about asserting this, however, if more appropriate items had been included in the questionnaire, and more relevant information thereby obtained.

This point, however, should not be taken too far. It can obviously not be regarded as a defect that urban varieties of English were not investigated by the Survey (with the puzzling exception of York, Sheffield, Leeds, and an area of inner London). The study of urban dialects, as well as of less traditional rural varieties, was a less urgent task, and could be left till later.

It can be noted, though, that this same historical bias has led to one defect in the atlas, as in a number of other atlases, that is a source of distress not only to a sociolinguist but also to any linguist. The particular linguistic defect that arises out of this diachronic bias is that 'phonology' is construed for the most part historically, and researchers interested in phonological systems, in phonological (as opposed to phonetic) change, and in what contrasts are and are not made in which areas, will have a difficult task. It *is* possible, by comparing maps for *grave* and *rain, loaf* and *snow, hear* and *mare*, to work out which areas probably do and do not preserve the historical contrasts of *made* and *maid, nose* and *knows, hear* and *hair* – and so on. But this is a difficult and cumbersome task because the main interest of the compilers lay in examining the phonetic reflexes of Middle English vowels and consonants. The mapping of phonological systems as such, however tentative, along the lines proposed by workers on the Scots atlas, would have been a very welcome addition.

THE MORE WE KNOW, THE MORE WE CAN FIND OUT

Another contribution that sociolinguistics could make to dialectology concerns the principle, mentioned above as having been argued for by Labov, that 'the more we know, the more we can find out'. This does not, obviously, mean that we should not venture to do linguistic or dialectological work in fields, areas or languages that are unfamiliar. It simply means that the more we know about a variety, the more insights we obtain about its nature and structure, and the more we know what questions to ask ourselves next in planning further research. Conversely, the less we know about a variety the less certain we are of what questions to ask about it, and the more likely we are to make mistakes – and the more need there is, therefore, to guard against these mistakes.

There are a number of mistakes of this sort that one can readily point to in the work of the Survey of English Dialects (SED) (see Orton *et al.*, 1962–) as illustrated in the *Linguistic Atlas of England* (*LAE*). One obvious example concerns the phonetic transcriptions. Very many of them are not sufficiently narrow or detailed, and potential contrasts may therefore have been missed. In other cases it is obvious that the field-workers' own preconceptions of what they were going to find have influenced what they heard. And in yet other cases, both faults combine to obscure the true facts in a serious and misleading way. For example, there are large areas of Norfolk where *fool* and *foal*, *cool* and *coal*, etc. are homophonous. The atlas, however, gives *foal* [foul] and *school* [sku:l] for Norfolk (see maps 2.1 and 2.2). The problem is that the (too broad) transcription system employed permits both [ou] and [u:] as approximations to the actual pronunciation, which is around [ʊu] for both sets of words. Preconceptions about phonological systems on the part of the field-worker – in this case that *foal* and *school* cannot possibly have the same vowel – have done the rest of the damage. The field-worker has failed to follow the advice of Moulton (1968) – and indeed there is no provision for this in the SED questionnaire – and ask informants for rhymes, thus avoiding errors of this sort. (Even this, of course, is not without its dangers as Labov, among others, has pointed out. A number of studies have shown that pairs of words which are normally distinct may be merged if informants' attention is drawn to them.) I am not suggesting that dialectologists inevitably fall into this trap. The field-worker for eastern Suffolk, Stanley Ellis, who carried out more interviews for the survey than anyone else, correctly transcribes *foal* and *school* with the identical vowel [u:]. Lowman, too, got it absolutely right. What I am saying is that when one is working with alien varieties one must be doubly on one's guard about preconceptions, about asking the wrong questions, and about failing to ask the right ones.

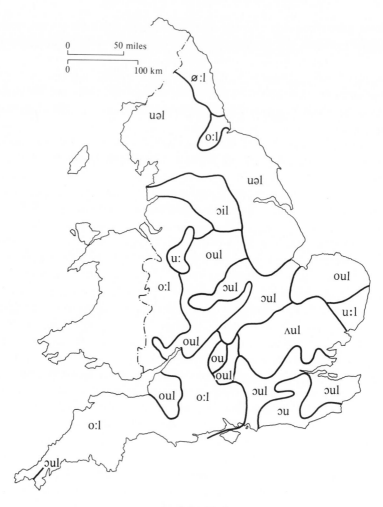

MAP 2.1   *Foal*

This point is borne out by other errors of this sort in the atlas. They appear to be particularly common in the case of the dialects of the south of England, which the atlas editors seem to be less interested in and less informed about generally. There is, for example, an important phonological problem concerning whether or not there is a contrast, in the south-west of England, between the /æ/ of *cat* and the /ɑː/ of *palm, path*. Wells (1982) and Hughes and Trudgill (1979) suggest that there probably is not. Many of the

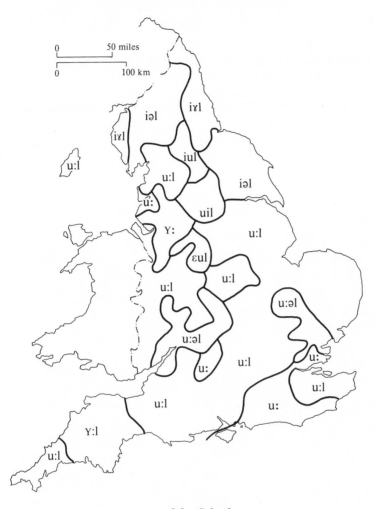

MAP 2.2 *School*

transcriptions in the atlas, however, suggest that they might be. Are these transcriptions wrong? The suspicion has to be that some of them, at least, are. And here again the dialectologist's historical bias causes problems. The only reliable way to resolve this issue would be to ask questions such as: are *lager* and *lagger* pronounced the same?; do *banana* and *manna* rhyme?; does *gala* have the same vowel as *pallor*?; and so on. Unfortunately, British dialectologists, at least, seem not to be interested in relatively recent words such as *lager* and *banana*, even though they occur very frequently in everyday modern usage.

The reliability of the atlas is in doubt also at other points. There are, for example, some faulty transcriptions which are easy to spot, especially those that turn up as 'field-worker isoglosses'. For example, maps 2.3 and 2.4, for the items *last* and *arm*, from the *LAE*, show a clear phonetic isogloss running between Norfolk, which has the back vowel [ɑ:] in these words, and Suffolk and

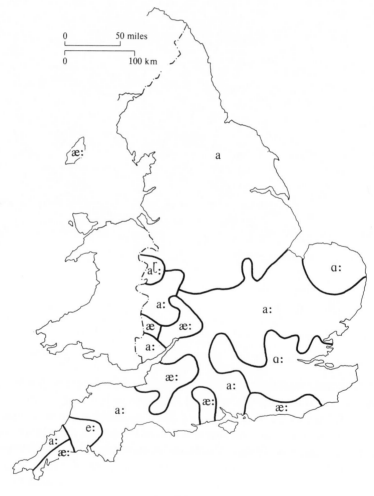

MAP 2.3   *Last*

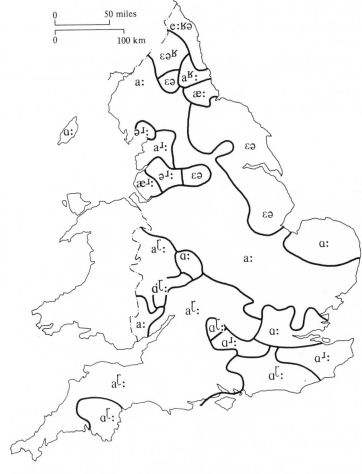

MAP 2.4 *Arm*

Cambridgeshire, which have [aː]. This [ɑː] in Norfolk would be
rather hard to explain – as can be seen, the only other instances of
this vowel occur in the regions of the two largest cities, London
and Birmingham – were it not for the fact that it is simply wrong.
The transcriptions made in Norfolk by Lowman in the 1930s (see
p. 89), my own work in the area, and my native speaker knowledge, suggest to me very strongly that the correct transcription
should be the front vowel [aː]. The isoglosses on maps 2.3 and 2.4

are simply lines drawn between the localities investigated by the Norfolk field-worker, who got it wrong, and those worked on by the Cambridge and Suffolk field-workers (including Stanley Ellis), who got it right.

A similar field-worker isogloss is illustrated in map 2.5, the map for *suet*. This shows that the second syllable of this word in Norfolk is pronounced with the vowel [ɪ], while the areas that surround Norfolk have instead the vowel [ə]. It is certain, once

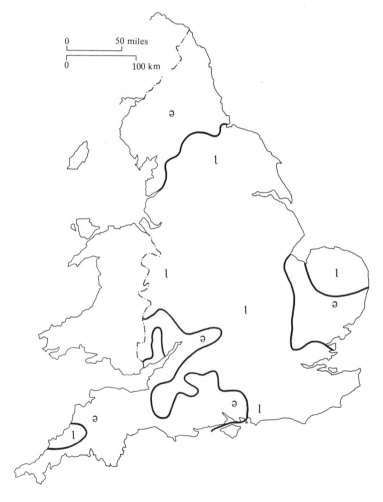

MAP 2.5 *Suet*

again, however, that the Norfolk transcriptions are incorrect. Norfolk dialect-speakers – and not just dialect speakers – do not say [sʉɪˀ] but [sʉəˀ].

This makes it seem as if I am conducting a vendetta against the Norfolk field-worker. I am not. There is no reason to suppose that he has done a worse job than anyone else. It is simply that this is the area that I know best and am therefore most qualified to spot mistakes in. Other users of the atlas should, however, have no real confidence about transcriptions for areas they are not familiar with, especially if the map looks odd in any way, unless two or more field-workers appear to agree. One has to be sceptical of anything which seems improbable.

The contribution which sociolinguistics can make to dialectology at this point is to (1) encourage dialectologists not only to use tape-recorders (and even spectographs) but also to trust them – tape-recordings were made in the Norfolk area but were obviously never employed by the editors. (2) Pilot studies should be conducted in each area under investigation and previous work on the locality studied and noted. (3) Wherever possible field-workers should be natives of the area, or people familiar with the local dialect. This is not always possible, of course, and even when it is there are some dangers – preconceptions are less likely to be wrong, but if they are wrong they are more likely to be adhered to. But generally speaking it is a help. (4) Greater attention should be paid to fine phonetic detail. It seems paradoxical, perhaps, that dialectologists should be criticized for lack of attention to phonetic detail, but the fact is that, at least in the English-speaking world, social differences in pronunciation of the type studied by sociolinguists and urban dialectologists are typically very slight. Attention to fine phonetic detail has been forced upon sociolinguists, for without it, many important aspects of social variation would simply be missed.

SOCIOLINGUISTIC METHODOLOGY

As far as the field-work methodology is concerned, it would be somewhat unfair to criticize the Survey of English Dialects (and indeed many other earlier surveys) too heavily for what may seem now, in retrospect, to be a lack of sociolinguistic sophistication.

Moreover, one of the atlas editors' own misgivings on this score seems to be completely unfounded: random sampling as a means of selecting informants would have been entirely inappropriate for work of this type – though they seem to think it might have been better or more sophisticated to use this method – since they were specifically *not* concerned to obtain informants who were representative.

However, it has to be observed that other and indeed much earlier dialect surveys were considerably more sociolinguistically sophisticated than this – a good and well known example is the work for the *Linguistic Atlas of New England.* It also has to be acknowledged that certain aspects of dialect methodology have actually probably influenced the data obtained by the SED. Dialectologists, for instance, have tended to argue, informally at least if not in print, that their selection of elderly rural informants avoids the problem of stylistic levels and of the 'observer's paradox' (Labov, 1972c) – approximately, that linguists want to observe how people speak when they are not being observed. Sociolinguists, on the other hand, as is well known, have tended to worry a great deal about the problems of the influence of the interviewer, the influence of the tape-recorder, and the difficulty of obtaining casual, vernacular speech. (Dialectologists and sociolinguists, of course, both tend to be most interested in the vernacular – dialectologists because the vernacular is the variety least influenced by the standard; sociolinguists, at least according to Labov, because the vernacular is systematic, regular, and the site of ongoing changes.)

There is evidence from the *LAE* that dialectologists may be wrong in this and that Labov's claim that there is no such thing as a single-style speaker (and therefore no informant who will always and only give the vernacular) is substantially correct. Maps 2.6 and 2.7, from the *LAE,* show that the majority of Norfolk localities are given as having *home* as [houm]. On the maps this looks very odd, since these Norfolk localities are surrounded by areas which have short vowels in this item, and have [hum], [hom], [hʌm], [ɔm] or [ɒm]. The Norfolk localities, moreover, are separated by these short-vowel localities from the other areas which have diphthongs or long vowels by as much as 200 miles (330 km) – a long way in English dialectology. The fact is, however, that the vernacular pronunciation in Norfolk *is* in fact [hum] = /hʊm/.

MAP 2.6 *Home* (1)

The problem that the field-worker encountered was that speakers in Norfolk, as no doubt elsewhere, also have available to them a more formal pronunciation of the type [houm ~ hʊum] = /huːm/. (A number of other words have this alternation also: *road* /rʊd/ ~ /ruːd/, *stone, bone, throat* etc.) The field-worker succeeded in obtaining only this more formal pronunciation, and not the vernacular. Informants who were more at ease, or an interviewer less obviously foreign or more obviously able to comprehend the

MAP 2.7   *Home* (2)

vernacular (another important requirement) might well have had better success.

This particular point has been very nicely illustrated indeed by Ellen Douglas-Cowie in her work in Northern Ireland. She arranged for one of the very experienced English field-workers on the SED to carry out interviews in her own native village – and the field-worker felt that he had done a good job, and that he had successfully obtained the vernacular. Douglas-Cowie then re-interviewed the same informants herself. The differences in the language obtained are startling (and amusing). It is clear that the English field-worker was a very long way indeed from obtaining vernacular speech. The 'observer's paradox', we can say, is always a problem, but it is a particular problem where speakers – as they are in large areas of northern Britain – are bi-dialectal.

A further, related, methodological problem is that it is especially difficult to obtain vernacular speech when what you are eliciting is one-word responses to a questionnaire. Labov has discussed this problem at some length, and points out that the amount of attention speakers devote to their speech correlates closely with the degree of formality of their speech. And it is certainly difficult to avoid directing informants' attention to their speech when you are asking them for one-word answers. One-word responses also typically produce citation forms,' and fail, naturally, to elicit features of connected speech. The one-word response syndrome is apparent in the *LAE*, not only in the map for *home* but also at a number of other points. One of these is the map for *butter*. In all areas of Britain – and this includes large areas of England and many rural dialects – where intervocalic /t/ can be realized as a glottal stop, the glottal stop pronunciation is stylistically marked as informal or very informal, and it is therefore relatively unlikely to occur in citation forms. The fact that the map shows very few glottal stops thus tells us very little. Recordings of spontaneous conversation of the type typically obtained by sociolinguists would be necessary for the true vernacular form to emerge. A similar problem is that of intrusive /r/ – which may be why this feature is absent from the Atlas. As a sandhi phenomenon there are relatively few opportunities (as in *thawing*) for it to occur word-internally, and the SED therefore elicited very few examples of this feature.

A further worry with one-word responses is that the greater attention this method focuses on the word being elicited may produce not only more formal pronunciations but instead, or as well, for some speakers, what can be called *hyperdialectisms*. These will occur where the informant is well-disposed towards the local dialect and the dialect survey, and where on-going linguistic changes make for fluctuation in the community and a certain amount of insecurity about what the local pronunciation actually is. For example, in the older English dialect of Norfolk there is a

consistent distinction between the two vowels /æi/ and /eː/ which
are merged in most other varieties of English (see also p. 12):

/æi/	/eː/
days	*daze*
maid	*made*
lays	*laze*

In recent years speakers have lost, or are losing, this distinction,
now pronouncing *daze* etc. with /æi/. However, when their attention is drawn to their local dialect by, for example, attempting to
elicit one-word responses to questions in overtly linguistic surveys,
the older monophthong /eː/ may return in *daze*, but also, unfortunately, in *days*, where it is not historically justified. Hyperdialectisms of this type are an interesting phenomenon, and may
in some cases have a permanent effect. One probable case of this
comes from the Arvanitika (Albanian) dialects spoken in the
Athens area of Greece (see chapters 6 and 7). Awareness that
Arvanitika /š/ corresponds often to Greek /s/ has led Arvanitika
speakers to introduce /š/ into items where in Albanian they originally had /s/:

	Albanian	Arvanitika
much	/šum/	/šum/
today	/sot/	/šot/

In dialectological work, however, they are a phenomenon that has
to be guarded against. (See further Trudgill, forthcoming.)

One, of course, cannot rely exclusively on tape-recorded conversation. Questionnaires are essential for obtaining lexical material,
and useful for obtaining rarely occurring features. Ideally the two
methods, the dialectological and the sociolinguistic, should be
combined.

GRADIENCE AND VARIABILITY IN SOCIOLINGUISTICS AND DIALECTOLOGY

One of the biggest problems of dialectology generally, and linguistic atlases in particular, is the isogloss. It has always been recog-

nized by sensible dialectologists that isoglosses are something of a fiction or distortion. It has not, however, always been recognized how much of a distortion they can be, or what difficulties they may produce.

Distortions can take a number of different forms. In the *LAE*, for example, there are a number of isoglosses separating [ɒ] from [ɔ]; [uː] from [ʉː]; [ei] from [ɛi]; and so on. The suspicion must be, however, that vowel quality actually changes gradually from location to location and that the placing of these isoglosses is therefore arbitrary and a simple artifact of the transcription system. The isogloss between [ɒ] and [ɔ] is drawn where it is simply because the symbols [ɒ] and [ɔ] have been assigned particular phonetic values.

The editors of the *LAE* also acknowledge that isoglosses usually mark transition zones rather than discrete breaks, even where phonetic continua are not involved. What the editors do not say is that the time-honoured dialectological system of getting one word from one informant once greatly reduces the amount of apparent variability in such zones – the point being that a different informant, a different sentence, or a different day might produce a different response – and thus masks many of the inadequacies of isoglosses.

In fact, however sophisicated one is about what exactly is implied by the drawing of an isogloss, the fact remains that the drawing of a line on a map implies that variation is geographically abrupt. It implies that one variant gives way to another at some particular point in space.

This problem has, I think, very rarely, if ever, been discussed in the literature, although the assumption of geographical abruptness is hardly one that can bear much scrutiny. Part of the conventional wisdom of philology has always been that variation is not abrupt, and the fact that linguistic variation most often ranges along a cline or continuum has now been reinforced by sociolinguistic work on creole-speaking communities, and urban dialects. Most dialectologists agree that transitions are gradual rather than abrupt, but introductory works on dialectology typically discuss dialect continua and isoglosses without pointing out that they are for the most part incompatible.

It has to be conceded that, in theory, the notions of the continuum and the isogloss could be reconciled. Transition zones, in traditional dialectology, contain *bundles* of isoglosses, consisting of lines which are in the same area but not, usually, contiguous. If one moved across this transition zone, one would have the impression of a continuum, since first one feature, and then another, and then another, would vary from place to place, giving an impression of gradualness. Study of a number of transition zones on the ground, however, suggests in fact that even this is a distortion of what often happens in transition zones (see Chambers and Trudgill, 1980).

For example, it is possible to draw isoglosses across England, based on the SED materials, dividing a northern area where words such as *dance* and *path* have the vowel /æ/, as in *cat*, from a southern area where they have the vowel /aː/, as in *palm, part*. If we draw an isogloss for every relevant word contained in the SED materials we get a bundle of isoglosses, giving an impression of a continuum, because no isogloss for a particular word coincides absolutely with any other isogloss for any other word. Our research shows, however, that the exact configuration of the bundle simply depends on the particular pronunciation that the particular field-worker obtained from a particular informant on a particular occasion for a particular word. On another occasion, or with another informant, he might have obtained a different response, since our investigations show that what actually happens in the transition zone is as follows. The southern /aː/ vowel is, or has been, gradually spreading north, with the consequence that in the transition zone most speakers alternate between the two vowels but:

(a) the /aː/ vowel is more common in middle-class speech than working-class speech;

(b) the /aː/ vowel is more common in formal styles than informal styles:

(c) the /aː/ vowel is more common in the speech of younger than older speakers;

(d) the /aː/ vowel is more common in some words than others;

(e) the /aː/ vowel is more common in some phonological environments than others;

(f) the /aː/ vowel is more common in the south of the transition zone than the north.

There are also the two additional complicating factors that:

(i) speakers are, obviously, not consistent in their use of one vowel or the other, but *some* may be consistent for *some* words, environments, styles, etc. And of course percentages of vowel use vary greatly;

(ii) the variation involves not only alternation between one vowel and the other but also the use of intermediate vowel qualities such as [æ:] and [a] (see also Chapter 4).

The overall picture, in other words, is very complex indeed, and not one which can accurately be portrayed by the use of isoglosses. Indeed, something of this complexity can even be gleaned from the SED itself, although not from the *LAE*, where the maps simplify and distort the situation. Map 2.8 (from Chambers and Trudgill, 1980), shows the boundary area between north of England areas which have /ʊ/ in *cup*, *but*, etc. and southern areas which have /ʌ/. Even the one-word response SED material shows that while some areas have exclusively either /ʌ/ or /ʊ/, these are separated by a corridor of variability which contains:

(i) mixed northern lects: /ʌ/ and /ʊ/ alternate, but /ʊ/ predominates;

(ii) fudged northern lects: /ʊ/ alternates with an intermediate vowel [ɤ];

(iii) fudged southern lects: /ʌ/ alternates with an intermediate vowel [ɤ];

(iv) mixed southern lects: /ʌ/ and /ʊ/ alternate, but /ʌ/ predominates.

The materials, of course, show variation between words. Conversational material would doubtless also show variation between different instances of the same word.

The solution to this problem is one that is relatively obvious to a sociolinguist: dialectology has to be made quantitative. Now, it has to be acknowledged that dialectology is already, in some respects, quantitative. A good example of quantification in dialectology is provided by *dialectometry*. For the most part, however, dialectometry works with the one-word responses to dialect survey questionnaires, and is concerned to quantify degrees of difference between apparently invariant and static varieties. Its isoglosses *are* quantified, but they are still isoglosses. And iso-

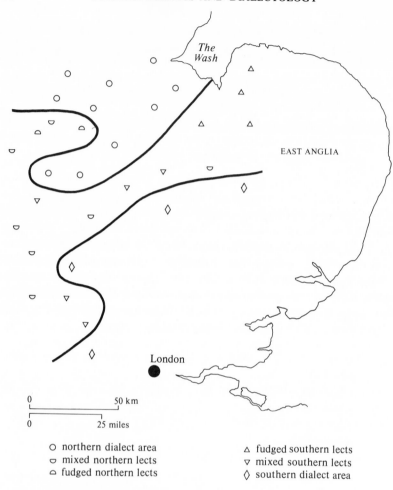

MAP 2.8   The elements of a transition zone, showing the distribution of lectal types. The northern line marks the beach-head of the innovation; the southern line its base

glosses, as we have seen – because they represent as a discrete break what is in fact a continuum, and as static what is in fact a dynamic situation – are inadequate.

What we therefore require is a transfer of sociolinguistic methodology to the geographical plane. (1) We need, in addition to traditional dialect study techniques, the recording of fluent, natural conversation. (2) We need the establishment and quantification of linguistic variables so that variability can emerge, and so that information can be produced based on many tokens rather than single tokens. (3) Then we require some method of portraying the results obtained cartographically in a manner that will parallel for regional variation the social variation portrayed in the style and social-class graphs employed by sociolinguists. We require, that is, some way of making dialect maps quantitative that will permit the handling of variability without too much distortion (see chapter 3).

CONCLUSION

Sociolinguistics, of the more linguistic sort, has much to gain from dialectology. Dialectology, on the other hand, also has much that can be learned from certain types of work in sociolinguistics. It can benefit from an increased emphasis on on-going linguistic changes and synchronic facts, without abandoning its interest in historical processes and conservative varieties. It can benefit from incorporating into its methodology some recognition of the fact that even older rural dialect speakers cannot be relied upon on all occasions to produce the vernacular. It can benefit from an increased acknowledgement that fine attention to detail and a very open-minded approach are helpful when dealing with unfamiliar varieties. Finally, it can benefit from paying increased attention to the heterogeneity of speech communities and the variability of speech. It was dialectology that first brought to our attention how full of variety languages are. It should have no difficulty therefore in handling the notion that idiolects, too, are full of variety. Similarly, dialectologists have for a long time been aware that isoglosses were often a kind of fiction. They should therefore have no difficulty in perceiving that the fiction is not necessarily always a helpful one. Theoretical linguists have for a long time worked with the fictional notion of the homogeneous speech community, and it has been left to sociolinguists to point out that this simple fiction is often an unhelpful and misleading one. They can do dialectologists the very same service by pointing out to them that the facts of regional variation are often very complex, *and* that this complexity can be coped with and put to good and insightful use. We attempt to illustrate this point in the following chapter, which we present as an example of sociolinguistically informed dialectology, or *geolinguistics*.

CHAPTER 3

Linguistic Change and Diffusion

Description and explanation in
Geolinguistics

William Labov's *Social Stratification of English in New York City* made a number of very important contributions to linguistic theory and practice.[1] Among these were the development of the concept of the linguistic variable, which provided linguists with a means of measuring and describing gradient and variable linguistic features, and the adoption of certain aspects of sociological methodology (particularly sampling and social class index construction), which permitted a detailed study of the covariation of linguistic and social phenomena. This in turn enabled us to achieve a clearer understanding of the nature of the relationship between language and various sociological parameters, and increased our knowledge about the social setting of linguistic change. In this chapter I want to argue that the linguistic variable, together with a number of methodological and theoretical insights from human geography, can similarly improve our knowledge of the relationship between language and geography, and of the geographical setting of linguistic change.

In section 1 I shall suggest some reasons for considering the improvement of descriptions and explanations of geographical variation in language. Section 2 will contain suggestions, based on the work of cultural geographers, for ways in which improvements

---

[1] I am very grateful indeed to R. L. Hodgart, who first interested me in this topic, and to Arne Kjell Foldvik, who first involved me in the study of Norwegian, and without whom the Brunlanes survey would have been impossible. I am also grateful to the large number of people who commented on earlier versions of this chapter, especially E. Afendras, C. J. Bailey, D. Bickerton, R. W. Fasold, A. K. Foldvik, W. N. Francis, T. Hagerstrand, P. Haggett, B. Jernudd, W. Labov, A. McIntosh, F. R. Palmer, S. T. Trudgill and J. C. Wells. My thanks are also due to Ingeborg Hoff for her help with aspects of the Norwegian data.

52

in descriptions can be effected, and section 3 will consist of an illustration of these improvements, based on empirical research carried out in a Norwegian speech community. In section 4 we shall examine suggestions for improvements in explanations, with assistance from data obtained in empirical studies made in East Anglia, England, and in section 5 we shall again illustrate these improvements with reference to the Norwegian data.

1 DESCRIPTION AND EXPLANATION IN LINGUISTIC GEOGRAPHY

Labov's methodology of correlating the variable linguistic data that he wishes to investigate to previously established sociological categories such as age, sex and social class has not been without its critics. De Camp (1971) has written:

a linguistic geographer would be properly horrified at the following suggestion: let us use state boundaries as preconceived pigeonholes for sorting the data from an American linguistic atlas, and then merely indicate the percentage of New York informants who say *pail* as opposed to *bucket*, the equivalent percentage for Pennsylvanians, for Virginians, etc. Why then have sociolinguists so often correlated their linguistic data to preconceived categories of age, income, education, etc., instead of correlating these non-linguistic variables *to* the linguistic data?

De Camp's objection is somewhat puzzling. In any study it is usual and sensible to hold constant those variables which one is not investigating (such as income and age), and study the (in this case) linguistic variation as it relates to these constants. It would be useful to correlate age and income *to* linguistic data, as De Camp suggests, only if one wanted to employ language as a tool for establishing or investigating the existence of particular social groups. However, this quotation does provide a useful introduction to one aspect of the subject under discussion here. I want to suggest that the (hypothetical) dialectological methodology felt by De Camp to be absurd bears a close resemblance to the kind of approach which linguistic geography ought to be adopting. I would like, in other words, to suggest that, far from sociolinguists learning from the example of dialectologists, as De Camp proposes, the reverse should be the case. Dialectologists, I would argue, should begin to consider the possibility of correlating their data, as geographers have done, with 'preconceived' geographical units. These units should not, however, be entities so disparate or non-comparable as American states.

The reasoning behind this suggestion is twofold. First, I want to argue that dialectologists should not be content simply to *describe* the geographical distribution of linguistic features. They should also be concerned to *explain* – or perhaps, more accurately, to adduce reasons for – this distribution. Only in this way will we be able to arrive at an understanding of the sociolinguistic mechanisms that lie behind the geographical distribution of linguistic phenomena, the location of isoglosses, and the diffusion of linguistic innovations. If we are to achieve this understanding we need to be able to say *exactly* why and how linguistic features, under linguistic change, are diffused from one location or social group to another. This does not mean to say, of course, that linguistic geography, hitherto, has not been concerned with explanations of this type. German dialectology, in particular, certainly has (see Bach, 1950; Moser, 1954; Wagner, 1927, amongst several others). Kurath (1972), too, contains many references to explanatory factors and studies. I merely wish to suggest that in certain respects dialectology as a whole has not been *sufficiently* concerned with explanation.

Secondly, I want to argue that this *relative* lack of interest in explanation in linguistic geography is the result of the fact that, paradoxically enough, the descriptions themselves have not been sufficiently full or accurate. That is, not only has dialectology remained, to some extent at least, in the descriptive stage, but, as Pickford (1956) has also pointed out, the descriptions provided have often been inadequate. It is not possible to provide explanations for phenomena for which there is insufficient information. I therefore want to propose that it may be possible to effect an improvement in our descriptions of geographical dialects – and hence in our ability to explain dialect phenomena – by adopting a geographical and sociolinguistic-influenced methodology not unlike that dismissed by De Camp. If such a methodology proves to be successful, then explanations may follow.

Let us first of all consider an example of the way in which inadequate descriptions, based on traditional methodology, may hamper explanation. Map 3.1 shows the geographical distribution of post-vocalic /r/ in England in the items *yard* and *farm* and is based on information contained in the publications of the Survey of English Dialects (Orton *et al.*, 1962). This map represents a description of the type normally provided by dialect surveys, and

MAP 3.1   Three areas with post-vocalic /r/ in *yard* and *farm*, after SED

one which is of considerable interest and value. However, if we are keen to achieve an understanding of some of the processes of linguistic change involved here, it is desirable that we should be able to explain why the isoglosses shown on the map are exactly where they are. In fact it proves very difficult if not impossible to do this. Say, for example, that we wish to explain the, on the face of it, rather surprising fact that the post-vocalic /r/ isogloss runs very close indeed to London. How do we explain the fact that the areas immediately to the south and west of London have been so little affected by the speech of the metropolis, which has probably been r-less as long as 300 or 400 years (see Wyld, 1956: 299)? The answer, of course, is that they *have* been affected. It is simply the case that our description is inadequate and fails to show this: except for the very small minority of conservative rural dialect speakers in this area, the isogloss drawn on the map is *not* in fact where it is shown to be, although where exactly it is we cannot at this stage say – except that it is well to the south and west somewhere, depending on age, social class, and similar factors. We cannot explain the current distribution of post-vocalic /r/ in the London area simply because we do not know what it is. (The map is also very inaccurate in other places: Liverpool and some other urban areas in the north-west, for example, are also r-less.)

Map 3.2 provides a second example. This map shows the distribution of uvular r in the languages of western Europe, in educated speech. The spread of the uvular r pronunciation in Europe is a rather remarkable phenomenon of considerable sociolinguistic interest, and one that we should like to be able to explain. This map, and the one that follows, map 3.3, have proved very difficult to compile – few full and accurate descriptions are available – and it is doubtless very inaccurate in many details.[2] I hope, however, that the main point will be clear: if we require an explanation for the current distribution of uvular r, map 3.2 is very misleading. The back (dorsal) pronunciation of /r/ is thought to have started in Paris (but see Moulton, 1952) in the seventeenth century (see, for example, Ewert, 1963 and Martinet, 1969) and we know that it had reached Copenhagen by 1780 (Skautrup, 1968). It is now standard in French, German and Danish, and partly so in Dutch, Norwegian and Swedish. It also occurs in areas not shown in map 3.2; it is found in the speech of a number of Italian speakers, particularly in the north-west, Turin, area; in certain varieties of Oslo Norwegian; in some types of North Frisian; in the north-

---

[2] I am including under the heading of 'uvular r' all uvular and velar pronunciations of this type, including trills, fricatives and frictionless continuants. The maps are based on the following sources: tape-recordings and reports from Reading University students studying abroad; my own tape-recordings and observations made in Belgium, Holland, Germany, Denmark and Norway; reports from colleagues and foreign students at the University of Reading; and information received from very many European dialectologists and linguists, including particularly R. Chevrot, J. Daan and A. Ellegård. I am very grateful to the very large number of people who helped in this way. Bibliographical sources consulted include the Reeks Nederlandse Dialectatlassen, the German Linguistic Atlas, and Sjöstedt (1936), Martinet (1968), Jørgensen(1960), Keller (1961), and Hildebrand (1965).

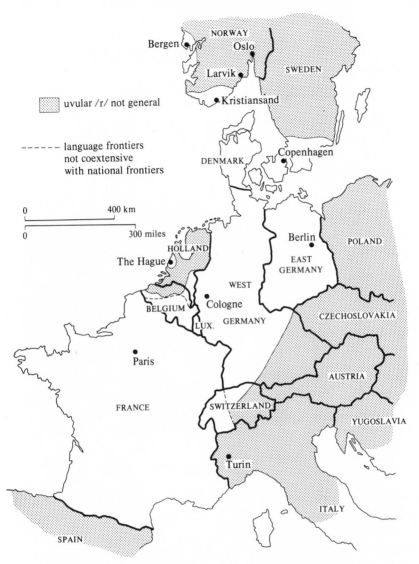

uvular /r/ not general

language frontiers
not coextensive
with national frontiers

0   400 km

0   300 miles

MAP 3.2   Uvular /r/ in Europe

east of England; and in parts of North Wales. Outside Europe,
uvular r also occurs in some varieties of Afrikaans, Hebrew and
Canadian French. It is not absolutely clear whether the British
pronunciations, or the occurrence of uvular r in certain varieties
of Portuguese and Spanish, are related phenomena or not.

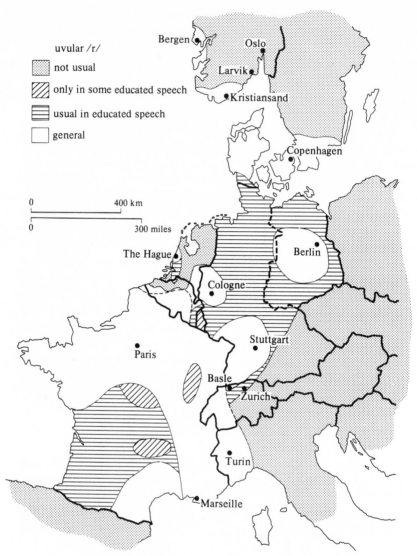

MAP 3.3   Uvular /r/ in greater social detail

But how exactly did uvular r achieve this distribution? Map 3.2 suggests that, for the most part, it spread as an innovation gradually across the countryside until it arrived at the configuration it has today. This is misleading, and it is misleading because the map is very incomplete. Map 3.2 fails to show how many people in a given area use a uvular r pronunciation, how often they use it, when and where they use it, and what sort of people they are. The social density of usage is not indicated, and map 3.2 is therefore as inaccurate as map 3.1: the speech of only one social group is portrayed.

The extent to which the explanation suggested by map 3.2 is false is indicated by map 3.3 which, although it itself is very incomplete, does show the distribution of uvular r in greater social detail. It is true that we still do not have a full or accurate description, but we have been able to add an extra dimension to the description which should improve any explanation we attempt to make. Map 3.3 suggests that the diffusion of this feature as an innovation has indeed taken place through gradual spread as far as large parts of France and adjacent areas of Belgium, Switzerland and south-west Germany are concerned, regardless of language frontiers. But it also indicates that, elsewhere, diffusion has taken the form of the jumping of uvular r from one large urban centre to another, particularly The Hague, Cologne, Berlin, Copenhagen, Kristiansand and Bergen. In map 3.2, in other words, the role of the urban centre in the diffusion of innovations is obscured. This is particularly undesirable since linguistic innovation diffusion of this type is doubtless a common phenomenon. Panov (1968), for example, provides interesting sociolinguistic data for the same type of process in Russian.

2   DESCRIPTION IN GEOGRAPHY

The contrast between maps 3.2 and 3.3 suggests that we are unable to attempt explanations of the geographical distribution of linguistic phenomena until our descriptions are full and accurate, and our dialect maps greatly improved. What, ideally, would such maps look like? Consider map 3.4. This map gives a full and accurate description of the distribution of a particular phenomenon in space at a particular time. For this reason it is susceptible of explanation: the spatial diffusion patterns of this phenomenon as an innovation are clear, and tell us much about the processes involved. This, I suggest, might well be what dialect maps should look like. Map 3.4 is taken from the work of the Swedish geographer Hägerstrand (1952). How was this map, and others like it, compiled? The technique is almost exactly the one rejected by De

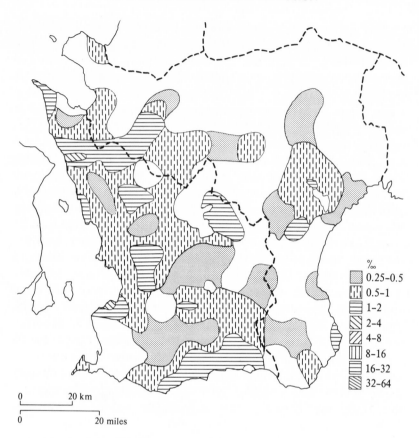

‰
⬚ 0.25–0.5
⬚ 0.5–1
⬚ 1–2
⬚ 2–4
⬚ 4–8
⬚ 8–16
⬚ 16–32
⬚ 32–64

0   20 km

0   20 miles

MAP 3.4   Southern Sweden: motor-cars per 1,000 inhabitants, 1918

Camp. The landscape is divided up into a number of carefully placed areas of uniform size and shape, and the investigator then measures the amount, number or percentage of the particular phenomenon in which he is interested in each area in turn. (In this case the areas used are hexagonal. Discussion of the relative merits of different shapes, as well as of the statistical and cartographical problems that arise in work of this kind, can be found in the Hägerstrand paper itself, as well as in, for instance, Haggett, 1965, and Robinson and Sale, 1969, chapter 7.)

Hägerstrand (1952) has written: 'When studying changes we cannot draw boundary lines and observe their displacements.[3]

---

[3] This has been done with linguistic data (cf. Daan 1971).

Instead we must ascertain *the spatial diffusion of ratios'*. That is, if the dialectologist were to adopt this approach, he would have to calculate the percentage of, say, post-vocalic /r/ employed in each geographical cell (at given points in time) in exactly the same way that Labov and others have calculated percentages for different social class cells. This methodology will, of course, be considerably more complex than the methods traditionally employed in linguistic geography: sampling of some kind, for example, will need to be used. However, as a result of the development of sociolinguistic urban dialectology we now have the techniques for carrying out work of this sort. It is only in this way, moreover, that we will be able to obtain information about the geographical distribution of linguistic features that is detailed enough to be of any value. We do not just require to know the geographical location of a linguistic phenomenon; we need to know its 'density' and social distribution as well.

In his work as a whole Hägerstrand (1965a, 1965b, 1966, 1967a, 1967b) has concentrated on the geographical diffusion of technical innovations, but his research has several important implications for a study of linguistic innovations. Hägerstrand (1952) is concerned – as we were above in our discussion of the spread of uvular r – with *patterns* of diffusion. His basic theme is that the diffusion of an innovation is the result of the interplay of exposure to information about the innovation and factors leading to resistance to its adoption, and it is worth noting that he considers interpersonal contacts to be much more influential than the mass media. (Much is often made, by writers on language, of the role of television, in particular, in the changing of speakers' linguistic habits. It seems to me that, while the media do play a part in the dissemination of new vocabulary and fashionable idioms, they have almost no effect at all in phonological or grammatical change. This is because they require only passive understanding on the part of the hearer or reader, and involve no interaction between innovator and potential receptors. Studies like many of those contained in Laver and Hutcheson (1973) may in the future be able to tell us more about what exactly leads speakers to modify their speech and adopt the linguistic characteristics of those they are interacting with, and what role this plays in linguistic change.) Brown and Moore (1971) write:

Hägerstrand posits that the destination of personal messages depends upon the sender's network of inter-personal contacts and that the configuration of this network is primarily dependent on the presence of various barriers. Attention is focussed upon terrestrial barriers, which impede communication, such as lakes, forests, difficult terrain, and the geographical distance separating two potential communicants (the latter is termed *the neighbourhood effect*). However, since the work of Karlsson (1958) and Duncan (1957) suggests that social barriers are functionally similar to terrestrial barriers, it is not unreasonable to consider social barriers as a part of the conceptual model.

Diffusion patterns are also mediated through a system of urban centres (*central places* – see Christaller, 1950) in any given area, 'where diffusion is primarily dependent on individuals in one central place communicating with those in another', which is the kind of phenomenon we have already seen illustrated in map 3.3. A time dimension can also be added to those studies by comparing maps of the same area at different points of time. A comparison, for example, of map 3.4 with map 3.5 is very revealing in this respect. The innovation can be seen spreading from a centre to surrounding areas, and then jumping to other members of the central place hierarchy at a greater distance (as also in map 3.3). In linguistic studies the time dimension can be added by investigations in *apparent time* of the type carried out by Labov (1966a).

Now, it is only right to concede that dialect geographers have of course been able to explain some linguistic phenomena in the same kind of way as geographers. It has sometimes been possible to show that isoglosses correlate with terrestrial or political barriers. And central places have been recognized in dialect theory as the source of *focal areas* (see Moser, 1954). However, although dialectologists have often been able to point to *where* certain innovations have *started*, they have not always been able to explain why these particular innovations, rather than those originating elsewhere, have been successful, nor why these innovations have *stopped* where they have. The exact location of isoglosses, and their exact configuration, is often unexplained. Geographers, on the other hand, have developed techniques for the fuller and more accurate description of the spatial distribution of phenomena which are of considerable value in achieving an understanding of diffusion processes, and which may be of some significance for linguists (see Brown, 1968, for references). However, we have also to concede that there may be important differences between technical innovations (like motor-cars) and linguistic innovations

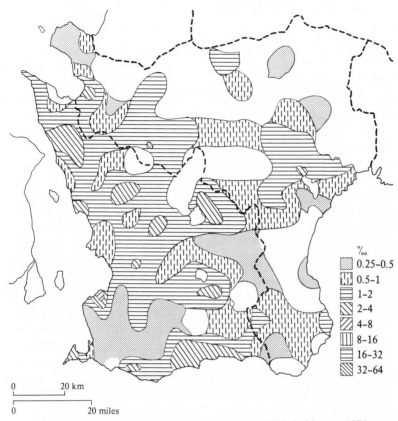

%o
0.25–0.5
0.5–1
1–2
2–4
4–8
8–16
16–32
32–64

0   20 km

0   20 miles

MAP 3.5   Southern Sweden: motor-cars per 1,000 inhabitants, 1970

which mean that the approaches cannot be identical in both cases. Linguistic change is a much more subconscious process, usually, than the adoption of a technical innovation, and is as yet very badly understood. It is also much harder to explain how and why linguistic innovations begin in the first place. This means that the linguistic geographer may be presented with rather more difficulties than the social geographer. But does it also mean that linguistic descriptions of this type are not possible? We report now on research carried out in conjunction with Arne Kjell Foldvik of the University of Trondheim into linguistic change in Norwegian. This work suggests, as does Jernudd and Willingsson (1968), that difficulties of this type should not prove to be an obstacle to obtaining full descriptions of linguistic data similar to those exemplified in the work of Hägerstrand.

3   DESCRIPTION – THE NORWEGIAN STUDY

Our Norwegian research was carried out in Brunlanes, a small rural peninsula near Larvik on the south coast of Norway (see map 3.3). It is an ideal area for the study of the diffusion of linguistic innovations: it is cut off on the west, south and east by the sea, while the northern area is for the most part uninhabited and without roads. Brunlanes is dominated by Larvik, a town of about 10,000 inhabitants, at its north-eastern corner, and all (or nearly all) land communications from Brunlanes lie through this town. Stavern, a town of 2,000 people, stands at its south-eastern corner, and two villages, Nevlunghamn (locally Hamna, 'the harbour'), and Helgeroa, at the south-west and north-west corners respectively. There were at the time of the study two metalled roads from Larvik towards Nevlunghamn, one direct and one, not yet completely metalled, via Stavern along the south coast. Apart from the two villages, the population of Brunlanes is distributed in farmsteads relatively evenly scattered across the countryside.

We were particularly concerned with linguistic change in this area, and especially with the diffusion of non-standard Larvik speech into the surrounding rural areas. One development of this type involves a phonetic change in the vowel /æ/. Eastern varieties of Norwegian have a basically nine vowel system, all of which occur short and long.

$$/y/ \quad /i/ \quad /ʉ/ \quad /u/$$
$$/ø/ \quad /e/ \qquad /o/$$
$$/æ/ \qquad /ɑ/$$

There are, in addition, three common diphthongs: /æi/, /æʉ/, and /øy/. The status of /æ/ is rather marginal compared to that of other elements in the system since in most cases it can be regarded as a realization of underlying //e// before //r// where no morpheme boundary intervenes (see Fretheim, 1970). It is, however, involved in surface contrasts in the accents under investigation here, and phonetic change of /æ/ appears to be closely linked, as a related change in phonetic space, to a similar change of /ɑ/. In much of the south-east of Norway, particularly in the Oslo area, back variants of /ɑ/ appear to be on the increase and to co-occur with lower and backer variants of /æ/. Popperwell (1963) gives [æ] and [ɑ] as typical educated Oslo pronunciations of /æ/ and /ɑ/, but the anti-clockwise movement of vowels that has affected Norwegian and Swedish accents for a considerable period of time appears still to be under way in the case of these two vowels, and preliminary research in Brunlanes showed that while older speakers tended to have [ɛ] as a realization of /æ/, younger speakers were more likely to have [æ] or even [a].

In Brunlanes, /æ/ occurs, as in educated Oslo speech, in:

(a) items with //e// + //r//
    her/hær/'here'
(b) reduced forms of pronouns with /æi/
    jeg/jæi/ > /jæ/'I'
(c) a few other items
    dæven/dæːvn/'the devil'

It also occurs in:

(d) items with //e// + //l//
    or //e// + //rd//
    where //l// and //rd// are realized as /ʈ/ (the so-called 'thick l') *ferdig* /fæːʈi/'finished'
(e) items which have /æʉ/ in educated Oslo pronunciation, which tend to have /æv/ in Brunlanes
    sau/sæv/'sheep'

(It would probably also be legitimate to consider the first elements of the diphthongs /æi/ and /æʉ/, where it does occur, as examples of /æ/, since they too appear to be involved in the same phonetic change. For the moment, however, these have been excluded.)

(f) plurals of masculine nouns, and certain other items with *-er* endings.
    gutt/gʉtt/'boy'
    gutter/gʉttær/'boys'
    cf. educated Oslo/gʉtter/

We examined only instances of stressed /æ/, so the majority of examples come under headings (a) and (d). Other things being equal, (d) variants tend to be more open than (a) variants. This was not taken into consideration in our calculations since we analysed a sufficiently high number of vowels for any skewing effect to be cancelled out.

We believe we have sufficient information from this study to suggest, albeit somewhat modestly, that it *is* possible to use techniques similar to those used by geographers for the description of linguistic data. An added bonus is that these techniques, together with the use of the linguistic variable, provide a very useful way of dealing with linguistically and geographically gradient phenomena. (Traditional dialectological techniques to permit the cartographical representation of isoglosses separating, say, *pail* areas from *bucket* areas. It is an altogether different matter, however, to portray a gradual phonetic change from [ɛ] to [a]. Moreover, once we have developed techniques for handling geographically gradient phenomena of this type, we can then be more honest about lexical differences such as *pail* and *bucket* and recognize that even in cases like this the transition from one area to another is usually a gradual one, and that in any case the difference between the two areas is more-or-less rather than either-or – the result of dynamic linguistic, social and geographical processes that should, where possible, be described in a more dynamic manner.)

The methodology adopted in Brunlanes was, first of all, to cover the area under investigation with a hexagon grid (see map 3.6), and then randomly to select one named locality in each cell and record some of the population at each locality. (There is little point in constructing a random sample for the linguistic study of farmstead clusters.) Interviews were carried out in the form of tape-recorded unstructured small group interaction sessions. These were mostly in fact small spontaneous coffee parties, and in nearly all cases casual speech, as characterized by Labov (1966a), was obtained throughout. Analysis was carried out on the speech of almost 40 informants, and several thousand examples of /æ/ were recorded. Informants are of both sexes. Social class was not taken into consideration, but the informants form a relatively homogeneous group, most of them being from farming families.

In our study of the geographical distribution of variants of /æ/ we set up (æ) as a linguistic variable, in the manner of Labov

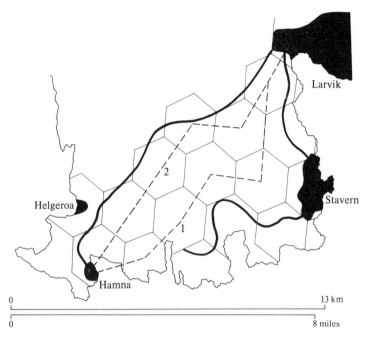

MAP 3.6   Brunlanes – hexagonal grid and west–east profiles

(1966a), with the following value scale:

$$(\text{æ}) - 1 = [\varepsilon]$$
$$(\text{æ}) - 2 = [\varepsilon\tau]$$
$$(\text{æ}) - 3 = [\text{æ}]$$
$$(\text{æ}) - 4 = [\text{æ}_1^{\llcorner}]$$
$$(\text{æ}) - 5 = [a_1^{\llcorner}]$$

Indices are calculated in such a way as to give scores of 000 for consistent (æ)–1 usage, 400 for consistent (æ)–5. It is then possible to calculate individual scores for (æ) for each informant, and then work out average scores for each cell, much as Labov and others have done for social class (and other) cells. Figure 3.1 gives the scores for many of the cells investigated: the profiles correspond to the two dotted lines shown on map 3.6. (Scores for Larvik have also been included for the sake of comparison, although these are based on tape-recordings of 'anonymous observations' (Labov, 1972c) in the town and on interviews with people known to us rather than with a sample of informants. The scores are supported

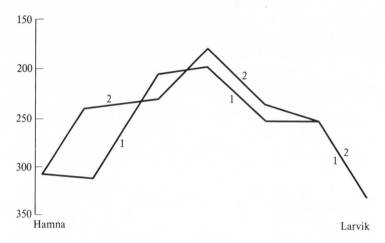

FIGURE 3.1   Brunlanes – west–east profiles, average (æ) scores

by descriptions provided by Steinsholt, 1964, 1972.)[4] Figure 3.1
suggests very strongly that, if a linguistic change is taking place in
Brunlanes, it takes the form of influence from Larvik, where the
average pronunciation seems to be around [æ̗], spreading to
neighbouring areas (the neighbourhood effect), but also jumping
to Nevlunghamn, from where in turn open vowels are spreading
out into the surrounding areas. (Nevlunghamn is no more than a
village (pop. 450) by, say, English standards, but it lies at the end
of the main road from Larvik, and is important as a harbour and
a boating centre. In Brunlanes it is a *central place*.)

We suspect, then, that a linguistic change is taking place in
Brunlanes in the case of the vowel (æ). We can confirm that this is
indeed the case by making a study of the pronunciation of this
vowel in apparent time. The way we propose to present the data
from this study is, as suggested above, to construct maps like
those presented by Hägerstrand and other geographers – such as
maps 3.4 and 3.5 – which we suggested were what dialect maps
ought to look like. Inevitably, in view of the fact that we have so
far investigated only one phonetic feature in a rather small area,
our maps are more suggestive than anything else. Their main

---

[4] Steinholt's two books, *Dialect conflict in Hedrum* and *Dialect conflict in Hedrum 30 years after*,
provide an excellent and unusual example of a study of linguistic change in real time. His research plots
the progress of Larvik dialect forms into the countryside to the north-east of the town during the period
from the 1930s to the present.

purpose is to demonstrate that this kind of work with linguistic data is both possible and desirable. The method recognizes that we are dealing, as with most linguistic features, with language as a dynamic phenomenon. We are dealing here with temporal, geographical, social and linguistic continua and, as Hägerstrand has said, 'the spatial diffusion of ratios'. Basically the method is very simple. (For refinements and complications see Robinson and Sale, 1969, chapter 7.) We have considered the (æ) index score for the locality sampled in each hexagonal cell to represent the hexagon as a whole, and selected one point in each hexagon – in this case the central point – to stand for each cell. The drawing of isoglosses then takes the form of interpolating lines (in the manner of contours) between the central points of the hexagons at distances appropriate to the average index scores of their cells. (If points x and y are mid-points of cells with average (æ) scores of, respectively, 180 and 240, and the mid-points are 60 mm apart on the map, then the (æ) 200 or (æ)–3 isogloss will pass between them at a point which is 20 mm from x and 40 mm from y.) Map 3.7

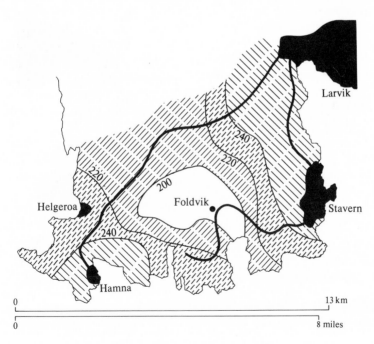

MAP 3.7   Brunlanes (æ), speakers aged 70 or more

shows a map constructed in this way for older Brunlanes speakers, with three 'isoglosses' or contours enclosing areas with average (æ) index scores equal to or less than, respectively, 200, 220 and 240. There is a central area marked off by the (æ) 200 isogloss, where the pronunciation of (æ) amongst this age-group is on average [æ] or closer. To the west and east are areas where the vowel is more open, and in the immediate neighbourhood of Nevlunghamn, Stavern and Larvik the average pronunciation can be seen to be between [æ] and [æ̞]. Map 3.8 gives similar information for middle-aged speakers, and map 3.9 for younger speakers. These three maps, when viewed together, provide a demonstration in apparent time of the linguistic change of this vowel, and show that this is a useful method of portraying cartographically linguistically gradient phenomena. They also illustrate very clearly the form that the spatial diffusion of this particular linguistic innovation is taking: more open vowels are spreading outwards from Larvik, Stavern and Nevlunghamn with younger speakers in these areas

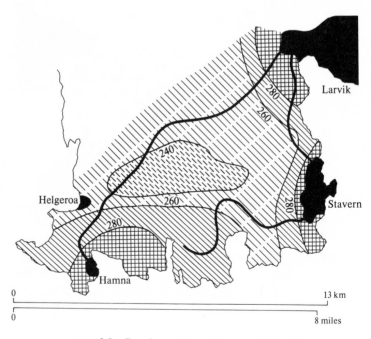

MAP 3.8   Brunlanes (æ), speakers aged 25–69

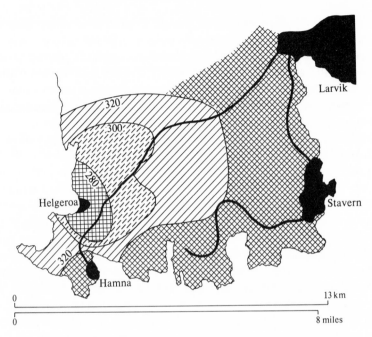

MAP 3.9   Brunlanes (æ), speakers aged 24 or less

having a pronunciation more open than [æ̞] and approaching [a̠]. These maps also tell us something else, however. They show that the central more isolated and conservative area with closer vowels in map 3.7 is displaced westwards in maps 3.8 and 3.9 so that, in the case of younger speakers, it is the Helgeroa area which is most resistant to the innovation. It can also be seen, in map 3.9, that Nevlunghamn, while itself still receptive to innovation, has much less influence on its surrounding areas than at earlier periods. The influence of Larvik and Stavern appears to be correspondingly greater. We can guess that these different patterns are due to changes in the Brunlanes transport situation in the lifetime of the present community, and to increasing centralization in education and other spheres. Sea transport has declined in importance since the development of the motor car and metalled roads, and Nevlunghamn has therefore declined in influence and in its contacts with Larvik. We shall discuss this point further in section 5, below.

Maps 3.7–3.9, then, represent our description of this one feature of Brunlanes Norwegian. It is incomplete in some respects, but we feel able to suggest that it is in many ways superior to traditional dialect maps. It is also, to return to the second main theme of this chapter, a form of description which provides much more readily for explanations. We see illustrated very clearly, for example, the jumping of the innovation from one central place to another, and the subsequent operation of the neighbourhood effect which was also portrayed, although less clearly, in map 3.3.

4   EXPLANATION IN GEOGRAPHY, AND THE EAST ANGLIAN STUDY

There are good reasons for arguing that linguists can learn from geographers, not only how to improve their descriptions in the manner just described, but also how to improve their explanations. Hägerstrand's later work has been concerned with a study of the diffusion processes which explain the spatial patterns of particular phenomena that have already been described. Hägerstrand (1967a) has said that:

the spatial order in the adoption of innovations is very often so striking that it is tempting to try to create theoretical models which simulate the process and eventually make certain predictions achievable.

He and others have been attempting to develop models of spatial diffusion processes in order to acquire an understanding of the forces behind the spread of various phenomena in space. I want to suggest that, if dialectologists adopt the descriptive methods of geographers and sociolinguists, as we have attempted in Brunlanes, they may then be a position to attempt to develop a similar geographical diffusion model for language. Together with Afendras (1969, 1970a, 1970b) and Jernudd (1968, unpublished) I believe this to be a desirable objective. The long-term aim would be to develop a model that would help us discover what factors are involved in the diffusion of linguistic innovations, and what is their relative importance: why exactly, for instance, has the diffusion of (æ)–4 and (æ)–5 from Larvik taken the precise form shown in maps 3.7–3.9 – why is Nevlunghamn a centre of innovation diffusion, but not Helgeroa? Even if this should eventually prove to be too difficult a task, the exercise will have been very fruitful. Only by constructing a model and then discovering where its predictions do not fit with the known facts will we be able to find out what factors are involved, and what is the relative significance of, say, different barriers. It is important to attempt this since at the moment we do not understand exactly what leads speakers to adopt or reject linguistic changes.

I am not, I must stress, able to make anything other than suggestions as to the form this model should eventually take. I want, however, to attempt to give some indication of the way in which a geographical diffusion model for language may be useful if dialectology is to provide more satisfactory explanations. We can take, as a first example, the *gravity model*, a simple model which geographers have borrowed from the physical sciences in order to investigate the interaction of two centres (as in studies of migration, for example). We can investigate the ways in which this model is and is not adequate for our purposes and, in so doing, provide some indication of the sort of steps that might be possible with a more satisfactory model.

In this section we shall first discuss gravity models with reference to empirical linguistic research carried out into the English spoken in East Anglia, since this region is in many ways less complex than the Brunlanes region of Norway. Then we will attempt, in section 5, to apply the particular model we select to an explanation of the Norwegian data we discussed in section 3, above.

Suppose, first of all, we take as a phenomenon that we wish to explain: why do linguistic innovations spread to centre *a* from centre *b* and not from centre *c*? For example, a number of linguistic innovations now appearing in the English of Norwich, in East Anglia, appear to originate in London speech (see Trudgill, 1974). Many younger speakers, for instance, now lack the distinctions /f/:/θ/, and /v/:/ð/, a well-known London phenomenon. The first thing we might like to explain here, because it appears to be relatively simple, is *why do linguistic innovations spread to Norwich from London* (and not, it seems, from anywhere else)? Now it is quite simple using the parameters of *population* and *distance* to develop a gravity model formula to calculate the strength of the influence of London on Norwich relative to that of other centres. We can begin with a rather simple formula sometimes employed by geographers (see Olsson, 1965 and Haggett, 1965:35, for further discussion and treatment of – often serious – problems):

Eq. 1: $\quad M{ij} = \dfrac{PiPj}{(dij)^2}$

M = interaction

P = population

d = distance

This is to be interpreted as a statement to the effect that the interaction (M) of a centre i and a centre j can be expressed as the population of i multiplied by the population of j divided by the square of the distance between them. If we take population in thousands and distances in miles, this gives us an index score for the interaction of London and Norwich as follows:

$$M \cdot \text{London} \cdot \text{Norwich} = \frac{8,000 \times 120}{(110)^2} = 080 \text{ approx.}$$

(The figure 080 here is, of course, purely an index score. Geographical studies are more usually concerned with producing real number answers, e.g. the number of persons migrating annually from one centre to another.) A similar calculation for Birmingham (England's second largest city) and Norwich, on the other hand, gives an index of 006. This might suggest, therefore, that the linguistic influence of London on Norwich is about 13 times greater than that of Birmingham. This, however, is a serious distortion of the facts: very few, if any, linguistic innovations spread to Norwich from Birmingham. There are two reasons why the index scores are misleading in this way. First we have not taken the communications network or terrestrial barriers (if any) into consideration. (These factors also appear to be important in explaining the differential behaviour of Nevlunghamn and Helgeroa in Brunlanes – see below.) Secondly, there is an important respect in which the diffusion of linguistic features differs from that of other innovations. In the case of language, we have to deal with particular resistance factors that are not met with in other fields. One such factor stems from the fact that it appears to be psychologically and linguistically easiest to adopt linguistic features from those dialects or accents that most closely resemble one's own, largely, we can assume, because the adjustments that have to be made are smaller. We must therefore attempt to take into consideration a factor we can label *prior-existing linguistic similarity*. This is not necessarily a function of distance: Norwich English is probably more like that of Canterbury than that of Peterborough, for example, although this is a difficult thing to measure. We shall therefore modify equation 1 to read:

$$\text{Eq. 2:} \quad Mij = s. \frac{PiPj}{(dij)^2}$$

where s is a variable expressing linguistic similarity. For Norwich phonology one might suggest a set of values something like the following:

$s = 4$ for other Norfolk varieties
3 for other East Anglian varieties
2 for other south-eastern varieties
1 for other varieties in England
0 for all others.

Already, then, by attempting to develop an explicit model of geographical diffusion, we have discovered (or, rather, been encouraged to consider), by reason of inadequacies in our initial formulation, the importance of an additional variable.

The formula must also be modified for another reason. At the moment it is an expression of the *interaction* of two centres. What we are interested in, however, is obtaining a measure of the *influence* of one centre on another. If we assume that interaction consists of influence in each direction proportional to population size, we can amend the formula as follows:

$$\text{Eq. 3:} \quad Iij = s \cdot \frac{PiPj}{(dij)^2} \cdot \frac{Pi}{Pi + Pj} \qquad \begin{array}{l} I = \text{influence} \\ Iij = \text{influence of } i \text{ on } j \end{array}$$

This yields indices of linguistic influence on Norwich as follows:

London 156
Birmingham 005

This appears to be a much more satisfactory expression of the relative linguistic influence of the two centres, since it seems that nearly all features new to Norwich English are also found in London speech.

There is, however, a more important respect in which our simple formula, even when combined with measures referring to barriers and the communications network, is seriously deficient. At the moment it will only operate correctly, in the explanation of the geographical distribution of linguistic features, for large isolated centres such as Norwich. We can exemplify this in the following way. In some respects Norwich English more closely resembles London English than it does that of the areas surrounding Norwich. Rural East Anglia, for example, is an 'h-pronouncing' region. Working class Norwich speech, on the other hand, is h-less. H-deletion, as an innovation, has jumped, as it were, from London to Norwich, while leaving the intervening areas unaffected. Equation 3 does predict this, but it fails to predict satisfactorily the order in which other, smaller East Anglian centres acquire this London-based innovation. We must therefore adapt the formula in some way to permit the inclusion of the competing pressures of different centres. We want, that is, to account for the failure of certain towns to adopt, as yet, h-lessness, in terms of competition between the influence of London and *earlier* Norwich speech. This will apply in principle to all of those of the urban centres in the area which are smaller in population than Norwich. For example, we have seen that Norwich receives significant linguistic pressure from London. Lowestoft (see map 3.1), on the other hand, will be influenced both by Norwich and London speech. In terms of our formula, equation 3, the influence of London on Lowestoft has an index of 060, while the influence of Norwich on Lowestoft is 025. Indices for the influence of the other main Norfolk centres, Yarmouth and King's Lynn, on Lowestoft are 050 and 001 respectively. This gives a combined Norfolk total of 076, which of course is greater than that of the London influence index. Similar indices for King's Lynn are:

$$
\begin{aligned}
\text{London} - \text{King's Lynn} &= 048 \\
\text{Norwich} - \text{King's Lynn} &= 011 \\
\text{Yarmouth} - \text{King's Lynn} &= 050 \\
\text{Lowestoft} - \text{King's Lynn} &= 001 \\
\text{Total Norfolk index} &= 062
\end{aligned}
$$

The fact that the combined Norfolk influence indices are higher than those for London in both cases suggests that there was no chance of Lowestoft, King's Lynn or other urban centres in the

Norwich area becoming 'h-less' while Norwich was still h-pronouncing. Once working-class Norwich speech had become h-less, however, the theory would predict that it was only a matter of time before these centres became similarly h-less. (This last point is important, of course: we must also build a *time-lag* factor into our model. Norwich has in fact been h-less for the last 70

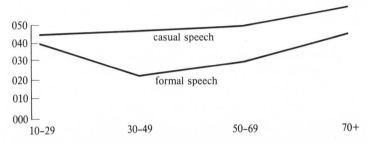

FIGURE 3.2   H-deletion in Norwich by age group and contextual style

years at least. Figure 3.2, after Trudgill (1974), shows that /h/ is not currently involved in linguistic change in Norwich – the pattern shown is typical of Norwich variables not subject to change.) Our theory would also predict that there would be a considerable period of time, while h-deletion was spreading from Norwich to the other centres, when the degree of h-deletion in these centres would be lower than that in Norwich. Research (see also chapter 4) into the speech of teenagers in Lowestoft and King's Lynn enables us to test this hypothesis by comparison with the initial Norwich data (Trudgill, 1974). In each case the sample consists of schoolchildren randomly selected from schools in the area in question. The results for h-deletion in four different contextual styles in each town are given in table 3·1 and figure 3.3. As predicted by equation 3, h-deletion is lower in King's Lynn than in Lowestoft. In both cases, moreover, it is lower than in Norwich. However, the Lowestoft formal speech and casual speech scores

TABLE 3·1   Percentage h-deletion in four contextual styles by teenagers

	Word lists	*Reading passage*	*Formal speech*	*Casual speech*
Norwich	006	022	050	061
Lowestoft	000	008	044	059
King's Lynn	000	005	022	031

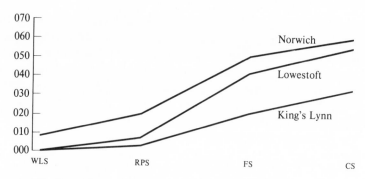

FIGURE 3.3 Percentage h-deletion by teenagers (WIS = word list style; RPS = reading passage style; FS = formal speech; CS = casual speech)

are only just lower than those for Norwich. This may simply be because sufficient time has now elapsed for h-deletion to have reached Norwich-type proportions in Lowestoft. On the other hand, it may be that we also have to take into consideration a factor we have so far ignored: Lowestoft is doubtless also subject to influence from Ipswich, which has a population roughly the same size as that of Norwich. The index of influences of Ipswich on Lowestoft is 005, very much lower than that of Norwich, but the point is that the influence of London and Ipswich *combined* (065), together with that of other towns in the area, may have outweighed that of the Norfolk centres – assuming, as seems reasonable, that Ipswich became h-less before Norwich did. It is clear, therefore, that our model needs to be considerably more complex than the simple formula of equation 3. We have to incorporate a measure of the *relative* strength of influence of different centres. We must subtract from the influence of one member of the central place hierarchy on another the influence of other members.

5   EXPLANATION – THE NORWEGIAN STUDY

We can now attempt to incorporate this relative-strength-of-influence factor into our study by applying the model as it has so far been developed to the Norwegian data illustrated in section 3. At earlier periods, it seems, sea traffic was in some respects more important in Brunlanes than road traffic. We will therefore apply the model developed above to produce indices of the linguistic influence of the centres Larvik, Stavern, Nevlunghamn and Helgeroa on each other using distances by sea (in kilometres). We will, in addition, compute scores for one of the farmsteads that we investigated, Foldvik, which lies in the central, conservative area of map 3.7. (Bearing in mind that sea traffic was presumably more important than land traffic because certain types of movement by land were relatively more difficult, we shall use d^3 rather than d^2 in our calculations of the land distances. This reflects the fact that, at earlier periods at least, the terrain was more difficult and the population less mobile in Brunlanes than in East Anglia.)

With s set at 1, the amended formula yields the indices of linguistic influence shown in table 3·2. This table makes it quite clear that, if the innovation of open (æ) vowels begins in Larvik, then the next place to be affected by this development will be Stavern. We can propose that, susequent to this, a chronological development will take place as follows. Larvik and Stavern now have open vowels, and their combined influences on the other centres will be as shown in table 3·3. (Computations are based on

TABLE 3·2   Indices of linguistic influence in Brunlanes; sea distances

| | Influence on: | | | | |
	Larvik	Stavern	Nevlunghamn	Helgeroa	Foldvik
Influence of:					
Larvik	—	10416	97	47	18
Stavern	2083	—	27	11	4
Nevlunghamn	5	7	—	16	0
Helgeroa	3	3	17	—	9
Foldvik	0	0	0	0	—

TABLE 3·3   Sea model – intermediate stages

	Influence of Larvik and Stavern	Subtract influence of other centres	Total
Influence on:			
Nevlunghamn	124	17	107
Helgeroa	58	16	42
Foldvik	22	0	22

TABLE 3·4   Sea model – final stages

	Influence of Larvik, Stavern and Nevlunghamn	Subtract influence of other centres	Total
Influence on:			
Helgeroa	74	0	74
Foldvik	22	0	22

the scores shown in table 3·2.) This demonstrates that Nev-lunghamn will acquire open vowels next. Table 3·4 indicates that Helgeroa will follow, with Foldvik last. In other words, the model predicts the following hierarchy for the diffusion of linguistic inno-vations in Brunlanes:

> Larvik
> Stavern
> Nevlunghamn
> Helgeroa
> Foldvik

This is precisely the picture illustrated in map 3.7. The model has, so far, been successful. But what of maps 3.8 and 3.9? In map 3.8 the order of the last three centres is

> Nevlunghamn
> Foldvik
> Helgeroa

and that in map 3.9:

> Foldvik
> Nevlunghamn
> Helgeroa

Foldvik, through time, is moving up the hierarchy relative to Helgeroa, and Nevlunghamn is moving down. How can we ex-plain this? The answer appears to lie in the switch in dominance from sea to land transport, with the advent of better roads and the motor car. (Earlier in this century Nevlunghamn and Helgeroa

TABLE 3·5 Indices of linguistic influence in Brunlanes; land distances

	Influence on:				
	Larvik	Stavern	Nevlunghamn	Helgeroa	Foldvik
Influence of:					
Larvik	—	772	14	30	18
Stavern	154	—	0	4	4
Nevlunghamn	1	0	—	20	1
Helgeroa	2	1	22	—	1
Foldvik	0	0	0	0	—

were important as harbours. This is not true today.) Table 3·5 gives index scores for linguistic influence in Brunlanes using land rather than sea distances, still employing d^3.

Once again it is clear that Stavern will be the first to be influenced by linguistic innovations spreading from Larvik. The next stage can be deduced from table 3·6. Here we can see that, this time, the third place to be influenced will not be Nevlunghamn, as with the sea model, but Foldvik. It is important to note that, although it is actually Helgeroa which has the highest score in the left-hand column in table 3·6, it is in fact Foldvik which receives most influence from Larvik and Stavern. This demonstrates the advantage of taking the competing influence of different centres into consideration. Table 3·7 shows, finally, that the next place to develop open vowels will be Helgeroa, with Nevlunghamn last.

We are now, therefore, in a position to present a comparison of predictions produced by the model with actual recorded data.

TABLE 3·6 Land model – intermediate stages

	Influence of Larvik and Stavern	Subtract influence of other centres	Total
Influence on:			
Nevlunghamn	14	22	0
Helgeroa	34	20	14
Foldvik	22	2	20

TABLE 3·7 Land model – final stages

	Influence of Larvik, Stavern and Foldvik	Subtract influence of other centres	Total
Influence on:			
Nevlunghamn	14	22	0
Helgeroa	34	20	14

This is done in table 3·8. This shows that map 3.7 coincides exactly with the predictions produced by the sea-distance model. Maps 3.8 and 3.9, on the other hand, appear to represent intermediate stages on the way to hierarchy predicted by the land-distance model. This last hierarchy continues the trend for Foldvik to rise and Nevlunghamn to fall, as a result of the change-over from the dominance of sea to the dominance of land traffic. We can therefore suggest that our linguistic diffusion model has been relatively successful in explaining the data concerning the diffusion of the linguistic innovation shown in maps 3.7–3.9. The model produces a perfect fit with the data obtained for the older speakers, and, while it does not coincide so exactly with scores for the younger informants, it appears to predict very accurately the change in the diffusion hierarchy which is currently taking place. Studies in a few years' time will be able to show whether Helgeroa has acquired, as predicted, more open vowels than Nevlunghamn.

TABLE 3·8 Linguistic diffusion hierarchies predicted by the model and illustrated in the maps

Model – sea distances	Map 3.7 older speakers	Map 3.8 middle-aged speakers	Map 3.9 younger speakers	Model – land distances
Larvik	Larvik	Larvik	Larvik	Larvik
Stavern	Stavern	Stavern	Stavern	Stavern
Nevlunghamn	Nevlunghamn	Nevlunghamn	Foldvik	Foldvik
Helgeroa	Helgeroa	Foldvik	Nevlunghamn	Helgeroa
Foldvik	Foldvik	Helgeroa	Helgeroa	Nevlunghamn

6 PROBLEMS AND CONCLUSION

There are many factors other than those we have discussed which an adequate model will need to incorporate. A measure of attitudinal factors, for instance, will clearly be required. If we are fully to understand the diffusion of linguistic changes we shall require to know the extent to which a feature has prestige or, as in the case of Norwegian (æ) or /h/ in East Anglia, covert prestige (Labov, 1966a: 108[5] – and see chapter 10). It is also important to know, not only the geographical location of origin of a linguistic innovation, but also which particular social group the innovation has arisen amongst. It may well be that uvular r, as an originally upper-class feature, has spread by means of mechanisms which do not apply in the case of working-class features such as /h/-deletion – it has certainly spread a lot further, and across language frontiers. In any case it seems likely that different processes might be involved at different social levels, because of different social interaction networks.

There are, too, other respects in which changes in language are rather more complex than the spread of technical innovations. Consider maps 3.2 and 3.3. Why should it be that uvular r is only partly standard in Dutch, while it is the usual standard pronunciation in French, German and Danish? One possible explanation is that we have to take the *linguistic system* into account as a resistance factor (dialectologists have long been aware of this type of resistance factor, of course). In Dutch there was already a uvular or velar fricative resembling the uvular r. Adoption of the innovation might therefore have led to a loss of phonological contrast, and resistance may therefore have been stronger than in other areas. (This does not imply that potential loss of phonological contrast *prevents* the adoption of [ʀ]. Clearly it does not, and in any case studies of sound change, notably those of Labov *et al.* (1972), have shown that preservation of phonological contrast is by no means the most important factor in the prevention or propagation of change. I simply wish to suggest that, other

[5] Attitudinal factors cannot be ignored. It may appear to be self-evident that linguistic innovations should spread outwards from a large metropolis such as London, until one remembers that many typically New York City forms appear to be confined to the city itself (Labov, 1966a: 499). This is clearly due to the fact that New York is, linguistically speaking, 'a great sink of negative prestige' (Labov, 1966a: 499).

things being equal, change may be slowed down by factors of this type.) Daan (personal communication) also reports at least one related instance of confusion, where *gril* 'caprice' was interpreted as *geel* 'yellow'. And a loss of contrast does appear to have occurred in certain Dutch accents.

Do geographical diffusion models have a useful future in linguistics? Map 3.10 shows one of the most important isoglosses in England. As far as I know, the location of the isogloss that

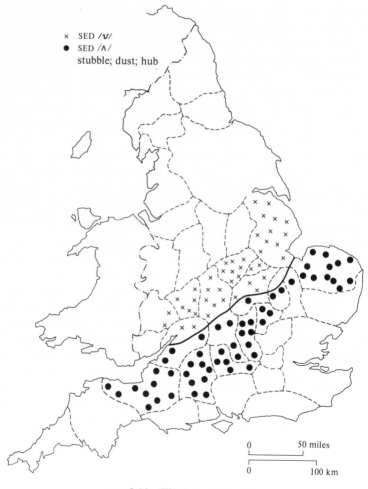

MAP 3.10   The /ʊ/ – /ʌ/ isogloss

separates those accents which have /ʊ/ in *butter, but,* etc., from those which do not has never been accounted for. If our model is to be of any value, it is precisely this kind of problem it needs to be able to handle. Why is this isogloss where it is? The first point to concede is that we are once again faced with a data problem. There are very many people north of this line who do not have /ʊ/ in these items, and we do not know who or where they are. We are also rather ignorant about the more important problem of where speakers have a phonological distinction between *cud* and *could* and where they do not (cf. chapter 2). Map 3.10 is valid only for broad phonetic descriptions of the most conservative rural speakers. But can a diffusion model explain even the distribution at this social level? A possible explanation is suggested by map 3.11. A comparison of maps 3.10 and 3.11 shows that the isogloss coincides to a large extent with the gap between the two most heavily urbanized areas of England. It also appears to be the case, from rough calculations, that the population of the areas of England north and south of this line are approximately equal. We can therefore perhaps explain the location of this isogloss, at this social level, in terms of the parameters of population and distance we used in the gravity model: we can explain it in terms of the balance of populations. This is as far as a London-based innovation could get before its progress petered out because the population 'behind it' would no longer support the distance.

A number of problems do arise with this explanation of course. Scottish accents also have the /ʌ/:/ʊ/ distinction that southern English accents have. Is this the result of a separate but almost identical innovation? Or did the London-based innovation jump to, say, Edinburgh, leaving the intervening Midlands and North unaffected? Or did the innovation perhaps start in Scotland? A second problem is that we require an explanation for why the /ʌ/:/ʊ/ isogloss has a very different configuration from the postvocalic /r/ isogloss of map 3.1. In terms of the model we have been discussing we are forced to say that either (a) the innovations began at different periods of time, when population distribution was different and distance a factor with a different kind of weighting because of different transport conditions; and/or (b) they began in different places; and/or (c) there are linguistic factors to take into consideration – perhaps the loss of /r/ in certain contexts is an entirely different phenomenon from the introduction into the

MAP 3.11 Urbanized areas in Britain (over 400 persons per square mile), 1951, from Dickinson (1967: 173)

system of a new phonological unit /ʌ/, and has different diffusion characteristics. Factors (a) and (b), at least, are probably valid. But, whatever the true explanation may prove to be, the main point is that our discussion of diffusion models, and of explanation generally, has meant that questions of this type are now being asked. In any case, if we can, however tentatively, explain one imperfectly plotted isogloss in this way, there is some hope of developing a more sophisticated model that will explain more sophisticated data.

In conclusion we can note, as Bailey (1971) has pointed out, that there has in the past several years been an increase in interest in language as a dynamic phenomenon. Wang and others (Wang, 1969; Chen and Hsieh, 1971), for example, produced work on lexical diffusion as a process, while Labov (1965, and elsewhere) dealt with some of the processes involved in the diffusion of linguistic innovations from one social class group to another. In both these cases, as Bailey (1973) argues, the time dimension is important. The geographical diffusion of linguistic features that we have been discussing in this chapter is the spatial counterpart to the other two types of process. Indeed, it constitutes both a reflection of these processes and proof that they take place. So far, however, even in 'wave theory' studies inspired by Schmidt (1872), linguists have generally been interested in the results of processes of this type rather than the processes themselves. A dynamic dialectology or geolinguistics making use of time-incorporating geographical diffusion models and sociolinguistic and geographical techniques that permit the handling of gradient phenomena, may be better able to describe and even explain some of the processes involved in the geographical diffusion of linguistic innovations.

CHAPTER 4

The Sociolinguistics and Geolinguistics of Vowel Mergers

Dialect contact in East Anglia

The loss of phonological contrasts through linguistic change is known to be rather common, and there are in particular many well-attested cases from many languages of loss of contrast through the merger of vowels that were formerly distinct.[1] In many of these cases, we have evidence from an earlier stage in the language when the vowels in question were distinguished, and we also have information on the later stage when the merger has been completed and what was formerly two (or more) vowels has now become one. Most often, however, we are not very well informed as to what went on in between, during the intervening period when the merger was being carried through. How exactly did the merger take place, and what exactly did speakers do while the merger was being completed? We are still, that is, rather ignorant about the actual mechanisms involved in vocalic mergers.

The same thing is also true of certain aspects of sound change in general. There has, for example, been a certain amount of controversy (see Postal, 1968; King, 1969, amongst others) as to whether sound change is best regarded as a gradual or a sudden process. The prevailing view today (see Labov *et al.*, 1972; King, 1975) would appear to be that sound change is essentially gradual. But it is legitimate to ask: if this is the case, what exactly is meant, in this context, by the term *gradual*? If speakers modify their language *gradually*, what exactly does this involve, and how exactly do they do it? In this chapter we shall attempt to begin to

---

[1] I am very grateful to J. K. Chambers for helpful comments on earlier versions of this chapter.

answer this question with reference to the problem of vocalic mergers using data from empirical sociolinguistic and geolinguistic research of various types.

If we examine the development of the English language, we can note (see Kurath, 1964) that the modern English vowel /ou/, as in *go, home*, has been involved in a vocalic merger and is the result of two different (main) sources in Middle English. The first is the monophthong ō [ɔː], as in *road, go*, while the second is the diphthong ou [ɔu], as in *flow, know*. (The distinction is still, of course, in most cases reflected in the orthography). Now if we are interested in what exactly happened while the merger that resulted in these two Middle English vowels becoming one was taking place, it is useful to note that there are some varieties of modern British English where the vowels are still distinct. For instance, in a study of the English spoken in Norwich (Trudgill, 1974) it was shown that speakers of this variety have a high back rounded vowel in items descended from the Middle English monophthongal forms: *road* /rʊud/; *go* /gʊu/, while items that had Middle English diphthongs have a wide diphthong of the type: *flow* /flʌu/; *know* /nʌu/ (see chapter 1). This means that there are minimal pairs such as the following:

/ʊu/	/ʌu/
moan	mown
rose	rows
sole	soul

(See also Wells, 1970.)

Further investigations have shown, however, that in many other parts of East Anglia, this vocalic contrast is now being lost; the two vowels are becoming merged. In this chapter we examine the mechanisms involved in this on-going vowel merger, and examine to what extent the description 'gradual' is an accurate one in this case. In doing this we shall draw on empirical studies of rural dialects carried out in Eastern England by Lowman (cf. Lowman

and Kurath, 1973) in the 1930s;[2] by the Survey of English Dialects, in the 1950s (see Orton and Tilling, 1969); and a study of
urban varieties carried out since 1974 (see Trudgill, n.d.).[3]

THE PROGRESS OF THE MERGER

Most of the evidence we have suggests that this East Anglian
merger has indeed so far taken place gradually. It has certainly,
for instance, been gradual geographically. Map 4.1 suggests that
the geographical progress of the vowel merger northwards and
eastwards from the London region is a genuinely gradual process.
South of line 1 on the map is an area where there is no trace at all
of the older distinction between *moan* and *mown*. Between line 1
and line 2 is an area where, in conservative rural dialects of the
1930s, the only trace of the distinction was the relic pronunciation
of one word, *go*, as /gʊu/. (Even today, some older speakers in
places as far south as Watford have /gʊu/.[4]) Between line 2 and
line 3 is a region where /ʊu/ occurred in several words of this type
in rural dialects in the 1930s but where by the 1950s it survived
only in *go*. Between lines 3 and 4, /ʊu/ appears in the 1950s rural
dialect records, as a relic pronunciation, in a number of words in
addition to *go*. (Even today /ʊu/ appears in *go* in a number of
urban centres in this area, such as Northampton.) And between
line 4 and line 5 the distinction survives, in the Survey of English
Dialects records, throughout the lexicon, but not consistently (see
below). Between lines 4 and 6, in the west, and lines 5 and 6 in the
east, the distinction is currently consistently preserved in rural
areas, but has suffered a marked loss in urban areas. And in the
region north of line 6, including Norwich, the distinction survives
today, even in urban areas, more or less consistently.

The change is also gradual socially. As table 4·1 shows, in the
East Anglian towns where the merger is not yet completed,
middle-class speakers are adopting the merger before working-
class speakers. The merger, we can say, is spreading from the
middle class downwards.

---

[2] Lowman's records were made available by R. I. McDavid Jr., to whom we are very grateful (see also
chapter 2).

[3] This research was financed by a grant from the SSRC, and field-work carried out by Tina Foxcroft.

[4] Recordings made by D. Sutcliffe.

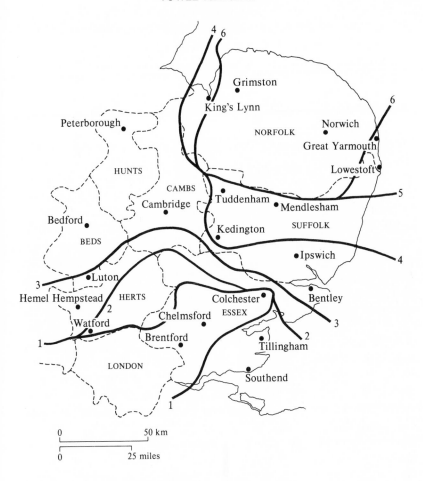

MAP 4.1   The East Anglian merger

It is also probable that the change is gradual stylistically, in that speakers adopt the merger in some stylistic contexts, and that it later spreads to others. In Norwich, as we have seen, the distinction is preserved more or less intact. But fig. 4.1 (from Trudgill, 1974) shows that, even here, some speakers use, on average, a smaller amount of phonetic distinction between the two lexical sets in more formal styles than in less formal styles.

TABLE 4·1   Degree of merger of /ʊu/ and /ʌu/

	Percentage informants		
	Merger consistent	Merger variable	No merger
Lowestoft (1975)			
middle class	30	40	30
working class	0	23	77
Great Yarmouth (1975)			
middle class	33	17	50
working class	0	40	60
King's Lynn (1975)			
middle class	33	20	47
working class	0	0	100
Norwich (1968)			
middle class	4	46	50
working class	0	0	100

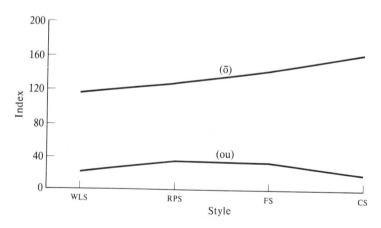

FIGURE 4.1   *moan* (ō) and *mown* (ou) in Norwich: lower middle class speakers (200 = [u]; o = [ʌu]; wLS = word list style; RPS = reading passage style; FS = formal speech; CS = casual speech)

STRATEGIES FOR VOWEL MERGERS

If we accept that this merger is taking place in a way that is in some sense gradual, we can then ask: how exactly does this happen? Two possibilities suggest themselves. First, speakers could employ what we might perhaps call the strategy of *transfer*. They could variably, and one by one, transfer lexical items from one lexical set to another. That is, they could begin, on occasions, to pronounce words such as *road* as /rʌud/ rather than /rʊud/, and gradually do this more and more often, and with more words.

Alternatively, speakers could employ a second tactic which we can call *approximation*. (Cf. the 'fudged lects' of chapter 2.) That is, they could gradually approximate the two vowels by bringing them closer together phonetically until, finally, they become identical. In the present case, this might involve the gradual lowering of the first element of the diphthong in words of *go* type, and/or the raising and rounding of the first element of the diphthong in words of the *low* type (see table 4·2).

TABLE 4·2   Transfer and approximation

Transfer:	road	/rʊud/ >	/rʌud/
Approximation:	road	[rʊud] >	[rɐud]
	rowed	[rʌud] >	[rɐud]

Transfer

If we examine the evidence, we see that quite a lot of it suggests that speakers actually adopt the first strategy. They transfer words from one lexical set to another, with different words being affected at different times. This process involves, that is to say, a form of lexical diffusion (and compare the 'mixed lects' of chapter 2).

Even in Norwich, which is in the centre of the geographical area which does not have the merger, at least one word has undergone this process. In the rural districts surrounding Norwich, the word *no* is pronounced /nʊu/ by many older speakers, especially when it is said emphatically. Norwich speakers, however, consistently pronounce *no* as /nʌu/ – except when it functions as an adverbial, in which case the /ʊu/ is retained. Thus we have:

/nʌu ðæs nʊu gʊd/
No, that's no good.

We can also note that throughout Norfolk all items which had Middle English ō in the context —/l/C as in *old, bolt, cold* now have /ʌu/ rather than /ʊu/. In some cases, that is, diffusion of the innovation may not be genuinely lexical but rather influenced by phonological conditioning. In other words, the change may also be *linguistically* gradual, in that it affects some environments before others (cf. Bickerton, 1975; Bailey, 1973). However, this change may well be of some antiquity (see Kurath, 1964) and cannot be relied upon as evidence here.

More convincing is the material provided by the Survey of English Dialects. Table 4·3 shows that, while Norfolk informants (Grimston – see map 4.1) have a clear contrast between the two lexical sets, and informants from southern Essex (Tillingham) have none, informants from geographically intermediate areas (Tuddenham and Bentley) have transferred some but not all of the /ʊu/ words to the /ʌu/ set.

TABLE 4·3   Transfer

	toad	*smoke*	*coal*	*oak*	*poker*	*own*	*grow*
Grimston	uː⊤	ʊ·⊤	ou̞	ou	ou	ɒu	ɒu
Tuddenham7ˑ	üː	üː	ʌʊ	ʌʊ	ʌʊ	ʌʊ	ʌʊ
Bentley	ɔʊ	ɔʊ	ʊu	ɔʊ	ʉuː	ɔʊ	ɔʊ
Tillingham	ʌʊ	ʌʊ	ʌʊ	ʌʊ	ʌʊ	ʌʊ	ʌʊ

(After the Survey of English Dialects)

Further illustrations of the strategy of transfer are provided by Milroy and Milroy (1978) for Belfast. They show that items such as *pull* and *took* alternate between /ʌ/ and /ʉ/, and that the lexical set involved in this alternation has diminished since the nineteenth century, certain words having been stabilized in the /ʉ/ set.

Transfer and diffusion

The strategy of transfer is a phenomenon which is well known to dialectologists. They observed early on that isoglosses for a particular phonological variant could be located at different points depending upon which lexical item was considered (see Bach, 1950). Thus, for example, the German /ɔks/ – /ɔs/ *Ochs* 'ox' isogloss does not follow the same line as that for /zɛks/ – /zɛs/ *sechs* 'six' or those for other similar items. Some dialects, that is, have transferred some lexical items but not others, and geographical differentiation of this type is simply the spatial reflection of lexical diffusion.

However, we also have to acknowledge that the probability is that speakers transfer items from one set to another spasmodically and irregularly. If this is so, then we can suppose that a dialect field-worker in Tuddenham or Bentley might, on some other occasion, have obtained examples of transfer in different or additional words. (This suggestion is supported by the occurrence, in the region currently under consideration, of the SED entries for Mendlesham, which has the word *toad* with both [ʌʊ] and [üː].) This also suggests that the bundling of isoglosses such as those for German *Ochs* and *sechs* may in some cases be an artifact of traditional dialect methodology. A more accurate picture might be of a consistent [-ks-] area and a consistent [-s-] area divided by a zone of variability within which speakers alternate between one pronunciation and the other (as illustrated in chapter 2).

Examples of supposed lexical diffusion must also, for the same reason, be treated with caution. If one were, for example, to attempt to draw an isogloss across England for northern /æ/ as opposed to southern /ɑː/ in items such as *after, past,* on the basis of SED material, then the location of this isogloss would depend very much on which word was examined. Lexical diffusion *may* be a factor here, but the variability may also simply be due to the pronunciation which the field-worker happened to elicit on the day. Indeed, observations of a relevant area of Lincolnshire[5] show that some speakers, at least, alternate between /æ/ and /ɑː/ in items of this sort, just as New York City speakers (Labov, 1966a) alternate between /r/ and zero in the set of *cart*, and Norwich

---

[5] Observations made by myself and J. K. Chambers.

speakers (Trudgill, 1974) alternate between /ʊu/ and /ʊu/ in the set of *boot*.

In any case, it is clear that transfer, no less than approximation, can be a gradual process.

Approximation

We have also to note that there is some evidence to suggest that the strategy of phonetic *approximation* is also often adopted. First, there are a few transcriptions in the rural dialect records which *may* represent intermediate articulations. One example is the notation used for the *low, know, snow* set in the SED locality Kedington, which alternates between [ʌʊ] and [ᴛoʊ].

Perhaps more significant than this, however, are the more detailed recordings made in Norwich. Here, 13 of the 60 informants recorded in 1968 produced some variability in their realizations of these two vowels. (These informants constitute the 46 per cent of middle-class informants shown in table 4·4.) One problem in dealing with realizations of this type is that the analyst is faced with what is in fact a phonetic continuum. The solution that was adopted in this case was to transcribe each instance as either definitely an example of East Anglian /ʌʊ/, definitely an example of East Anglian /ʊu/, or as something intermediate. Most often these intermediate vowels have as a first element a rounded vowel in the mid-central region resembling that of RP/ɵʊ/.

TABLE 4·4   Vowel approximation in Norwich

	Percentage vowels		
	/ʌu/	*Intermediate*	/ʊu/
4% middle-class informants:			
low class	0	100	0
go class	0	100	0
46% middle-class informants:			
low class	72	28	0
go class	1	52	47
50% middle-class informants + 100% working-class informants:			
low class	100	0	0
go class	0	0	100

Table 4·4 shows exactly what happened in the case of this group of speakers. (The other speakers, it can be seen, have either the received pronunciation (RP) no-contrast system, or the consistent East Anglian system.) The variable speakers have *no* transfer of /ʌu/ items to the /ʊu/ class. There is minimal (1 per cent) transfer of /ʊu/ items to the /ʌu/ class. The major strategy is that of approximation: a minority – 28 per cent – of /ʌu/ items have an intermediate vowel; and a majority of the /ʊu/ items (52 per cent) have an intermediate vowel.

Merger and approximation

If we accept that approximation, as in the case of these middle-class Norwich informants, can take place, we have also to consider the possibility that 'intermediate' does not necessarily mean *merged*: vowels may approach each other without actually becoming identical. In fact, some recent work of Labov and his associates (Labov, 1975; Nunberg, 1975) deals with a number of cases where precisely this has taken place – where, during the course of linguistic change, distinct vowels have become phonetically closer without actually merging. However, the most interesting point to emerge from this work is that it seems that, if the approximation is close enough, speakers will themselves perceive the vowels as identical *even when they are not*. This at first somewhat startling discovery has important implications for historical linguistics (see Labov, 1975). It may, for instance, provide an explanation for how lexical sets such as those of *meat* and *mate*, in earlier forms of English, appear on the basis of all the available evidence to have merged and then, at a later stage, to have split again. The suggestion is that they may have actually never merged at all. What happened was perhaps simply that the approximation became so close that speakers perceived – and therefore reported – the vowels as being identical. Since, however, they were *not* actually identical, the lexical sets remained distinct and were therefore able, later on, to diverge again.

We do not as yet have any data of this type for East Anglian /ʊu/ and /ʌu/, but a case of exactly the same type is provided by the apparent merger in Norwich of the vowels of the sets of *beer* and *bear*. All except the very oldest of Norwich informants report that these two vowels are identical (see Trudgill, 1974). Local dialect poetry also uses the two vowels as rhymes:

> Bor, ha' yew sin that marrer layin' by the pulpit stair?
> They reckon tha's the biggest we'a had in forta year!

and

> Ah, more'n once I'a stopped there jus' to hear
> Their lovely songs that fill the evenin' air.

and

> The Plough, o'course, stood out right clear;
> The Saven Sisters tew, were there;
> I see the Hunter artra Hare,
>   An plenty more
> Ole friends I'a know'd fer many a year,
>   An looked out for.   (Kett, 1975)

TABLE 4·5   /ɪə/ and /ɛə/ in Norwich

Informant	beer	bear
1 (age 92)	[bɪiʲə]	[bɛiʲɛ]
2 (age 67)	[be·ə]	[bɛ·ə]
3 (age 45)	[bę:]	[bɛ:]
4 (age 26)	[bę:]	[bę:]

However, as table 4·5 shows, it is only younger informants who have genuinely identical pronunciations.

There is also a further development which, on the face of it, is very surprising. This is that many, particularly teenage informants, actually have vowels in the set of *beer* which are more open than those of *bear*. That is, the two vowels appear to have passed each other in phonetic space. (Figure 4.2, from Trudgill (1974), also suggests the same development, but this is based on grouped and averaged index scores; 0 = [ɪə], 200 = ɛː]). It is not entirely clear how this development should be possible. It may be that, as in the cases reported by Labov, there are small phonetic differences between the two lexical sets which remain unnoticed not only by the native speakers who make them but also, in this case, by the analysing linguist. If this is so, then these differences (as the transcriptions given in table 4·5 suggest) must involve features other than tongue-height, such as secondary articulations or articulatory setting (see also Knowles (1978) on the inadequacy of some

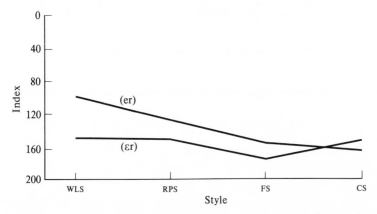

FIGURE 4.2   *beer* (er) and *bear* (ɛr) in Norwich: upper working class speakers

phonetic transcriptions for sociolinguistic work). Alternatively, it might be that speakers have been able to keep these vowels phonologically or physiologically distinct through 'knowledge' of pronunciations used by older speakers in the speech community or through stylistic alternations. Whatever the explanation, it is clear that approximation may be a complex kind of process, and that reports of mergers should be treated with caution.

EXPLANATIONS

In the case of East Anglian /ʌu/ and /ʊu/ we appear to have established that the two merger strategies – transfer and approximation – can both be adopted. In the northern part of East Anglia we find *approximation*, centering around an RP-like vowel [ɵu]. This results, in the case of some middle-class Norwich informants and some rural Suffolk speakers, in an indeterminate situation which, as we have just noted, must be treated with caution. The urban speech of Ipswich, however, appears (see table 4·6) to have achieved a more advanced, more stabilized situation than that of the more northerly city of Norwich. In Ipswich, an intermediate [ɵu]-type vowel is consistent in all items, except that phonological conditioning has led to [ʌu] occurring as an allophonic variant before /l/. The process of merger through approximation is here, that is, genuinely complete, suggesting that this is also a possible future development for Norwich.

TABLE 4·6   Working-class informants, 1975 survey

	road	rowed	roll
Norwich	[ʊu] = /ʊu/	[ʌu] = /ʌu/	[ʌu] = /ʌu/
Lowestoft	[ɵu] = /ʊu/	[ʌu] = /ʌu/	[ʌu] = /ʌu/
Ipswich	[ɵu] = /ou/	[ɵu] = /ou/	[ʌu] = /ou/
Colchester	[ʌu] = /ou/	[ʌu] = /ou/	[ʌu] = /ou/

In the southern part of East Anglia, on the other hand, items from the original /ʊu/ class are *transferred* to the /ʌʊ/ class, in some cases leaving behind a number of relic forms with /ʊu/. This gives /ʌu/ in most of the rural Essex dialects and in the urban dialect of Colchester.

Two final questions therefore remain to be answered. First: why, under approximation, is the vowel /ʊu/ affected much more than the vowel /ʌu/ (see table 4·4)? The answer may well be that, in southern England, the vowel [ʊu] is *conspicuous* in that it is phonetically very different from the vowels used by other speakers outside East Anglia in words of this set. The contrast between Norwich *boat* [bʊuʔ] and advanced London [bæɐ̈ʔ] is very marked and often noted by speakers from both areas. Attention, conscious or subconscious, is therefore directed more to this lexical set than to the other. (Norwich /ʌu/ is of course much closer to the London form.)

Secondly: why do some speakers adopt the strategy of transfer, and others approximation? One clue is provided by the fact that it is *middle*-class speakers from the *north* of the region who use approximation, and *working*-class speakers from the *south* who use transfer. This suggests rather strongly that the difference is the result of different targets. Speakers in the north of East Anglia are not directly exposed to or influenced by London speech a great deal, but middle-class speakers in this area are influenced by the prestige accent RP – which happens to use a vowel intermediate between the two East Anglian vowels. Speakers in the southern area, on the other hand, are exposed, through geographical proximity, to London speech, which in its less advanced forms has a vowel very like the /ʌu/ already found in East Anglia. Hence the strategy of transfer. This hypothesis is strengthened by data from King's Lynn. This town is on the periphery of linguistic East Anglia and also, crucially, has a large London overspill population. Table 4·7 shows that some speakers here adopt one strat-

TABLE 4·7   King's Lynn

	Informant				
	1	*2*	*3*	*4*	*5*
nose	[ʊu]	[ɵu]	[ɵu]	[ʊu]	[ʌu]
knows	[ʌu]	[ɵu]	[ʌu]	[ɵu]	[ʌu]

egy and some the other. Some speakers, we can assume, are taking RP as their model, while others are responding to the London model which , because of the overspill policy, they are also directly exposed to.

The suggestion is, then, that although the consequences of transfer and approximation may be phonological, the inital impetus, and the choice between the two strategies, may well often be phonetic in origin. What is involved, initially, is simply the imitation of particular pronunciations in individual words. Imitation, however, is not a helpful explanation for what takes place where mergers are not the result of external influence. What, for example, occurred in the first variety of English to merge the vowels of *go* and *low*? The Norwich merger of *beer* and *bear* (see table 4·5) cannot be ascribed to any external influence and, like similar developments described by Labov *et al.* (1972), is clearly taking place through approximation. It may be, then, that transfer takes place only where influence from external varieties is involved, that is, as a result of dialect contact.

But even the merger of *beer* and *bear* raises a further difficulty. Why does the approximation that is occurring in this case involve principally the lowering of the vowel of *beer* rather than the raising of that in *bear*? Labov's work suggests that there may be widespread or even universal tendencies of sound change, possibly articulatory or acoustic in origin, at work in developments of this kind. One of the strongest of his findings, however, is that tense vowels tend to become closer, lax vowels more open – which does not fit the present case. There may, alternatively, be explanations concerned with phonological space, phonological patterning, or articulatory setting. However, we have to concede that, in our present state of knowledge, when it comes to establishing exactly what factors are involved in changes of this type, we remain rather ignorant. (Or, as they may continue to say in parts of East Anglia for some time yet, we simply /dʊunt nʌu/.)

CHAPTER 5

Language Contact and Language Change

On the rise of the creoloid

In the previous chapter we examined the phenomenon of dialects in contact. In this and the following chapters we look at some aspects of the phenomenon of languages in contact.

At the 1972 Congress of Linguists, William Labov presented a paper entitled 'On the use of the present to explain the past' (Labov, 1975). Using the present to explain the linguistic past is obviously a very sound and useful principle, and indeed Labov's paper is a very exciting and important one. Clearly, if there are general tendencies at work in change in human language, we must expect that those tendencies we can reveal to be at work today must have been at work at earlier periods also, if only because we must assume that human beings are, in most important respects, approximately the same now as they were then. I want to suggest in this chapter, however, that the present is in some important respects obviously very different from the past, and that these differences may have linguistic consequences.

Before we can examine these consequences, however, it is necessary to consider the proposition that linguistic changes may come in two rather different types. Some forms of linguistic change may be relatively 'natural', in the sense that they are liable to occur in all linguistic systems, at all times, without external stimulus, because of the inherent nature of linguistic systems themselves – and it is here of course that the stability of the nature of human beings is relevant. Other types of linguistic change, on the other hand, may be relatively 'non-natural', in the sense that they take place mainly as the result of language contact. They are, that is, not due to the inherent nature of language systems, but to processes that take place in particular sociolinguistic situations.

102

It is certain, I think, that contact has an important explanatory role as far as *rate* of linguistic change is concerned. Other things being equal (and they are not always equal, of course – I am thinking in particular of attitudinal factors), we can suppose that varieties whose speakers have frequent contact with speakers of other varieties will change more than varieties whose speakers have infrequent external contact.

There are many well-known examples of this and it is of course a principle familiar to dialectologists and other students of spatial linguistics that geographically peripheral areas tend to be less innovating. If we compare related languages such as Faroese and Norwegian, we can note that in most (but not all) respects, Faroese is much more conservative than Norwegian. *Conservative*, of course, means that Norwegian and Faroese, having a common ancestor, differ because of linguistic changes that have taken place, most of them having taken place in Norwegian rather than in Faroese. And the Faroes, I think we can say, are a much more isolated place than Norway. Norwegian, in its turn, is relatively more conservative, in most (but not all) respects, than Danish. And non-standard varieties of English spoken in southern Scotland are certainly more conservative, in most respects, than those spoken in south-eastern England. Both Denmark and south-eastern England are closer to the European centre of things than, respectively, Norway and Scotland. And so on. (There are certainly also counter-examples, but as a general rule this principle seems fairly sound.)

But what of contact as an explanatory factor in an examination of *type* of linguistic change? (I am not thinking here of the more obvious types of borrowing and interference.) If the proposition that contact leads to 'non-natural' change is correct, then we would expect that in those cases where low-contact conservative varieties are *not* more conservative – that is, where they have undergone change which related but less conservative varieties have not – then these changes will tend to be of the 'natural' type.

This raises the problem of what 'natural' can mean in this case. If we accept that natural changes are those due to the inherent nature of language, then there would probably be agreement that sound changes of the type discussed by Martinet and by Labov, *et al.* (1972) as well as more obvious candidates like phonological assimilation, come into this category. If we then again compare

Norwegian and Faroese, we see that Faroese has undergone some changes that most varieties of Norwegian have not, and that one of these is indeed a diphthongization of long vowels of the type [aː] > [ɔə] which bears a very close resemblance to one of the sound-change types suggested as typical by Labov *et al.* Similarly, one of the few respects in which Norwegian is more innovating than Danish is in a chain shift of vowels, [ɔː] > [oː], [oː] > [uː], [uː] > [ʉː], [ʉː] > [yː], again of the type discussed by Martinet, and by Labov *et al.* (As far as grammatical change is concerned, one respect in which Norwegian has been more innovating than Danish is in the development of double marking of the definite article: *den store mannen* 'the big man-the', an interesting example of an increase in redundancy which we shall mention again shortly.)

Correspondingly, we would expect high-contact, innovating varieties of language to have undergone more 'non-natural' changes. If we examine how modern Norwegian differs from Faroese, we note the following: Faroese preserves three cases throughout the nominal system, while Norwegian has two cases in the pronominal system only; Faroese has a number of distinct verb conjugations, while Norwegian does not; Faroese has three different noun declensions for each of the three genders, while Norwegian has only one; Faroese has 11 different inflected verbal forms, while Norwegian has only 5 – and so on.

Now it is important for our thesis to argue that developments of this type are relatively 'non-natural'. Yet we have to recognize that some earlier linguists and philologists regarded this type of change as being perfectly and indeed particularly natural, and in some cases as an inevitable part of some kind of evolutionary process. The development of Norwegian, *vis-à-vis* Faroese, could be seen as part of a much wider pattern in which we observe that the most striking changes that have taken place, to varying degrees, in West European Indo-European languages (and elsewhere) involve a movement from relatively synthetic to relatively analytic structure. And this is true whether we compare modern German with Old High German, English with Old English, modern Romance with Latin, or modern continental Scandinavian with Old Norse. In all these instances, as is very well known, we find a reduction in cases and an increase in prepositional usage; reduction in conjugations, declensions and inflected forms; increase in periphrastic verb forms; more restrictions on word order; and so on.

Can such a widespread tendency genuinely be said to be 'non-natural'? Bailey and Maroldt, in an important paper, 'The French lineage of English' (1977), point out that changes of this sort are of the same type, although less extreme, that we know to occur under pidginization. Pidginization, of course, represents the language contact situation *par excellence*, and one where the move from synthetic to analytic is very clear indeed.

It is therefore legitimate to suggest that these changes are, in our sense, 'non-natural', and that it is, on the contrary, the movement from analytic to synthetic that can more convincingly be argued to be 'natural'. There are well-attested examples where for instance, the development of case-endings or of personal inflections on verbs can be shown to have arisen out of cliticization and morphologization processes which are probably initially phonetic in origin, and where 'ease of articulation' can be used as a, very natural, explanation. (We can also note that the development of post-clitics into fully-fledged case endings leads to an increase in redundancy – the marking of grammatical categories several times in the same noun phrase, for instance – similar to the Norwegian development of the double definite article mentioned above.)

There does therefore seem to be a *prima facie* case for accepting the proposition concerning 'natural' and 'non-natural' changes as worthy of examination. In low-contact situations we might expect: a slower rate of change; more 'natural' linguistic changes; a possible increase in redundancy; and even a possible move towards a more synthetic structure. In high-contact situations, on the other hand, we expect: a faster rate of change; more 'non-natural' changes; a reduction in redundancy; and a move towards a more analytic structure. (For further discussion, see Trudgill, forthcoming.)

Why exactly should this be? Why should sociolinguistic contact situations lead to the 'non-natural' type of change illustrated in the contrast between Faroese and Norwegian – and what exactly is 'non-natural' about it? Obviously, in many contexts, the process of levelling or koinéization plays an important role. Where varieties in contact are related and similar, they may retain what they have in common, and lose what is different. (Bailey and Maroldt point to contact between English and Scandinavian as a factor in changes in English grammatical structure.)

But it is also possible to argue that linguistic change of the synthetic to analytic type represents a clear case of simplification, and then go on to argue that surely simplification in language is a natural process. I think, however, that we have to point out that this is a rather particular form of simplification, and one which is particularly typical of contact situations. We have to ask, with reference to this form of simplification: *simplification for who?* Probably not simplification for the native speaker, or, in any serious way, for the young child. Rather it is simplification for the *adult non-native learner*. Hence the link between the imperfect learning by adults that takes place during pidginization, and the drive towards 'non-natural' changes of this particular simplification type that occurs in high-contact varieties of non-pidgin languages (see also chapter 6).

It is usual for laymen to claim that some languages are easier to learn than others. Linguists have tended to play down this suggestion, and to point out that it depends on what your point of departure is: Spanish is easier for an English speaker to learn than Chinese, but for a speaker of Thai it might be the other way round. However, I think it is legitimate to suggest that some languages actually are easier for adults to learn, in an absolute sense, than others. If one were given a month in which to learn a language of one's choice, I think one would select Norwegian rather than Faroese, Spanish rather than Latin, and Sranan rather than English. These are languages which, relatively speaking, have experienced more contact, and have undergone more changes of the 'non-natural' type.

We know that, during pidginization, restriction in function leads to linguistic reduction, and that contact leads to imperfect learning and hence to admixture and simplification. Under creolization, the reduction is 'repaired' by expansion, while the admixture and simplification remains, as in Sranan (unless decreolization takes place, as with Jamaican Creole). But other contact situations give similar results. We know of many creole-like varieties which demonstrate mixture and simplification but which have probably never been pidgins. A useful term for varieties of this type is *creoloid*, a term first used, I believe, by Loreto Todd, and John T. Platt. A good example is Afrikaans which, relative to Dutch – and it is important to note that this term is essentially relative – shows significant simplification and mixing.

Norwegian is, relative to Old Norse, also a creoloid. And Middle English, Bailey and Maroldt might want to argue, is a creoloid, relative to Old English.

Creoloids, then, are languages which show relatively large numbers of changes of the 'non-natural' type, as a result of linguistic contact, and which may be relatively easier, for this reason, for adults to learn. We have therefore to consider that the sort of linguistic situation which gives rise to the type of simplification most typical of creoloids may have been much more common in recent centuries than at earlier periods. Increased geographical mobility, and increased world population, have probably led to an increase in contact situations, and thus, perhaps, to an increase in non-natural changes and relatively more analytic linguistic structures. It is not entirely out of the question, that is, that, although for demographic and sociolinguistic rather than straightforward linguistic reasons, our philological forbears were right when they pointed to a kind of evolutionary trend in linguistic change.

CHAPTER 6

Language Contact in Greece

Reduction and simplification in the Albanian dialects of Attica and Biotia

It is not too widely known that a majority of villages in the Athens area of Greece are inhabited by people of Albanian rather than Greek ethnic origin.[1] These people are not recent immigrants, but the descendants of Albanians who entered the country at various times, for the most part between the eleventh and fifteenth centuries (see chapter 7). These Greek Albanians long retained a clearly separate ethnic identity, apparently, but gradually this identity has been eroded. Today they refer to themselves not as Albanians but as *Arvanites*, and call the language they speak not Albanian but *Arvanitika*. They are also very concerned to explain to outsiders that they are not only Arvanites but Greeks as well (see chapter 7). The result of this development is that the main, perhaps only, identifying characteristic of the Greek Albanians is now their language.

This chapter is based on work carried out in these Arvanitika-speaking villages[2] which was designed to investigate the nature and extent of Arvanitika language-maintenance, Greek interference in Arvanitika, and Greek–Arvanitika language switching (Trudgill and Tzavaras, 1975). One of the clearest findings to emerge from this study is that Arvanitika is, very probably, a dying language. Table 6.1, which is based on responses to a questionnaire administered to a sample of the population of almost all relevant villages in Attica and Biotia (see chapter 7),

[1] I am very grateful to F. R. Palmer, P. H. Matthews, Paul Fletcher, Michael Garman, Arthur Hughes, and George A. Tzavaras for their comments on earlier versions of this chapter.

[2] This work was financed by a grant from the SSRC. It was carried out by myself and George A. Tzavaras, a Research Assistant trained in linguistics and fluent in Greek, Arvanitika, and English (see chapter 7, fn. 1).

TABLE 6·1   Comprehension of Arvanitika

	age-group:						
	5–9	10–14	15–24	25–34	35–49	50–59	60+
Comprehension							
Not at all (%)	11	1	0	0	0	0	0
Some (%)	89	99	14	0	0	0	0
Quite well (%)	0	0	86	100	9	0	0
Very well (%)	0	0	0	0	91	100	100
	100	100	100	100	100	100	100
n =	123	241	239	224	276	298	302

Total informants: 1,703

shows very clearly the extent to which the ability to understand Arvanitika is diminishing in these communities. As self-reports, these responses are open to some doubt, but they are paralleled by the results of a translation test also administered to informants, and by many observations (for details, methodology and discussion, see Trudgill and Tzavaras, 1975 and chapter 7).

The dying out of a language in this way may have interesting linguistic consequences, and a study of its latter stages may be able to tell us something of value about certain aspects of linguistic change (see Dorian, 1973). Perhaps somewhat flippantly, I entitled an earlier version of this chapter 'creolization in reverse'. The sociolinguistic justification for this (we shall discusss below whether there are also linguistic justifications) is that the situation we are dealing with here involves the loss by a language of its native speakers, whereas creolization involves the 'acquisition of native speakers by a language' (Sankoff and Laberge, 1974).

REDUCTION AND SIMPLIFICATION

The processes of pidginization and creolization have been subject to considerable attention in recent years (see particularly Hymes, 1971), although actual studies of creolization and, especially, pidginization in progress are few and far between. All workers in the field, however, are agreed that both linguistic and sociolinguistic factors are at work in these processes, and that definitions of the terms have similarly to include parameters of both types. All writers on pidgins, for instance, recognize that they are mixed, reduced and simplified languages, *and* languages of restricted use.

Most linguists are also agreed that pidgins as languages are in some sense 'inadequate'. In the words of Labov (unpublished) 'pidgins do not provide all the features which native speakers seem to demand of a language'. (This is not a problem, of course, since pidgins, by definition, do not have native speakers.) But what exactly is meant by terms such as *reduction, simplification* (both very common in the pidgin and creole literature) and *inadequacy*? This is an important question, both from the point of view of our understanding of linguistic change, and because a few linguists appear to be prepared to suggest that the *inadequacy* of pidgins may carry over to their descendant creoles which, of course, do have native speakers (e.g. Craig, 1971; Whinnom, 1971). It is also the case that there is considerable confusion in the literature over the terms *reduction* and *simplification*, many writers using them interchangeably.

A first step to answering this question and to sorting out the confusion has been taken by Hymes (1971), who suggests a distinction between *reduction*, which refers to changes in inner form, and *simplification*, which should refer to outer form, as different types of *loss*. (*Reduction* can be characterized, in a preliminary way, as the actual loss of some part of a language, while *simplification* can be thought of as an increase in regularity.)

Whinnom (1971) makes a similar distinction between *impoverishment* (which is probably at least approximately equivalent to Hymes's *reduction*) and *simplification*, and isolates four defining criteria for a pidgin: *impoverishment, simplification, stability and unintelligibility*. Mühlhäusler (1974) shows how these features can be used in the typological classification of mixed languages of various kinds, after the manner of table 6.2.[3] (Note that pluses and minuses should ideally be replaced by numbers indicating differences of degree; that unintelligibility refers to mutual comprehension with the source language; and that Hymes's term *reduction* will be used, rather than *impoverishment*, throughout this book.)

Table 6.2 is of course inadequate in many ways and should be regarded as merely suggestive. It does suggest, however, that the

---

[3] See chapter 5 for the term *creoloid*.

TABLE 6·2 Typological Classification of Mixed Languages (after Mühlhäusler)

	Reduction	Simplifi-cation	Stability	Unintelli-gibility
Lingua-franca use	+	+	+	−
Pre-pidgin	+	+	−	−
Pidgin	+	+	+	+
Creole	−	+	+	+
Post-creole	−	+	−	−
Creoloid	−	+	+	−

distinction between reduction and simplification is a useful one. It also suggests that simplification takes place in cases where languages are learnt in contact situations by adults (although not only in these cases, of course), and that reduction is found only in the case of languages which have no native speakers and are of restricted use.

This chapter therefore addresses itself to the questions: Is the distinction between reduction and simplification a valid and clear-cut one? Is it possible for reduction to take place independently of simplification? (Table 6.2 gives no instances, but this would provide further evidence for a distinction between the two processes.) Can languages which have native speakers demonstrate reduction? (Table 6.2 again gives no instances, but cf. Craig, 1971, and Whinnom, 1971.) And are the suggested connnections between restriction and reduction, and between imperfect learning and simplification, legitimate?

Our initial hypothesis concerning Arvanitika, based on observations of it in use, is that it is subject both to restriction (it is increasingly replaced by Greek) and reduction, but not to simplification. The suggestion is, that is, that it is linguistically as well as socio-linguistically a case of 'creolization in reverse', since it demonstrates the features shown in table 6.3. (Arvanitika, like the

TABLE 6·3   Creolization in reverse

	Reduction	Simplifi-cation	Stability	Unintelli-gibility
Creoles	−	+	+	+
Arvanitika	+	−	−	−

Gaelic discussed by Dorian, is unstable, in that it is in a state of considerable flux, with no real norms for usage. Influence from Greek is considerable, and the language of younger speakers is rather radically different from that of older speakers. It remains, however, to a certain extent mutually intelligible with Albanian.[4])

We can therefore use data gathered in the Arvanitika speech community to test this hypothesis and to help in answering the questions we have just posed. If it is indeed true that Arvanitika, relative to Albanian, is reduced but not simplified, then we will be able to suggest that the distinction is a valid one, and that natively spoken languages can in some circumstances be subject to reduction. It might also be possible to link 'inadequacy' to reduction, and suggest that since, unlike pidgins, creoles are not reduced, they are not in any meaningful sense 'inadequate'. (Languages which do demonstrate reduction, such as Arvanitika, may on the other hand be relatively 'inadequate'. This again, however, would not constitute a problem for Arvanitika speakers. It would merely be a reflection of the fact that they are increasingly employing Greek.)

REDUCTION

Reduction can perhaps best be described as the 'actual loss of some part of the language – or more precisely a loss of some part of a component of the grammar without resulting complication of another component to make up for this loss' (Mühlhäusler, 1974). Mühlhäusler, in one of the fullest available discussions of simplification and reduction, suggests that the most obvious place where reduction can take place is in the vocabulary, but that phenomena such as the loss of optional permutation transformations and of surface case might perhaps also constitute reduction. Mühlhäusler also states that 'the question that is involved is what cannot be said in a pidgin, or at least not equally well'. This 'equally well' point is necessary, because skilful users of a pidgin are often able to compensate for its lack of resources through circumlocutions and constructions such as the probably apocryphal 'him fellow big box you fight him he cry' = *piano*. But it also presents a consider-

---

[4] There are difficulties, apparently, but a few of our informants listen to Albanian radio, and some related stories from the Second World War of co-operation between Arvanites in the Greek army and Albanians, against the Italians in Albania.

able problem, since it is very difficult, as we shall see below, to know exactly what 'well' can mean in a case like this.

Labov (unpublished) has shed some light on this problem, with particular reference to time and tense. He points out that tense is not obligatory in pidgins, whereas in many other languages it is obligatory and forms an important component in redundancy. This does not mean, however, that pidgins are unable to express time and temporal relations, since this can be done through the use of time adverbials. On the face of it, then, lack of tense might appear to be an example of simplification rather than reduction, since this does not constitute an example of something that 'cannot be said in a pidgin'. There are reasons, however, for arguing that this kind of phenomenon is genuinely an example of reduction. First, it can be claimed that temporal relations are much more *fully* specified through the combination of tense *and* temporal adverbials (see Crystal, 1966, for some of the more subtle aspects of temporal expression in English). Secondly, as Mühl-häusler has argued, the loss of 'alternative ways of saying the same thing' can quite properly be regarded as, at the very least, stylistic reduction. And, thirdly, Labov has pointed out that the obligatory expression of tense in non-pidgin languages is by means of morphs that in normal conversation are unstressed and subject to phonological reduction to differing degrees. According to Labov, therefore, 'there is no basis for arguing that tense markers express the concepts of temporal relations more clearly than adverbs of time' but 'the most important property which tense markers possess, which adverbs of time do not, is their stylistic flexibility'. (Labov cites evidence for this, in fact, only from English and English-based pidgins and creoles, but it is supported by Kay and Sankoff's (1974) suggestion that propositional qualifiers – such as negators and markers of time and aspect – are limited in their scope since they occur in surface structure in pidgins exterior to the propositions they qualify or not at all.) We can therefore suggest that, in addition to loss of vocabulary, loss of tense is also a candidate for the label of *reduction*.

SIMPLIFICATION

Simplification can be taken to refer to 'an increase in regularity' in a language (Mühlhäusler, 1974) and, like *reduction*, should be used only relatively, with reference to the source language. Drawing on earlier works on this topic, Mühlhäusler isolates two different aspects of simplification. The first aspect is an increase in morphophonemic regularity, including the loss of inflections and affixes and increase in invariable word forms. This parallels Ferguson's (1959) discussion of simplicity, where he lists: simpler morphophonemics; few obligatory categories marked by morphemes of concord; symmetrical paradigms; and strict concord and rection. The second aspect is an increase in the 'regular correspondence between content and expression'. This can refer to lexicalization, or lexical and morphological motivation or transparency (Ullmann, 1962). It is not, for example, unreasonable to regard Tok Pisin /hos man/ and /hos meri/ as simpler than English *stallion* and *mare*, or the opposition /planti/ – /no planti/ as simpler than the opposition *many* – *few* (cf. chapter 5).

A third possibility that we also have to reckon with is, as Mühlhäusler points out, that the loss of marked categories from a language, and their replacement by unmarked categories, should also perhaps be regarded as simplification. A phonological system with fewer marked elements, for example, might legitimately be regarded as more simple.

RESTRICTION IN ARVANITIKA

Our initial hypothesis, then, is that Arvanitika, since it has no history of being learnt by adults in a contact situation, will not demonstrate the features of simplification found in the case of pidgins and creoles. It will, on the other hand, have some features of reduction since, unlike creoles, it is now subject to increasing restriction in use.

Our evidence on the restriction in use of Arvanitika comes from two sources. First, observations we made over several months in the villages showed that there were clear age-group differences in the use of Greek and Arvanitika. Greek–Arvanitika bilingualism is now the norm for all age-groups, but there are many situations where older speakers employ Arvanitika and younger speakers Greek. The pattern appears to be that the oldest Arvanites use Arvanitika for most purposes except the most formal (and for communication with non-Arvanites). Middle-aged speakers and younger adults indulge in a considerable amount of switching according to factors such as formality, location, subject-matter, the presence of outsiders, and the linguistic ability of interlocutors. Many younger adults, though, will often use Arvanitika only if the situation is one that is particularly homely or informal, or if they are talking to elderly people who they know prefer conversing in Arvanitika (see chapter 7).

The second source of information on this topic comes from the responses to the questionnaire. A number of the questionnaire items have some relevance here, but perhaps the most helpful is the question: *which language do you find it easier to express yourself in?* This factor will clearly both influence and constitute a reflection of language use. Responses to this question, by age-group, are given in table 6.4, and suggest very strongly that Arvanitika is indeed subject to increasing restriction in use. They are, of course, once again merely self-reports, but they do tally very well both with our observations and with the figures given above in table 6.1.

TABLE 6·4   Language easier to express oneself in

	Percentage		
Age	Greek	Both	Arvanitika
5–9	100	0	0
10–14	100	0	0
15–24	94	6	0
25–34	95	4	1
35–49	18	73	8
50–59	0	93	7
60+	6	38	56

REDUCTION AND SIMPLIFICATION IN ARVANITIKA

Our approach now will be to discuss the linguistic consequences of this restriction in use, and of the contact situation generally, by examining some of the points at which Arvanitika appears to diverge significantly from modern Albanian. Many of these differences are fairly clearly due simply to interference from Greek, and

these will not be discussed here. Other differences are not so readily explicable, however, and we shall discuss whether those of
them that might be described as some form of *loss* can legitimately
be ascribed to reduction, to simplification, or to other factors.

1   As we have seen, the form of reduction most typical of
pidgins, and most easily recognized, is loss of vocabulary. As far
as it is possible to tell, there are many Albanian lexical items that
do not occur in Arvanitika, and certainly many that were un-
known to our informants. It is difficult, however, to argue that this
is a genuine case of reduction, since in nearly every case the corresponding Greek item was known and used by our informants in
speaking Arvanitika. It would, of course, be possible to claim that
reduction in Arvanitika has led to the necessity of adopting Greek
vocabulary. It is more reasonable, however, to recognise these
Greek items as loan-words that are now an integral part of Arvanitika. The Arvanitika lexicon, that is, has been subject to interference or substitution, but not to reduction.

2   This point becomes clearer if we compare the lexicon as a
whole with the situation to be found in the case of Arvanitika
relational words. The possession of a small number of prepositions and other relational words is a well-known characteristic of pidgins (see, for example, Clyne, 1968). When compared to
Albanian, the Arvanitika of younger speakers has undergone considerable reduction as far as items of this type are concerned. In
some cases, Albanian prepositions and other forms have simply
been replaced by the corresponding Greek forms, in which case we
have the same problems as in 1, above. In a number of other
cases, however, forms have apparently been lost altogether and
are replaced, not by Greek items, but by other Albanian forms of
similar meaning or function. The result is a loss of contrast. For
example:

	Albanian	*Arvanitika* (younger)
while	/jatə/	/kur/
when	/kur/	/kur/
about (adv. & prep.)	/rotuł/	/tor/
round (prep.)	/torə/	/tor/
near (adv. & prep.)	/pərcark/	/tor/

Developments such as these would appear to represent clear cases of reduction, since there are now distinctions that younger Arvanites cannot make, or at least do not make in Arvanitika.

3 Another relatively clear case of reduction is provided by the Arvanitika verbal system, at least if we accept the suggestion that the loss of tense is a form of reduction. Arvanitika has by no means lost tense altogether, but it has, especially in the case of younger speakers, lost tenses, and is clearly in the process of losing others. On the basis of analysis of spontaneous conversation, translation tasks from Greek, and direct questioning, we were able to establish that, while the compound verb forms of Albanian for the most part survive, the only other forms in full use are the present and past definite indicative. Our evaluation of the situation as a whole appears in table 6.5. Of the forms that remain in full use, only the present and past definite are inflected. (The present subjunctive is almost identical in form to the indicative.) The other fully used forms involve inflected forms of the verbs *to be* and *to have*, with past participles.

TABLE 6·5 The Arvanitika verbal system

	Indicative		Subjunctive		Conditional		Optative		Admirative	
	A	P	A	P	A	P	A	P	A	P
Present	U	U	U	U	M	M	L	L	L	L
Imperfect	M	M	M	M	—	—	—	—	L	L
Past definite	U	U	—	—	—	—	—	—	—	—
Perfect	U	U	U	S	U	S	L	L	L	L
Pluperfect	U	U	U	S	—	—	—	—	L	L
Future	U	U	—	—	—	—	—	—	—	—
Futurum exactum	U	S	—	—	—	—	—	—	—	—

A = active; U = in use; M = moribund; P = passive; S = some loss; L = lost.

In the case of the loss of the indicative forms, we can claim that we have a straightforward case of reduction. Most Arvanites now use past definite forms rather than the imperfect, and when complete loss has taken place, as it almost certainly will, Arvanitika will no longer be able to express the original distinction by means of tense. (This applies also to the loss of the imperfect subjunctive, which is in fact identical in form to the indicative.)

The other cases, however, are not so clear. What loss there is, for example, of the perfect and pluperfect subjunctive forms results in the use of the corresponding indicative. It could be argued that this is merely a form of simplification, since the alternation between subjunctive and indicative forms is mostly automatic and depends on the type of clause or conjunction involved. No contrast is lost, therefore. It does, moreover, involve the loss of a marked category.

However, there are in fact a number of cases where which mood is used is optional, for example in temporal clauses after conjunctions such as /posá/ *as soon as*. At the very least, then, we could consider this to be an example of stylistic reduction.

The three remaining moods present us with even greater difficulty. Clearly, something has been lost, or, in the case of the conditional, is being lost, from the language. But, just as clearly, this is not a question of something that 'cannot be said'. What Albanian expresses through the admirative mood,[5] Arvanitika deals with lexically, as do English and Greek. Optative mood is replaced by periphrastic forms based on the Greek model and employing the Greek impersonal form /makari/. Thus:

Albanian	*Arvanitika*	*Greek*	
/pifša/	/makari tə pi/	/makari na pjo/	*may I drink*
/pifšim/	/makari tə pimə/	/makari na pjiume/	*may we drink,*
			etc.

The conditional, too, is often replaced by periphrastic constructions employing /preps/ *it is necessary*, which is derived from the Greek impersonal form /prepi/. (The present conditional in Albanian is formed by prefixing the invariable form /do/ *will*, which is also used in the formation of the future, to the imperfect subjunctive: Albanian /do tə pija/; Arvanitika /do pii/. The loss of the conditional is thus at least in part connected with the loss of the imperfect.)

In all three cases we see the tendency to replace synthetic by analytic forms which is commonplace under pidginization, and is of course well attested in linguistic change generally (and cf. Dorian, 1973). The problem here is to decide how to categorize

---

[5] Admirative forms can often be translated by forms such as 'Look, I'm going!' or 'My word, you're going!'

developments of this type. They do represent, in a sense, loss from the language, but Arvanitika is apparently just as able to express the notions involved as is Albanian. It is also difficult to argue that Arvanitika does not do it so 'well' as Albanian. Reduction, therefore seems to be ruled out.

The question then is, do these changes qualify for the label of simplification? (They probably do represent simplification for the learner – cf. chapter 5 – but this is not entirely what is meant by *simplification* in this sense, and certainly cannot be used as a yardstick, since reduction also simplifies the task of the learner.) It is again difficult to argue that these changes make for an 'increase in regularity', but they do on the other hand involve the loss of inflexions, the loss of marked categories, and, possibly, an increase in the 'regular correspondence between content and expression'.

A way out of this problem is indicated by Mühlhäusler, who suggests a distinction between simplification in one component of a language with corresponding complication elsewhere, and *overall* simplification. In this case we can tentatively suggest that we are faced with, not overall simplification, but simplification *with cost* – the addition, in this case, of a certain amount of syntactic complexity. If this is so, then it requires a modification to our initial hypothesis, since we have now found not only reduction in Arvanitika, but also simplification-with-cost.

4 Further evidence is obtained by an examination of Arvanitika nominals. The noun in Albanian has four morphologically distinct case forms: nominative; accusative; genitive/dative; and ablative. It also has what is variously described as a postponed definite article or as distinct declensions for definite and indefinite forms. In Arvanitika, the genitive definite and indefinite forms are no longer distinct, the indefinite forms of Albanian having been replaced by the definite. This development, which applies equally to the declension of adjectives, is illustrated in table 6.6.

It does not represent an increase in regularity, or the loss of a grammatical category. It does, on the other hand, mean the loss of a distinction, and as such should possibly be considered as an example of reduction. Arvanitika can no longer, in some instances at least, distinguish between definite and indefinite in the genitive case, and this should therefore perhaps qualify as an (admittedly minor) example of something that 'cannot be said'. However, we have to recognize that this example also has some characteristics

TABLE 6·6   Noun declension

		Indefinite		Definite	
		Albanian	Arvanitika	Albanian	Arvanitika
sing.	N	mal	mal	mali	malтə
	A	mal	mal	malin	malтə
	G	mali	malit	malit	malit
	Abl	mali	–	malit	–
pl.	N	male	male	malet	maletə
	A	male	male	malet	maletə
	G	maleve	malevet	malevet	malevet
	Abl	maleš	–	malevet	–
		mountain (m)			
sing.	N	plak	plak	plaku	plaku
	A	plak	plak	plakun	plakun
	G	plaku	plakut	plakut	plakut
	Abl	plaku	–	plakut	–
pl.	N	plec	plec	plect	plectə
	A	plec	plec	plect	plectə
	G	plecve	plejvet	plecvet	plejvet
	Abl	plecš	–	plecvet	–
		old man (m)			

of simplification. It does, for instance, involve the loss of inflexional endings. It is possible, therefore, that we should regard this as a case of reduction *and* simplification.

A further instance of loss in the nominal system is also shown in table 6.6. There is no evidence in our Arvanitika data of any distinct forms for the ablative. (This is distinct in Albanian, in fact, only in the indefinite plural.) The crucial point, then, is what Arvanitika does instead. As far as we can tell, the ablative is now in fact replaced by prepositional phrases.

We can ascribe this development, which again is of a type well attested in linguistic change generally, either to the influence of Greek, or to the sociolinguistic situation as a whole. But how shall we classify it? It is an example of the loss of surface case which Mühlhäusler suggests might qualify for the label of reduction. But it also appears to be almost entirely parallel to the developments that have taken place with the optative and admirative verb forms. That is, simplification has taken place, but with compensation elsewhere in the system. This, then, is probably therefore once again to be categorized as simplification-with-cost.

Albanian also has a series of connecting particles which link nouns and following adjectives, or nouns and following genitives. These particles exhibit agreement of number, gender, case and definiteness with the preceding noun. Thus:

/park i cytetit/ *park* + particle + *of the city* = *city park*
/burə i mirə/ *man* + particle + *good* = *good man.*

The system of connecting particles in Arvanitika, when compared to that of Albanian, has been subject to loss. The definite and indefinite forms are now identical in Arvanitika, the Albanian indefinites having replaced the definites (see table 6.7). This development is almost certainly of recent origin, since a few older speakers did preserve distinct forms for the definite accusative (shown in parentheses in table 6.7. This also applies to the feminine genitive form /sə/, the alternation between /sə/ and /tə/ in some varieties of Albanian being phonologically conditioned).

At first sight this might appear to be another straightforward case of reduction since, as in the case of the genitive above, the distinction between definite and indefinite is now lost. However, since the connecting particles, as just stated, agree with the preceding noun, the distinction is in fact maintained: it is apparent from the form of the noun whether it is definite or indefinite. This, therefore, is simply a case of loss of redundancy.

TABLE 6.7   Connecting particles

	Definite				Indefinite			
	Masc.	Fem.	Neut.	Pl.	Masc.	Fem.	Neut.	Pl.
Albanian								
N	i	e	e	e	i	e	tə	tə
A	e	e	e	e	tə	tə/sə	tə	tə
G	tə	tə/sə	tə	tə	tə	tə/sə	tə	tə
Arvanitika								
N	i	e	tə	tə	i	e	tə	tə
A	tə (e)	tə (e)	tə (e)	tə (e)	tə	tə	tə	tə
G	tə	tə (sə)	tə	tə	tə	tə (sə)	tə	tə

We can note that the loss of connecting particles in Arvanitika is probably linked to the fact that, as in Albanian, adjectives of non-Albanian origin do not take connecting particles. Because of the large number of Greek loans in Arvanitika, connecting particles here will be much less frequent than in Albanian. Which features are actually lost under reduction and simplification, moreover, will probably be connected with frequency of occurrence, and the indefinite particles are probably more common in Albanian than the definites, since there are a number of linguistic contexts in which they alone can occur.

The problem, however, is: how are we to categorize this particular instance of loss?

5   There are two further examples of loss which can be used to shed some light on this problem. The first concerns the future, which in Albanian (Tosk) is formed, as we have already noted, by adding the invariable form /do/ *will* to the form of the present subjunctive. Thus /pi/, *he drinks*, pres. indicative; /tə pijə/, pres. subjunctive; /do tə pijə/, future. (The forms /tə/ is often to be translated as English *that*, and corresponds approximately to Greek /na/.) The equivalent Arvanitika forms are: /pi/, pres. indicative; /tə pii/, pres. subjunctive; /do pii/, future. Arvanitika, that is, has lost the particle /tə/ in this construction. We can be reasonably sure that this loss is a fairly recent development, since we did obtain forms such as /do tə jap/ *I shall give* from our oldest informant (102 years).

It seems legitimate to ascribe this loss of /tə/ to the influence of Greek, since the future in Greek is also formed by adding the invariable form /θa/ to the subjunctive, without an intervening /na/:

    Albanian: /do tə pi/ *I shall drink*
    Arvanitika: /do pi/
    Greek: /θa pjo/

We can also argue, however, that this is precisely the sort of development that also occurs under pidginization: the loss of redundancy (and cf. Dorian, 1973). (/tə/ is clearly redundant here, since /do/ serves unambiguously as a marker of the future.)

Loss of redundancy *per se* is not in fact included in any of the definitions of simplification we have discussed above. It is probable however, that we ought to consider developments such as the loss of /tə/ as examples of simplification. Loss of gender, declensions, conjugations, and inflexional endings generally, usual in pidginization, are examples of what can perhaps be referred to as loss of paradigmatic redundancy. Since these are taken to be typical examples of overall simplification, cases of loss of syntagmatic redundancy, like the loss of /tə/, should probably also be regarded in the same way.

A second case of the same kind of phenomenon is provided by certain types of interrogation in Arvanitika. Interrogative constructions in Albanian are introduced generally either by interrogative pronouns or by the interrogative particle /a/. The interrogative particle does not exist in Arvanitika. Thus:

    Albanian: /a ke par'a/
    Arvanitika: /ke par'a/   *Do you have money?*
    cf. Greek: /exis left'a/

Here again we can point to the possible influence of Greek, but we can also note the loss of syntagmatic redundancy. Interrogation is now signalled, in constructions such as these, by intonation alone rather than by both intonation and the interrogative particle. This again, therefore, is a candidate for the label of overall simplification.

The loss of the definite/indefinite distinction in the case of the connecting particles can be regarded in the same way. The particles still act as links between nouns and following adjectives, but definiteness is now indicated only in the noun rather than both the noun and the particle. This is not such a clear case of simplification as the previous two, since they involve the complete loss of an element from particular constructions (/tə/), or from the language altogether (/a/), whereas in this instance we have simply the loss of a distinction. The principle, however, appears to be the same in each case (although it is possible that the loss of /a/ and of the particle distinction should both be regarded as reduction *as well as* simplification. Note, too, that this loss also resembles Ferguson's criterion of fewer obligatory categories marked by morphemes of concord).

CONCLUSION

A study of the linguistic loss undergone by Arvanitika relative to Albanian shows that there are some clear examples of reduction: the loss of relational words; and the loss of the imperfect. There are also cases of the replacement of synthetic by analytic forms: the loss of the optative, admirative, and conditional; and the loss of the ablative. These involve simplification in one component of the language with compensation elsewhere, and we have therefore referred to them as examples of simplification-with-cost. There are also three cases of loss of syntagmatic redundancy: the loss of /tə/ in certain constructions; the loss of the interrogative particle /a/; and the loss of the definite connecting particles. As cases of loss of redundancy they are probably to be regarded as legitimate examples of overall simplification. We should also note, however, that there are no examples of the loss of paradigmatic redundancy commonplace in pidgins. In Arvanitika the three genders remain distinct, as do the separate declensions and conjugations. Irregular verbs and plural formations also remain irregular.

There are, in addition, a number of instances of loss which are difficult to classify. The loss of certain forms of the subjunctive was tentatively described above as stylistic reduction, but it does also represent the loss of a marked category and also, perhaps, of syntagmatic redundancy, and may therefore rather be simplification. The loss of the indefinite genitive is perhaps an example of both reduction *and* simplification. And this may also be true of the loss of /a/, and of the loss of the definite/indefinite distinction in the case of the connecting particles.

We can therefore suggest that while the distinction between reduction and simplification might appear to be a useful one, particularly in the treatment of pidgins and creoles, it is by no means a clear-cut distinction or one that is easy to apply in practice. It may be, to employ Hymes's distinction, that loss of inner and outer form may sometimes be, as it were, two sides of the same coin, and that it may often therefore be difficult to distinguish one from the other.

In attempting to answer the questions we have posed in this chapter, we have to acknowledge that a comparison of Arvanitika with Albanian without a study of colloquial Albanian as it is used in comparable situations must be unsatisfactory. We also have to recognize that we have examined data from only one language that is losing its native speakers. It is nevertheless possible to attempt to draw some conclusions.

We cannot be sure, for instance, that it is in fact possible for reduction to take place independently of simplification, or that they are entirely separate processes. We can note, however, that in the case of Arvanitika, *overall* simplification is rare. It also seems that a certain amount of reduction *can* take place in languages which have native speakers. It appears, however, that the reduction to which Arvanitika is currently subjected is simply keeping pace with the extent to which Arvanites are now becoming native speakers of Greek. The term 'native speaker', that is, is not particularly helpful in this situation. Even if reduction is to be linked to 'inadequacy', and even if it were possible to argue that the Arvanitika of younger speakers expresses certain things less 'well' than Albanian, this does not mean that they suffer from 'language deficit' or 'double semilingualism' (Hansegård, 1968). It is possible that Arvanitika as it is used by younger speakers is less adequate than Albanian in providing 'all the features which native speakers . . . demand of a language', but it is also the case that it is precisely these speakers who are most fluent in Greek, and who use it most.

Finally we have to say that even if 'creolization in reverse' is an accurate term sociolinguistically, it is much less so linguistically, since the parallels are by no means complete. A certain amount of simplification, as we have seen, has taken place in Arvanitika, while its reverse, complication, does not normally take place during creolization. This also leads us to note that it is not possible in fact to separate the factors *restriction in use* and *imperfect learning* one from the other, since the former inevitably leads to the latter. Young Arvanites no longer hear so much Arvanitika as did their parents, and thus perhaps learn the language less fully. It is probably to be expected, therefore, that reduction will be accompanied by simplification.

The situation of this dying language, however, is still distinct from that of a language undergoing pidginization. It does have native speakers. Its restriction in use is not so severe. Younger speakers, even though they may learn the language 'imperfectly', remain in full contact with more fluent speakers. And the contact situation is merely a bilingual one, whereas true pidginization (Whinnon, 1971) typically involves at least three linguistic communities. For this reason, reduction in Arvanitika is much less drastic than that which takes place during pidginization, and simplification is minimal and confined to simplification-with-cost and minor forms of loss of syntagmatic redundancy.

CHAPTER 7

Language, Contact, Language Shift and Identity

Why Arvanites are not Albanians

It is well known that language can act as an important defining characteristic of ethnic group membership, and in many communities the link between language and ethnicity is strong, and obvious.[1] It also has to be recognized, however, that a simple equation of ethnic and language group membership is far from adequate. There are, obviously, many examples of situations where a separate ethnic identity is maintained even though a distinctive language has been lost (see Fishman, 1968). Examples include the British Jewish community, and the Catholic community in Northern Ireland. (In some cases of this sort, dialect or accent differences within a single language may serve as identifying characteristics – Trudgill, 1974b, chapter 3.) More puzzling, perhaps, are cases where language distinctiveness appears not to be accompanied by any awareness of a separate ethnic identity. To what extent, for example, do Gaelic-speaking Scots form a separate ethnic group within Scotland?

It is not easy to determine what factors are involved in the establishment of these varying attitudes to language and ethnic group membership. However, the examination of sociolinguistic situations in which attitudes of this type appear to be undergoing change may perhaps be revealing. One such situation, which illustrates quite clearly the complex nature of the relationship between language and ethnicity, is the bilingual situation that currently obtains in the Attica and Biotia areas of Greece.

[1] We are very grateful to Paul Fletcher, Michael Garman, Howard Giles and Arthur Hughes for their comments on an earlier version of this chapter. The chapter is co-authored by George A. Tzavaras. Tzavaras also carried out all the field-work on which this chapter is based, and I gratefully acknowledge his work, cooperation and expertise. Chapters 6 and 7 would have been impossible without him.

As we have seen, the majority of villages in the immediate vicinity of Athens are (or were) Albanian rather than Greek-speaking. The Arvanites (see p. 108) who inhabit these villages are descended from Albanians, some of whom appeared in Greece as early as the eleventh and twelfth centuries, and the main expansions took place between 1350 and 1450 (when Albanians were invited to settle and cultivate the land in uninhabited and depopulated areas), and again during the second half of the eighteenth century (when many were brought in by the Turkish rulers of Greece). In Attica and Biotia Albanian-Greeks today number perhaps 140,000, and form the majority of the population of most of the villages concerned. They are, therefore, typically a rural rather than an urban people.[2]

These Albanians for a long time retained a clearly separate ethnic identity, apparently. (In nineteenth century travel literature, for example, they are often noted and discussed as a distinct people.) Gradually, however, this identity has been eroded, particularly in the wave of hellenization that followed the War of Independence, and again, in this century, in the aftermath of the Greek Civil War (which ended in 1949). A number of different factors appear to have played a part in this process of (partial) assimilation. Both Greeks and Albanians were (and are) members of the Greek Orthodox church, and the clergy of this body have typically tended to play down the fact of ethnic differences and to emphasize the religious similarities. The occupation of Greece by Turkey, a Moslem power, underlined this point, and helped to unite the two ethnic groups in the face of the common foe. Population movements also meant that formerly Albanian areas became mixed and hellenized to various degrees.

In more recent years the cultural, economic and political dominance of the Greeks has been instrumental in the progressive breaking down of Albanian ethnic identity, especially since this has been coupled, particularly since 1949, with deliberate governmental policies emphasizing Greek nationality and national unity. Education, too, has played an important role: there are no Albanian schools in Greece, and the Greek educational tradition tends to emphasize links with the classical hellenic past. Arvanites are

---

[2] Elsewhere in Greece there are other Albanian-speaking areas, including especially parts of the Pelopponese, Epirus and certain of the islands.

not literate in Albanian, and indeed many are surprised to learn that it is possible to write it.[3]

Today the main identifying characteristic of the Arvanites is their language. (In fact, it may well be their only distinguishing characteristic, with the possible exception of a number of cultural traditions for rituals such as weddings and funerals, and distinctive family names.)

This chapter is based on research carried out, between 1973 and 1975, in the Arvanitika-speaking villages (see p. 108), the principal aim of which was to investigate the extent of Arvanitika language maintenance, the degree and nature of Greek–Arvanitika language switching, and linguistic change and interference in Arvanitika[4] (see also chapter 6). In this chapter we shall focus on problems the Arvanitika-speaking community reports itself as having experienced as a result of being a linguistic and ethnic minority; their attitudes to the language and its use, many of which appear to have formed at least partly as a result of these problems; and the implications these attitudes have for the study of the relationship between language and ethnicity.

One of the clearest findings to emerge from this research is that Arvanitika, as we saw above, is a dying language, in that younger Arvanites are increasingly shifting to Greek. This shift from Arvanitika is in part reflected in and in part caused by a change in attitudes to the language that is currently taking place in the villages, and a related change in attitudes to ethnic group membership. During the course of the research, these attitudes were examined through the administering of a questionnaire to a total of 1,703 Arvanites drawn, as a judgement sample,[5] from all the relevant villages. The questionnaire, which was also designed to obtain information on language ability and use, was administered

---

[3] For further information on the background to the current situation, see Biris (1960); Phurikis (1931, 1932–3); Triandaphillidis (1938); Vakalopulos (1973).

[4] Arvanitika is a dialect of Tosk, or southern Albanian. Arvanitika and other varieties of Albanian are mutually intelligible to a fair degree, but there are difficulties, partly due to the large amount of interference from Greek in Arvanitika. Many Arvanites have a slight Arvanitika accent when speaking Greek, but many do not. This appears to be a regional feature rather than an ethnic one, since many Greeks who are not Arvanites also have some of the same accent features if they come from certain of the villages.

[5] Random sampling proved not to be possible because of the necessary cooperation with the authorities this would have involved, and the difficulty of working with ethnic minorities under the then Greek government. We are confident (see Trudgill and Tzavaras, 1975) that the sample is nevertheless a representative one.

orally, in Greek (as being the language appropriate for this type of activity), by an interviewer who was himself an Arvanitis (and known to be such by the interviewees).

One of the purposes of the study was to investigate the social, educational and other problems faced by Arvanites as a linguistic minority in Greece. The study showed, however, that while there clearly are problems, the era of really serious difficulties is now over, and that the current generation of Arvanitika speakers is not likely to be faced with any great problems of a practical nature – largely because they are fluent in Greek, and for the most part assimilated to Greek culture.

One of the items in the questionnaire that dealt with this point was: have you had any problems as a result of being an Arvanitika-speaker? This elicited, from a majority of informants, a number of responses of the type: speaking Arvanitika 'makes you feel embarrassed'; 'girls don't like it'; 'it makes people think you're not Greek'. With older speakers there was the additional problem: 'the children don't like me to speak it, and this upsets me'; 'we quarrel with the children about it'. Other responses, however, did reveal a number of perhaps more serious problems. Some answers, for example, showed that a number of Arvanites had suffered from what they regarded as discrimination, particularly during military service, and at school. There were reports, for example, that army officers attempted to stop the speaking of Arvanitika, and that Arvanites were given the worst jobs to do. Discrimination of this type, however, appears to have led to a determination, on the part of those who had experienced it, that their children will not suffer in the same way – because they will speak Greek. A few, on the other hand, did regret hostile attitudes to Arvanitika on the part of other Greeks, but even these could not conceive of actually doing anything about this.

As far as problems in school are concerned, information on this topic was obtained principally in response to the questionnaire item: what happened/happens in school? With the exception of those who had attended school only for a short time or not at all, our oldest informants reported that they had had difficulties, particularly in those cases where they had had to go to school in non-Arvanitika-speaking towns such as Thebes and Levadhia. There had been problems of discrimination – two informants reported that they had walked out of school after the teacher had called them 'dirty Arvanites'. There had also been linguistic problems, particularly in lessons concerned with the writing of Greek. They had had difficulties with Greek grammar, and problems arose because they would tend to use Arvanitika words in some cases rather than Greek ones.

Middle-aged informants had no trouble with the Greek language in school, because they were fluent bilinguals. They did have trouble, however, because teachers regarded them as 'foreigners', and actively discouraged the speaking of Arvanitika. Many of the informants resented this, particularly where Arvanites were humiliated in front of non-Arvanites in 'mixed' schools. Some, however, now believe that the teachers were right because 'after all we're not Albanians' and they were 'in school to learn Greek'. Male informants in this group reported that they used to speak Arvanitika during games, in the playground, and for chatting up girls, but spoke Greek in class.

Younger informants have in some cases come to resent unfavourable attitudes to Arvanitika expressed by some of their teachers. (This was particularly true of boys, who also complained of the same sort of attitude on the part of girls.) Generally speaking however, they have no problems, since they speak Greek most of the time, except when they are 'telling dirty jokes and smoking in the toilets'. Boys stated that they would not talk to girls in Arvanitika, but that they did show off sometimes by swearing in Arvanitika or by having competitions to see who knew most words – and that the girls liked to watch them doing this.

It seems, then, that for the most part social and educational problems are a thing of the past, and that those that remain are fairly trivial. Increasing fluency in and use of Greek means that younger Arvanites have far fewer problems of this type than their elders.

ATTITUDES

The item in the questionnaire that most directly tapped overtly expressed attitudes to Arvanitika was: do you like to speak Arvanitika? Responses to this question are given in table 7·1. It can be

TABLE 7·1   Do you like to speak Arvanitika?

	Percentage		
Age	Yes	Indifferent	No
5–9	1	10	89
10–14	16	17	67
15–24	17	41	42
25–34	30	67	3
35–49	46	53	2
50–59	67	31	1
60+	79	21	0

seen that, generally speaking, younger informants (in their overt attitudes at least) are antagonistic to Arvanitika, middle-aged informants indifferent and older informants favourable. This, of course, does not augur well for the future of Arvanitika. It is true that from these figures alone we cannot be certain that this pattern of attitudes is not one that is repeated in every generation, nor that more covert attitudes may be rather different. However, this sort of pattern is repeated in many other cases, and appears to be borne out by actual behaviour.

For example, a related question was: do you think speaking Arvanitika is a good thing to do? Responses, given in table 7·2, are very similar, except for a switch on the part of the 10–14 group from 'no' to indifferent and an increase in 'yes' responses on the part of older speakers. Few people under 35, it can be seen, appear to attach much value to speaking Arvanitika.

TABLE 7·2   Do you think speaking Arvanitika is a good thing to do?

	Percentage		
Age	Yes	Indifferent	No
5–9	1	10	89
10–14	17	73	10
15–24	18	48	35
25–34	32	66	3
35–49	64	35	1
50–60	95	4	1
60+	86	14	0

Reasons given by informants for these attitudes included those based on (a) the inherent superiority of Greek: 'Greek is a better language'; 'more classical'; 'more expressive'; (b) the inherent inferiority of Arvanitika: 'Arvanitika isn't nice'; 'you can't write it'; 'it isn't a real language'; (c) arguments to do with ethnic group membership: 'we're Greeks'; 'we're not Albanians'; and even 'we're not Turks'; and (d) more practical considerations: 'we don't want our children to speak Arvanitika'.

Arguments in favour of Arvanitika, from those who expressed this point of view, consisted of those based on (a) the superiority of Arvanitika: 'it's more expressive than Greek'; 'it's more picturesque'; it's more suitable for some topics'; and (b) attitudes to ethnic group membership and stereotypes: 'it's the language of our fathers'; 'it makes Athenians nervous'; 'only queers speak Greek'.

Responses to other questions bear rather less directly on language attitudes, but are nevertheless of some importance. One such question was: do/would you want your children to speak Arvanitika? A majority of informants aged under 35, who are or will be soon those engaged in rearing the next generation, declared (see table 7·3) that they were against their children speaking this language. It is of some interest, too, that of those answering 'no', 72 per cent were female. This tallies well with many other reports that women in many societies are less favourably disposed to low status forms of language than men (see Thorne and Henley, 1975).

TABLE 7·3 Do/would you want your children to speak Arvanitika?

Age	Percentage	
	Yes	No
10–14	16	84
15–24	29	71
25–34	46	54
35–49	56	44
50–59	67	33
60 +	66	34

We have to recognize that these figures are based on what are simply overt responses to a questionnaire, but they are borne out by the behaviour we actually observed: when children are present, nearly all adults automatically speak Greek. (One informant told us that when children get to be about 15, then adults feel they are able to use Arvanitika or Greek in front of them, as they please.) These figures, then, are very relevant to the maintenance of Arvanitika: a large section of the population are, at least publicly, not concerned that the language be retained.

A similar kind of picture emerges from the question: is it an advantage or disadvantage to you to be an Arvanitika speaker?

Younger speakers (see table 7·4) consider it to be a disadvantage, and gave reasons of the type already reported: problems with children, with the opposite sex, with 'making a bad impression' and so on.

TABLE 7·4   Is it an advantage or disadvantage?

Age	Advantage	Neither	Disadvantage
	Percentage		
5–9	1	17	82
10–14	12	38	50
15–24	34	50	16
25–34	40	49	11
35–49	56	36	8
50–59	67	33	0
60+	97	3	0

Those citing the advantages of being an Arvanitika speaker stated: 'there's something you know that others don't'; 'it's good for jokes and secrets': 'it's good for getting co-operation of other Arvanites'; 'you feel closer to people'; 'you can talk to the old people'. (The most convincing illustration of the advantages of speaking Arvanitika was given by one man who owed his life, he felt, to this ability. With the Greek army in Albania during the war, he became separated from his company and was stopped by some Italian soldiers. However, some Albanians who were with the Italians, finding that he could speak their language, told the Italians that he was an Albanian, secured his release, gave him shelter and helped him return.) The age-group differentiation shown in table 7·4 may perhaps be due in part to a change in economic and social circumstances, but it is certainly also due to the general pattern of increasing denigration by Arvanites of Arvanitika.

ETHNICITY

We have already seen that the practical problems of the linguistic minority are today for the most part fairly trivial. Sociopsychological problems, on the other hand, are more difficult to assess. There is certainly a conflict between overt attitudes of the type 'Greek is better than Arvanitika' and more covert attitudes which sometimes emerge in statements such as 'only queers speak Greek'. A number of teenage boys reported that if they attempted to change a conversation from Arvanitika into Greek they ran the risk of being called *eksipno* 'clever boy' or *pustis* 'queer' (these terms are in fact Greek).

The Arvanites' attitude to ethnic group membership, particularly as this relates to language, is also a rather paradoxical one. To the question: are you proud to be an Arvanitis?, 97 per cent of all informants answers 'yes'. However, all were also very concerned to point out that being an Arvanitis did not mean that one was not also Greek, and were distressed that outsiders sometimes think that they are not 'good Greeks'. Thus, to the question: is it possible to be an Arvanitis and a Greek at the same time?, 98 per cent answered 'yes' – including many who replied 'of course'. (The 2 per cent who answered no stated that they were Greeks and not Arvanites.) There is clearly, then, a certain apparent conflict of ethnic identity – of being a Greek and an Arvanitis.

However, there are also significant age-group differences in attitudes to ethnic group membership, as revealed by answers to the question: are Arvanites better than other Greeks? Table 7·5 shows that there has been a notable decline in the self-image of Arvanites. It is worth noting, too, that of those answering better, 67 per cent were male, while of the few that answered worse, 77 per cent were female. Many of those claiming superiority for the Arvanites stated that they were more hospitable, extroverted, good-hearted, generous, straightforward and trustworthy than other Greeks. Those answering worse, on the other hand, claimed

TABLE 7·5   Are Arvanites better than other Greeks?

	Percentage		
Age	Better	Same	Worse
5–9	7	82	11
10–14	1	95	4
15–24	7	84	9
25–34	46	49	5
35–49	93	7	0
50–59	73	24	3
60+	96	2	2

that Arvanites were more demanding, quarrelsome, moody, excitable, impolite and blasphemous.

We have seen, then, that our informants are very concerned to stress the fact that they are Greeks. Younger Arvanites, moreover, are not at all inclined to feel superior to other Greeks (and are more concerned to be assimilated into the mainstream Greek culture). We have also seen that what prestige the Arvanitika language has is mainly of the 'covert prestige' type (and that its connotations of toughness and friendliness are more favourably reacted to by male than by female speakers – see chapter 10). This low status is also reflected in the fact that a majority of younger Arvanites are not concerned that their children should learn to speak Arvanitika.

One interesting problem is how this lack of desire for the next generation to learn Arvanitika (and a third of even the oldest speakers share this view) is reconciled with the universal pride in being an Arvanitis. One explanation is provided by table 7·6, which gives responses to the question: is it necessary to speak Arvanitika to be an Arvanitis? With the exception of the under-15s, a majority in each age-group feels that the language is not a necessary requirement for ethnic group membership. (Informants answering 'no' explained that you are an Arvanitis if your parents are Arvanites and/or you were born in an Arvanitika-speaking village.) We feel, in the long run, that this view is an unrealistic one, in that language is now the main distinguishing characteristic of Arvanites.

TABLE 7·6 Is it necessary to speak Arvanitika to be an Arvanitis?

Age	Percentage	
	Yes	No
10–14	67	33
15–24	42	58
25–34	24	76
35–49	28	72
50–59	33	67
60+	17	83

The majority response of table 7·6 may be due in part to the fact that geographical origin and 'birthplace' is still an important component of ethnic identity. If one says one is from, for example, the village of Villia, this may be as good as saying that one is an Arvanitis. But the response is probably due much more, in fact, to an attempt to reconcile a desire for the maintenance of a separate Arvanitis identity with a recognition of the fact that younger speakers do not use a great deal of Arvanitika, and that it can be a social disadvantage for them to do so. It may be the response, that is, of a culturally threatened minority who are sufficiently small and isolated to see no hope of reversing the linguistic tide. The under-15s, on the other hand, are probably being more realistic since they are less concerned with the maintenance of a separate Arvanitika identity. They are prepared to concede that it is necessary to speak Arvanitika to be an Arvanitis because, although they are aware that Arvanitika is dying out, they do not regard the loss of the language or of the ethnic identity as undesirable. It seems, that is, that with younger people conflicts of this type are being resolved in favour of a Greek identity and the Greek language (cf. Le Page's stress on identity, chapter 8).

One aspect of this is a phenomenon we have already noted: the strong pressure many children exert on their parents – often successfully – not to speak Arvanitika, particularly in public. (These attitudes have parallels with those demonstrated by second-generation immigrants in, for example, the USA – see Weinreich, 1974; Wolfram, 1973). It seems, too, that the parents, in many cases, accept that the children's attitudes are probably correct. They are persuaded that Arvanitika is a less worthy language than Greek, and acknowledge that their children are better educated than they are themselves. The success that the children have, then, in altering their parents' speech habits appears to be the result of these factors combining with the desire, on the part of the parents, for their children to be upwardly socially mobile, and the recognition that it is ability in Greek, not Arvanitika, that will enable them to achieve this.

We can note, too, that there are no signs at all of any Arvanitika revival movement. Those who would be unhappy about the disappearance of the language do not feel this particularly strongly, and are in any case often unreasonably optimistic that it will survive. They are, moreover, for the most part older rather than younger Arvanites, since it is precisely the younger people (who in other parts of Europe and elsewhere are the most actively involved in the cause of ethnic minorities) who most strongly espouse the urban way of life and the hellenization that typically accompanies it. The most likely outcome, then, is that Arvanitika, although it is currently spoken by perhaps as many as 140,000 people in Attica and Biotia, as well as elsewhere in Greece, will quite probably die out completely in the next two or three generations. Certainly, any revival movement linked to Albania and Albanian is currently out of the question, since this would be unacceptable to most imaginable Greek governments, as well as to most Arvanites, who tend to look down on Albanians. It is possible, however, that the more covertly held favourable attitudes towards Arvanitika – its association with toughness, honesty and comradeship – may aid its survival longer than we have supposed.

At the beginning of this chapter we noted that the relationship between language and ethnicity can take a number of forms, and we raised the question of why, in some cases, the link between the two may not be a strong one. In the present case we have noted that the connection between language and ethnic group membership is not especially strong, and that it appears currently to be weakening.

In attempting to explain this phenomenon we can note the following factors. Modern Albanian-Greeks, as we have seen, perceive themselves as being both Greeks and Arvanites, and not as Albanians. In this they resemble other linguistic minorities such as, for example, many French Canadians, who regard themselves as an ethnic group separate from other Canadians, but not as French. In the case of the Arvanites, we can note, as explanatory factors, the geographical separation of the Arvanitika-speaking villages of Attica and Biotia from Albania, and the absence of cultural, religious and political ties with Albania. We should not, that is, regard this aspect of the phenomenon as any more surprising than the fact that, say, English-speaking Australians do not regard themselves as, from an ethnic point of view, particularly British.

The Arvanites, however, differ quite clearly from the French Canadians and other similar groups in (a) the extent to which they identify themselves as Greeks and in (b) the lack of importance they appear to attach to their language as symbol of ethnic group membership.

We noted above that (b), which is most typical of older Arvanites (see table 7·6), is probably the result of the fact that, while they are keen that a distinct Arvanitis identity should be maintained, they recognize that younger Arvanites do not speak much Arvanitika. To claim that Arvanitika is an essential component of the Arvanites' identity would therefore be to suggest that their children and grandchildren are not really Arvanites.

Attitude (a), on the other hand, is more typical of younger Arvanites (see table 7·5). (They are, as a consequence, more realistic (table 7·6) about the role of language in maintaining a separate ethnic identity.) This phenomenon is not so readily accounted for, but we can suggest the following factors. First, the attempts by Greek governments to stress Greek unity and nationality have been particularly strong since the Second World War, and have been mediated to a considerable extent through the educational system. Radio and television have perhaps also played a part. Younger people have therefore had more exposure to these influences than their elders.

Secondly, the relative lack of tolerance of or encouragement for ethnic diversity in Greece has been greatly aided by urbanization. Arvanitika, like most other minority languages in Greece, is almost exclusively a rural language. Because of the rather large and obvious differences between rural and urban standards of living, values and ways of life in Greece, Arvanitika is stereotyped not only as rural, but also as backward, old-fashioned, unsophisticated and uneducated. Younger Arvanites who aspire, as most of them appear to, to a middle-class way of life and a high standard of living, therefore also aspire to a Greek identity and to ability in the Greek language. It is, of course, possible that greater educational opportunities will eventually bring greater awareness, as it has elsewhere, of the value of cultural and ethnic diversity. For the time being, however, there is no evidence that this kind of development is about to take place.

CHAPTER 8

Acts of Conflicting Identity

The sociolinguistics of British pop-song pronunciation

Anyone with an interest in British rock and pop songs will have observed that there are 'rules' concerning the way in which the words of these songs are pronounced.[1] The label 'tendencies' might be more appropriate than 'rules' in some instances, but in any case it is clear that singers of this form of music employ different accents when singing from when they are speaking, and that deviations from their spoken accents are of a particular and relatively constrained type. This phenomenon of employing a modified pronunciation seems to have been current in popular music for some decades, probably since the 1920s, and has involved a number of different genres, including jazz, 'crooning', and so on. It became, however, especially widespread and noticeable in the late 1950s with the advent of rock-and-roll and the pop-music revolution.

Analysis of the pronunciation used by British pop singers at around that time, and subsequently, reveals the following rules and tendencies. (We ignore features such as the pronunciation of -*ing* as [ɪn] which are typical of most informal styles.)

1   The pronunciation of intervocalic /t/ in words like *better* as [t] or [ʔ], which are the pronunciations used by most British speakers, is generally not permitted. In pop-singing, a pronunciation of the type [d̪] (a voiced alveolar flap of some kind) has to be employed.

[1] I would like to thank the following for comments on an earlier draft of this paper; for the loan of their records; for messages run; and/or for information provided: Jim Birnie, Neil Brummage, Alice Davison, Georgia M. Green, Jean Hannah, Chuck Kisseberth, Margi Laff, Jerry L. Morgan, Mark Seidenberg, and Bruce Sherwood.

141

2   It is not permitted to pronounce words such as *dance, last* with the /aː/ that is normal in speech in south-eastern England. Instead they are pronounced with the /æ/ of *cat* (as in the north of England, although the realization is usually [æ] rather than the northern [a]). In addition, words such as *half* and *can't*, which are pronounced with /aː/ by most of those English speakers, of north and south, who have the /æ/–/aː/ distinction, must also be pronounced with /æ/. Thus:

	cat	dance	half
South-eastern England	/æ/ = [æ]	[aː]	/aː/
Northern England	/æ/ = [a]	/æ/	/aː/
Pop-song style	/æ/ = [æ]	/æ/	/æ/

3   Words such as *girl, more* tend to be pronounced with an /r/ even by those English English speakers (the majority) who do not have non-prevocalic /r/ in their speech.

4   Words such as *life, my* tend to be sung with a vowel of the type [aˑ] although they are normally pronounced by a majority of British speakers with a diphthong of the type [aɪ ~ ɑɪ ~ ʌɪ].

5   Words such as *love, done* tend to be pronounced with a vowel of the type [əˑ] rather than with the [ä ~ ɐ] typical of the south of England or the [ʊ ~ ɤ] typical of the north.

6   Words such as *body, top* may be pronounced with un-rounded [ɑ] instead of the more usual British [ɒ].

There are, of course, British varieties which do have these features: most English northern and midland varieties have /æ/ in *path* and a few have /æ/ in *can't*, while some south-western English and most Scottish varieties have no /æ/–/aː/ distinction and may have an [æ]-like vowel in all those words; many south-western English varieties have [d] in *better*; many western, north-western and Scottish (and other) varieties do have non-prevocalic /r/; some north-western accents do have /aɪ/ as [aˑ]; many mid-land and south-western varieties have [ə], although not usually [əˑ], in *love*; and some East Anglian and south-western varieties have [ɑ] in *body*. The point is, however, that no single British variety has all these features, and the vast majority of singers who use these forms when singing do not do so when speaking. There can be no doubt that singers are modifying their linguistic behaviour for the purposes of singing.

EXPLANATIONS FOR LINGUISTIC MODIFICATION

An interesting question, therefore, is: why do singers modify their pronunciation in this way? One theory that attempts to deal with language modification of this kind is the socio-psychological *accommodation theory* of Giles (see Giles and Smith, 1979). This, briefly, attempts to explain temporary or long-term adjustments in pronunciation and other aspects of linguistic behaviour in terms of a drive to approximate one's language to that of one's interlocutors, if they are regarded as socially desirable and/or if the speaker wishes to identify with them and/or demonstrate good will towards them. This may often take the form of reducing the frequency of socially stigmatized linguistic forms in the presence of speakers of higher prestige varieties. The theory also allows for the opposite effect: the distancing of one's language from that of speakers one wishes to disassociate oneself from, or in order to assert one's own identity.

Accommodation theory does go some way towards accounting for the phenomenon of pop-song pronunciation. It is clearly not sufficient, however, since it applies only to conversational situations. And we cannot assume that pop musicians adjust their pronunciation in order to make it resemble more closely that of their intended audience, since what actually happens is in many respects the reverse.

Another, less elaborate way to look at this problem is simply to discuss it in terms of the sociolinguistic notion of 'appropriateness'. As is well known, different situations, different topics, different genres require different linguistic styles and registers. The singing of pop music in this way, it could be argued, is no different from vicars preaching in the register appropriate to Church of England sermons, or BBC newsreaders employing the variety appropriate for the reading of the news. Certainly 'appropriateness' is obviously a relevant factor here. But, equally obviously, it is not on its own enough to provide an explanation for why it is this type of singing which is regulated in this way, nor why it is characterized by this particular set of pronunciation rules and tendencies rather than some other.

A more helpful approach, it emerges, is the theory of linguistic behaviour developed by Le Page. Indeed, the pronunciation of pop-song lyrics provides a useful site for a microstudy which exemplifies many aspects of Le Page's thinking. This theory, expounded by Le Page in a number of writings (see Le Page 1968, 1975, 1978; Le Page *et al.*, 1974) seeks to demonstrate a general motive for speakers' linguistic behaviour in terms of attempts to 'resemble as closely as possible those of the group or groups with which from time to time we [speakers] wish to identify'. (There are, obviously, similarities with accommodation theory here, but, as we shall see below, Le Page's approach is both more detailed and more helpful.)

In Le Page's terms, British pop singers are attempting to modify their pronunciation in the direction of that of a particular group with which they wish to identify – from time to time (i.e. when they are singing). This group, moreover, can clearly, if somewhat loosely, be characterized by the general label 'Americans': the six pronunciation rules and tendencies outlined above are all found in American accents, and are stereotypically associated by the British with American pronunciation. (If there were any doubt about the identity of the model group, this could be confirmed by reference to the words of pop songs themselves which, even if written by British composers for British consumption, tend to include forms such as *guy* (= *chap, bloke*), *call* (*phone*) etc., which are still Americanisms for many British speakers today, and were certainly Americanisms in the 1950s and 1960s.

The next question therefore is: why should singers attempt to imitate what they consider to be an American accent? The reason for this is reasonably apparent, even if somewhat intuitively arrived at, and without empirical verification. Most genres of twentieth-century popular music, in the western world and in some cases beyond, are (Afro-)American in origin. Americans have dominated the field, and cultural domination leads to imitation: it is appropriate to sound like an American when performing in what is predominantly an American activity; and one attempts to model one's singing style on that of those who do it best and who one admires most.

There are parallels here with other musical genres: British folk singers often adopt quasi-rural accents; and singers of songs in the reggae style often attempt Jamaican accents. We also have to note that, in many European countries at least, it is not a particular variety of English but simply English itself that has become associated with pop music: at one time, for example, many West German pop groups had English-language names and sang songs, written by Germans, in English – a phenomenon which cannot be entirely explained by a desire to conquer international markets. (It is difficult to think of precise parallels of cultural domination in fields other than music, but one candidate might be the quasi-English accents adopted by American Shakespearean actors even when acting in plays set in, for example, Verona.)

CONSTRAINTS ON LINGUISTIC MODIFICATION

British pop singers, then, are aiming at an American pronunciation. The end-product of this language modification is, however, by no means entirely successful. One obvious measure of their lack of success is that many American listeners are utterly unaware that this is what British singers are trying to do. The results of this modification, too, are complex and subject to change.

This also can be accounted for in Le Page's theory. The theory provides for the fact that, in modifying our linguistic behaviour, our performance as speakers 'is constrained by considerations which fall under one or another of four riders to the general hypothesis'. We will discuss these riders in turn. The first of Le Page's (1978) riders is that our modification of our linguistic behaviour is constrained by:

(i) the extent to which we are able to identify our model group.

We have already seen that British pop singers have, presumably without giving it too much conscious thought, successfully identified their model group as 'Americans', and that they attempt, again presumably for the most part below the level of conscious awareness, to model their language behaviour on that of American singers. More detailed study, however, suggests that they have not been especially successful in identifying *exactly which*

Americans it is they are trying to model their behaviour on. Comparison with the linguistic behaviour of American pop singers is instructive at this point, for there is a strong tendency for them, too, to modify their pronunciation when singing. Modifications made by American singers include (a) the use of the monophthong [aˑ] in *life*, etc. by singers who have diphthongs in their speech (i.e. the same modification made by British singers); and (b) the *omission* of non-prevocalic /r/ in *car*, etc. by singers who are normally *r*-ful in their speech. A good example is provided by Bob Dylan, who is from Minnesota, in the American Mid-West, and who has /ai/ = [ai] and non-prevocalic /r/ in his speech. His singing style incorporates frequent use of [aˑ] and r-loss:

> You may be an ambassador [æmˈbæsədə]
> To England or [ə] France
> You may like [laˑk] to gamble
> You might [maˑt] like [laˑk] to dance
> ('Gotta serve somebody', *Slow Train Coming*, 1979)

These two features suggest that the model group whose pronunciation is being aimed at by American singers consists of Southern and/or Black singers, since the combination of [aˑ] = /ai/ and r-lessness is most typical of the varieties spoken by these groups. The reason for this is again clear: it is in the American South and/or amongst Blacks that many types of popular music have their origins. (This is most obviously true of jazz, rhythm-and-blues, and rock-and-roll.) Cultural domination therefore causes singers with White non-Southern accents to modify their pronunciation when singing.[2]

This leads us to suppose that it is these same groups whose accents British singers too are aiming at, since they also, as we have already seen, have the [aˑ] = /ai/ feature in their singing styles. This supposition is strengthened, first, by the fact that other features of Southern and Black pronunciation, in addition to [aˑ], can be heard to occur from time to time in British pop songs:

1   pronunciations such as *boring* [bourɪn], and the occasional rhyming of words such as *more* with words such as *go*;

---

[2] There are other (e.g. choral) American singing styles which are deliberately r-less. These, however, have /ai/ as [aɪ], and are probably modelled on Eastern and/or English English accents.

2 the occasional inhibition of the pronunciation of linking /r/,
   as in *four o'clock*, without the insertion of a pause or glottal
   stop;
3 the pronunciation of /ɪ/ as [ɛ ~ ǽ] before /n/, /ŋ/, as in *thing*
   [θǽŋ], in imitation of the Southern and Black merger of /ɪ/
   and /ɛ/ before nasals.

Secondly, it is also confirmed by the occurrence, even in songs
written by British pop musicians, of grammatical features associated with Southern and Black dialects:

1 *copula deletion*
   'He livin' there still'   (Beatles *White Album*)
   'My woman she gone'   (Dire Straits
                                          Dire Straits)

2 *3rd-person -s absence*
   'She make me cry'   (Stranglers
                                          Rattus Norvegicus)

   'Here come old flat top'   (Beatles *Abbey Road*)
3 *negativized auxiliary*
      pre-position
   'Ain't nothin' new in   (Supertramp *Breakfast*
      my life today'   *in America*)

If this is so, then in one respect the British singers are in error.
Blacks and Southerners are typically *r*-less. This fact is, as we have
seen, recognized by many American singers, who (variably) delete
non-prevocalic /r/ when singing even though their speech is *r*-ful.
British singers, on the other hand, do the reverse: they insert
non-prevocalic /r/ in singing even though their speech is *r*-less.
(This contrast between British and American singers was particularly marked in the late 1950s when singers such as Cliff Richard,
who were to a considerable extent imitators of Elvis Presley,
attempted the pronunciation of non-prevocalic /r/ in their songs,
even though Elvis himself was for the most part *r*-less.) We do not
deny, of course, that some Southern varieties are *r*-ful. Nevertheless, it is possible to argue that, in their performance of pop songs,
British singers exhibit a certain lack of success in identifying who
their model group is. The two perceptions – that the model group
consists of (a) Americans in general, and (b) Southerners and/or

Blacks in particular – conflict when it comes to non-prevocalic /r/, since in the case of the particular model group being aimed at, the stereotype that 'Americans are r-ful' is inaccurate.

Le Page's second rider also turns out to be relevant for our study of the linguistic behaviour of British pop singers. This rider states that our linguistic behaviour is constrained by:

> (ii) the extent to which we have sufficient access to [the model groups] and sufficient analytical ability to work out the rules of their behaviour.

There is evidence that British singers' analytical abilities are in fact sometimes not sufficient. This is provided, again, by the case of non-prevocalic /r/. Like, for example, many British actors attempting to imitate r-ful rural accents, British pop singers often insert non-prevocalic /r/s where they do not belong. This is a form of hypercorrection. Singers know that, in order to 'sound like an American', one has to insert an /r/ after the vowels /aː/ as in *cart*; /ɔː/ as in *fort*; /ɜː/ as in *bird*; /ɪə/ as in *beard*; /ɛə/ as in *bared*; and /ə/ as in *letters*. The problem is that some singers have not mastered the principle behind where this should and should not be done; they are liable to insert an /r/ after the above vowels even where an /r/ is not required, as in *calm, taught, ideas, Americas* (*bird* and *bared*-type words are not a problem, since these vowels occur only before a potential /r/). The correct strategy to follow (except in the case of the word *colonel* – which does not occur too often in pop songs) is to use the orthography, which always has r where an /r/ is required. Phonologists must find it interesting, however, that, in spite of the sure guide that orthography provides, mistakes do occur – strong counterevidence to the claim that all r-less accents have underlying /r/ plus an r-deletion rule. Clearly, speakers who make mistakes of this type do not have underlying /r/. (It is possible (see Knowles, 1978) that we should distinguish between two types of hypercorrection: that due to an inability to perform r-insertion correctly in the heat of the moment, although the speaker actually knows how it *ought* to be done; and that due simply to ignorance of where it should be done. Ignorance, however, seems to be the main factor, since in some cases hyper-American /r/s are repeated again and again in the course of the same song.) Examples of complete lack of success in analysing the model accent correctly include:

1   Cliff Richard, 'Bachelor Boy' (1961):
    'You'll be *a bachelor boy* ...' /ər bæčələr bɔi/ – repeated
    many times.
2   Kinks, 'Sunny Afternoon' (1966):
    '... *Ma and Pa*'   /maːr ən paːr/
3   Paul McCartney, 'Till there was you' on *With the Beatles*
    (1963):
    'I never *saw them* at all'   /sɔːr ðɛm/.

Le Page's rider indicates that sufficient contact with the model
group might diminish this kind of mistake, but even close personal
contact with speakers of American English seems in this instance
to have relatively little corrective influence. One explanation for
this may be that Americans are unlikely to offer any overt, accurate correction of hyper-American /r/ because they (like Scots) are
used to the idea that 'English people put in *r*'s in the wrong place'.
They are, it appears, unable to distinguish between the *intrusive*
/r/, which occurs only before a following vowel (as in *Ma* in the
above example (2) from the Kinks), and is a normal part of everyday pronunciation in many Australasian, English (and indeed
some American) English accents, and *hyper-American* /r/, as in *Pa*
in the Kinks' song, which occurs before consonants and pauses,
and is found only in singing. Indeed, even well-known American
phonologists have been heard to assert that 'British speakers say
America /ə'mɛrɪkər/'. (There are in fact some English English accents which do genuinely have /r/ in *last* etc. and/or *vanilla* etc.
(see Orton *et al.*, 1978; Wells, 1982), but none of the pop singers
guilty of hyper-American /r/ speaks one of these varieties, so far as
I know.)
    Le Page's fourth rider (we shall return to the third shortly) is:

(iv) our ability to modify our behaviour (probably lessening as we get older).

We have already touched on this point in our discussion of hypercorrection: it is possible that imperfection in imitation is due to
lack of ability. We can further demonstrate the validity of this
rider by pointing to the fact that most of the modifications British
singers make in their pronunciation are variable, irregular, and
inconsistent. We can assume, for instance, that many singers
would pronounce all non-prevocalic /r/s if they could. It is simply
that, in the flow of the song, they are not consistently able to do

so. It is also of interest to observe that some phonological environments cause more difficulty than others. Most difficult, apparently, is the insertion of non-prevocalic /r/ in an unstressed syllable before a following consonant, as in *better man*. Here, fewest /r/s are pronounced by British singers. Correspondingly, it is in exactly the same environment that *fewest* /r/s are *deleted* by American singers.

The observation that non-prevocalic /r/ is only spasmodically inserted in singing can be confirmed quite simply by counting. For instance, in spite of a strong impression, to British listeners, that they are in this respect successfully imitating Americans, the Beatles, on their first British LP, *Please Please Me* (1963), manage to pronounce only 47 per cent of potential non-prevocalic /r/s.

CHANGING PATTERNS OF LINGUISTIC MODIFICATION

To count /r/s in this way is to acknowledge that, in British pop music, (r) is a linguistic variable in the Labovian sense. Employing the concept of the linguistic variable in this way, to examine this and the other features typical of British pop-song pronunciation, opens up the possibility of examining Le Page's theory in more detail, especially in so far as it allows for the possibility of accounting for conflict and change.

It permits, for example, the quantitative comparison of the pronunciation of pop songs from the late 1950s and early 1960s with that of later periods. This turns out to be very instructive. For example, an analysis of four LPs from the period 1963–5 (the first two British albums produced by the Beatles and Rolling Stones respectively) gives an overall (r)-count, based on 372 tokens, of 36 per cent (i.e. 36 per cent of potential non-prevocalic /r/s were pronounced). On the other hand, analysis of four British albums, selected at random, from 1978 and 1979, (Dire Straits *Dire Straits*; Supertramp *Breakfast in America*; Clash *The Clash*; Sham '69 *Hersham Boys*) gives an (r)-count, based on 546 tokens, of 4 per cent. Obviously it would not be legitimate to draw any conclusions from such a haphazard and small-scale comparison. At the same time, it does suggest that something has happened to pop-song pronunciation, and it does tally well with casual observations to the effect that things have changed.

This is further reinforced by figure 8.1. This figure portrays the (r) scores per album for ten of the eleven LPs released by the Beatles in Britain between 1963 and 1971, and paints rather a surprisingly dramatic picture. During the Beatles' recording life there was a very considerable falling-off in non-prevocalic /r/ usage. From a high of 47 per cent in 1963 this falls to a low of 3 per cent in 1970.

The same pattern is repeated in figure 8.2. This graph deals with the same ten Beatles records, together with scores for four records by the Rolling Stones. In addition to (r) scores, it also shows the percentage of intervocalic /t/s realized as [ɖ] = (t), and a less dramatic but equally clear picture emerges. (In calculating (t) scores, both environments such as *better* and *get a* have been

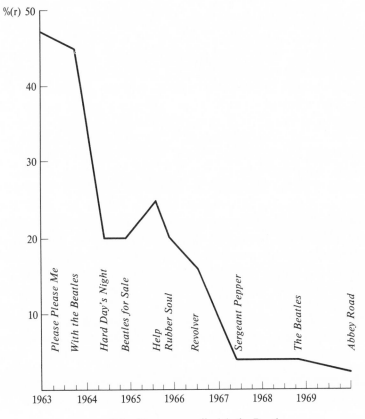

FIGURE 8.1   Non-prevocalic /r/: the Beatles

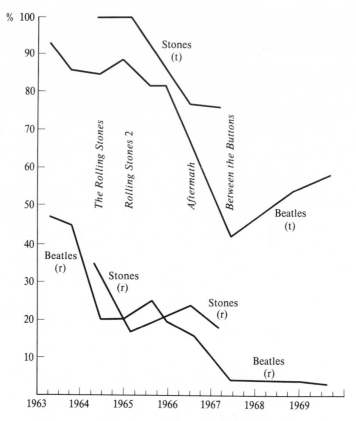

FIGURE 8.2   (r) and (t): the Beatles and the Rolling Stones

included. The phrase *at all* has been omitted from calculations since British speakers, unlike Americans, have for the most part resyllabified this as *a#t all*. In the case of (t), the phonological environment which causes British singers most difficulty is as in *adversity, nobility*, where there is some variability even in American English.)

Other quasi-American features, too, can be shown to have declined in frequency. We can draw no conclusions from the Beatles' pronunciation of *dance, past*, etc. as their native northern (Liverpool) English accents have /æ/ in these words in any case. It is, however, possible to detect a change in their treatment of items such as *can't* and *half* which have /æ/ in the USA but /aː/ in the north as well as the south of England. The progression is:

	Album	*can't, half*
1963	Please Please Me	/æ/
1963	With The Beatles	/æ/
1964	Hard Day's Night	/æ/
1964	Beatles for Sale	/æ/
1965	Help	/æ/
1967	Sergeant Pepper	/æ/ ~ /aː/
1968	The Beatles (White Album)	/æ/ ~ /aː/
1969	Abbey Road	/aː/

(The Rolling Stones, on the other hand, have always been /æ/-users, their lead singer Mick Jagger consistently scoring 100 per cent on all albums.)

So what has happened? One factor that may be important in examining the performance of a group such as the Beatles is that it could be argued that their change in pronunciation reflects a change in genre. Their early songs are often clearly in the rock-and-roll mould, while later songs tend to be more complex, contemplative, poetic, and so on. The subject-matter of the songs changes, too, and the later songs, now written entirely by themselves, show an increase in more obviously British themes and locales. (It may also be of some relevance that songs written by British composers tend, naturally enough, to have r-less rhymes of the type *bought–short* (Beatles *Revolver*), *Rita–metre* (Beatles *Sergeant Pepper*) (cf. Zwicky, 1976).) The particular 'image' that particular groups try to project will also be a factor.

But it is also clear that, from around 1964 on, British singers generally began trying less hard to sound like Americans. Why should this have been? Within the framework provided by Le Page, we can say that the strength of the motivation towards the American model has become weaker. If this is the case, then this change can in turn be ascribed to developments within the world of pop music itself. The enormous popularity of the Beatles, which extended to the USA by 1964, and, in their wake, of other Liverpool-based (and other British) groups, led to a change in the pattern of cultural domination. For a while, it was Britain that dominated America in this field, and, while this is no longer the case, the *strength* of American domination was permanently weakened. British pop music acquired a validity of its own, and this has been reflected in linguistic behaviour.

CONFLICTING MOTIVATIONS

Le Page's third rider is:

(iii) the strength of various (possibly conflicting) motivations towards one or another model and towards retaining our own sense of our unique identity.

As we have just seen, the strength of the motivation towards the American model diminished from 1964 on. Imitation of this model, however, was not in conflict with any other, and the American model remained the sole motivation there was for pop singers to modify their pronunciation. British singers were indeed trying *less hard* to sound like Americans; but it cannot be said that they were actually trying to sound *more British*. Nor does it actually appear to be true, although it was often claimed to be the case at the time, that from 1963 on singers from elsewhere tried to imitate a Liverpool accent. (The Beatles themselves sounded both more American, as we have seen, *and* more Liverpudlian on their early records than on their later records. Obviously Liverpool features included: the heavy aspiration/affrication of voiceless stops (*passim*); the rhyming of *gone* and *one* (*With The Beatles*); the rhyming of *aware* and *her* (*Rubber Soul*); the pronunciation of *book*, etc. with long /uː/ (as late as *Sergeant Pepper*); the pronunciation of *hang a ...* and *long ago* with [ng] (*Revolver*).)

In more recent years, however, especially since 1976, this situation has changed. A new and conflicting motivation *has* arisen. This new motivation is most apparent in the performance of music by pop groups categorized under the heading of 'punk-rock' and/or 'new wave'. The music of 'punk' groups is typically loud, fast and aggressive, and the songs concerned, often, with themes such as violence, underprivilege, alienation, and rejection. The songs are also frequently – in non-punk mainstream societal terms – in bad taste. The intended primary audience is British urban working-class youth.

'Punk-rock' singers, like their antecedents, modify their pronunciation when singing. Analysis of their pronunciation, however, shows that there has been a reduction in the use of the 'American' features discussed above, although they are still used, and an introduction of features associated with low-prestige south of England accents. These features, crucially, are employed in singing even by those who do not use them in speech. They include:

1 the use of wide diphthongs, as /ei/ = [æɪ] *face*, and /ou/ = [æʉ] *go*;
2 the pronunciation of /ai/ as [ɑɪ] *sky*, and of /au/ as [æu ~ ɛu] *out*;
3 the vocalization of /l/, as in *milk* [mɪʊk];
4 the (occasional) deletion of /h/;
5 the use of [ʔ] realizations of /t/ not only finally, as in *get*, but also intervocalically, where it is most socially stigmatized and conspicuous, as in *better*.

The use of these low-status pronunciations is coupled with a usage of non-standard grammatical forms, such as multiple negation and third-person singular *don't*, that is even higher than in other sub-genres of pop music, and the intended effect is assertive and aggressive. There is also clearly an intention to aid identification with and/or by British working-class youth, and to appeal to others who wish to identify with them, their situation and their values. The 'covert prestige' (see chapter 10) of non-standard, low-prestige linguistic forms is clearly in evidence, and the overall motivation, conflicting with that towards the American model, is clearly towards a working-class British model, and towards retaining, although at a group rather than individual level, a sense of a unique (and non-American) identity. (Note that accommodation theory – see above – might be applicable here.)

The continued use in punk-rock of 'American' forms, however, shows that the assertion of a unique British working-class identity is not the whole story. The old motivation of sounding American has not been replaced by the new motivation, but remains in competition with it. Not only, for instance, are American pronunciations retained, but American locutions, such as *real good*, continue to be employed. Moreover, many obvious British features are not employed – intrusive /r/, for example, is extremely rare, even on recent recordings. And at points where the two pronunciation models are in direct conflict, such as the realization of /ai/, forms like [a·] and [ɑɪ] alternate, even in the same song.

We therefore have, in Le Page's terms, conflicting motivations towards different models – the American and the British working class. This conflict, however, is not equally apparent in all types of British pop music. This is clearly revealed in Table 8.1. This table is based on data from seven albums only, and can again therefore be no more than suggestive. These albums are nevertheless possibly quite representative of those produced by many other singers and groups. The albums are: Rolling Stones *Some Girls* (1978); Supertramp *Breakfast in America* (1979); Dire Straits *Dire Straits* (1978); Stranglers *Rattus Norvegicus* (1977); Clash *The Clash* (1978); Sham '69 *Hersham Boys* (1979); and Ian Dury *Do It Yourself* (1979). The Rolling Stones, Supertramp and Dire Straits represent the 'mainstream' pop-music tradition, while the other performers represent the newer, punk-rock-oriented school. Information is given in the table on the percentage of non-prevocalic /r/s pronounced = (r); the percentage of intervocalic /t/s realized as [ɖ] = (t); the percentage of /æ/ rather than /aː/ in the lexical set of *path*, *dance* (except for Supertramp and Dire Straits, whose singers are from the north of England); and the percentage of intervocalic /t/s pronounced as a glottal stop.

It can be seen from Table 8.1 that the Rolling Stones, so far as their pronunciation is concerned, are still at the no-conflict, semi-American stage typical of the mid-1960s (and indeed it has always been apparent that Mick Jagger has more self-consciously than most in many respects modelled his singing style on that of Black American rhythm-and-blues singers.) The Stones' (r) and (t) scores are, however, still much lower than they would have been in the early 1960s.

TABLE 8·1   Usage of 'American' and 'British' features (percentages)

	'American'			'British'
	(r)	(t)	/æ/	[ʔ]
Rolling Stones	19	46	100	0
Supertramp	7	81	–	0
Dire Straits	1	92	–	0
Stranglers	0	88	80	0
Clash	6	71	24	10
Sham '69	1	57	50	9
Ian Dury	0	5	0	22

The two newer mainstream groups, Supertramp and Dire Straits, represent the phase after the weakening of American influence. This is apparent from a comparison of their (r) scores with that of the Rolling Stones: the very low (r)-count is typical of nearly all recent British singers. These two groups, however, still heavily favour the 'American' realization of (t) – unlike the Rolling Stones (their low score on *Some Girls* may be influenced by one particular song where the word *pretty* is repeated many times with [tʰ]). It seems, in fact, that British singers now have considerable freedom in the extent to which they feel obliged to conform to the earlier 'American' norm for (t). (It is perhaps relevant that the Supertramp record was recorded in the USA, is entitled 'Breakfast in America', and expresses sentiments such as 'Like to see America / See the girls in California ...'.) The supposedly 'punk' group the Stranglers also come out as having an orientation only towards the American model, in that they closely resemble the 'mainstream' groups in their linguistic behaviour. (This is probably of more interest to rock musicologists than to linguists, but it is interesting to note that The Stranglers have been one of the groups accused of having 'sold out' and of not being 'really punk'. Perhaps giving your records Latin titles does not help here either.)

The Clash and Sham '69, on the other hand, can clearly be placed, on phonological grounds alone, in the punk-rock category. In their scores the conflict between the 'American' and 'British' motivations is clearly portrayed. Scores for (r) and /æ/ are low, and [ʔ] is quite heavily used (scores for word-final [ʔ] would be considerably higher than these intervocalic (t) scores). And, interestingly enough, the orientation towards the 'British' model receives overt recognition in one of the songs on the Clash album, which is entitled 'I'm so bored with the USA'. On the other hand, 'American' forms are still used extensively. Punk-rock singing style is probably the only accent of English where the combination of *can't* /kaːnt/, *high* [ha ·] and *face* [fæɪs] is possible.

The scores given for Ian Dury are interesting in a different respect. These show no real signs of any conflict at all: his single model is clearly that of the speech of working-class London. Not too much, however, should be concluded from this as far as pop-song pronunciation in general is concerned. Dury is in some respects on the fringes of the pop-music tradition, and his bawdy and amusing lyrics owe perhaps as much to the comic tradition of the music hall as to pop. His extensive usage of [ʔ], for instance, can certainly be attributed in part to the aggressive style of punk-rockers, but it can also be attributed to the music-hall tradition which has often used Cockney pronunciation for comic effect. (A similar interpretation has to be placed on pronunciations used in the Kinks' 'Little bit of real emotion' (1979) where [lɪʔɫ bɪʔ əv] alternates, in the chorus, with [tʰ] and [ɖ] allophones of /t/. The effect of this is certainly not aggressive, and is perhaps more whimsical than anything else.)

CONCLUSION

British pop singers, then, have attempted to model their linguistic behaviour, when singing, on that of Americans. Their success in this has been constrained, first, by their ability to identify their model group: there has been some confusion as to which American accent it is that is being imitated. Secondly, their analytical ability has not always been sufficient to work out the rules of American linguistic behaviour, with the result that hyper-American /r/s occur. Thirdly, their ability to perform these modifications, even where analysis is correct, is far from perfect, so that American forms occur only inconsistently. Finally, as a result of the rise in the influence of British pop music, the strength of the motivation towards the American model was reduced, around 1964, and there was a drop in the frequency of occurrence of these American forms.

More recently, the past few years have seen the rise of a new sub-genre within pop music, often labelled 'punk-rock'. Groups who perform this type of music typically cultivate a more aggressive, urban working-class image. This has led to the development of a motivation towards a new model: southern English urban working-class youth. This motivation has not replaced the motivation towards the American model, but coexists – and conflicts – with it. This conflict leads to a style of pronunciation where stereotypically American forms combine with stereotypically English working-class forms.

Le Page's work has already helped us to understand that the selection of linguistic forms from different codes may be due to split motivation, and that a combination of different linguistic features may be very functional in retaining a balanced public and self-image. In Belize, for example, the split may be between 'how to behave if you want eventually to get a job outside the country' and 'how to behave as a good Belizean' (see Le Page, 1978).

In British pop music, motivations towards different models have changed and shifted in the past two decades. The result is that the particular combination of 'American', neutral, and 'British' forms used may currently vary from singer to singer (and even from song to song). Singers in the mainstream pop tradition show for the most part motivation only towards the 'American' model, albeit much more weakly than was the case twenty years ago. A few singers, like Ian Dury, may show an orientation almost exclusively towards a 'British' model.

Many punk-rock singers, however, are like Belizeans. For them there is a genuine split in motivation. The conflict is between a motivation towards a supposedly American model, and a motivation towards a supposedly British working-class model – which can be glossed as a conflict between 'how to behave like a genuine pop singer' and 'how to behave like a British urban working-class youth'. The combination of linguistic forms that is typically found in punk-rock singing is an attempt to find a balance between the two.

Le Page's theory is an attempt to find a general motive for speakers' linguistic behaviour. In developing this theory, Le Page finds it 'necessary to emphasise the phatic and self-expressive more than the communicative function of language'. Pop-music is a field where language is especially socially symbolic, and typically low in communicative function, high on the phatic and self-expressive. It is not surprising, therefore, that the factors isolated in his work by Le Page are so clearly apparent in pop-music singing. We must expect that, in more typical and less restricted forms of language use, the location of these factors will be a much more complicated task. We must also expect, however, that it will be possible.

On the other hand, it is also certain that any inadequacies in the theory that are apparent in its application to pop-song pronunciation will also prove to be inadequacies elsewhere. One of these inadequacies is the following: even in the narrow field of pop-song pronunciation it is not possible, in terms of this theory (or any other), to explain why *particular* (in this case 'British' or

'American') consonantal, vocalic or other variants are retained, rejected or selected, and not others. We therefore await theoretical refinements, since it may be the case that until we are better able to account for why, say, the Clash (*The Clash* 'Remote Control') sing [kɑːnt gɛɖ ə'hɛd] (rather than [kænt gɛɖ ə'hɛd] or [kɑːnt gɛʔ ə'hɛd]), we as sociolinguists may perhaps not be able to make too much progress either.

CHAPTER 9

Social Identity and Linguistic Sex differentiation

Explanations and pseudo-explanations
for differences between women's
and men's speech

It has been known for some considerable time that in some societies language is involved in covariation, not only with parameters such as social stratification, social context and age, but also with the parameter of sex. The fact that the speech of men and women may differ in interesting ways was initially noted in only a rather small number of linguistic articles and discussions, and research tended to concentrate either on non-urbanized communities or on relatively peripheral aspects of the subject (see Jespersen, 1922, chapter 13; Sapir, 1929; Haas, 1944; Hertzler, 1954; Fischer, 1958; and the summary of other work in Crystal, 1971). In the past two decades, however, a number of studies have appeared which present accurate, structured data illustrating the form that sex differentiation takes in the linguistic communities of complex urbanized societies. Early work of this type was based on sociolinguistic investigations into varieties of urban American English (see Labov, 1966a; Levine and Crockett, 1966; Shuy *et al.*, 1967; Wolfram, 1969; Fasold, 1968). More recent studies of other varieties – and very many could be cited – include Trudgill (1974a), Milroy (1980), and Cheshire (1982); and see also chapter 10.

The results of all these sociolinguistic studies, and they are by now very numerous, have one very striking feature in common. They are all agreed that women, allowing for other variables such as age, education and social class, produce on average linguistic forms which more closely approach those of the standard language or have higher prestige than those produced by men.

It is important to stress the point that this type of differentiation is *on average*. All the studies that have been made of urbanized societies indicate that this aspect of sex differentiation in language is a matter of sex-preferential tendencies – the speech of men and women differs only in general and by degree. Differences are not sex-exclusive. (This point has sometimes been misunderstood. Spender (1980), for example, writes, with reference to Trudgill (1974b), that 'Trudgill maintains that there is a feminine and a masculine linguistic variety'. This has actually never been maintained, of urbanized western societies, by anyone.)

Nevertheless, this phenomenon is one that requires explanation, and over the past several years a number of explanations have been advanced, some of them in print, some informally, many of them controversial, and most of them speculative. Amongst them we may include the following:

1   One 'explanation' lies in suggesting that the phenomenon of sex differentiation in language actually does not exist (and therefore does not have to be explained). Spender (1980) writes that 'it might be possible that women do speak "better" than men, ... but at the moment the available evidence is not convincing'. The evidence from sociolinguistic studies is, as we have seen, in fact utterly convincing and overwhelming. It is the single most consistent finding to emerge from sociolinguistic studies over the past 20 years. This phenomenon may be found by some people to be embarrassing and undesirable, but there can be absolutely no doubt that it does exist.

2   Another attempt to 'explain away' this finding involves the, on the face of it very reasonable, suggestion that the phenomenon is due to the fact that field-workers in sociolinguistic studies are male. (See, e.g., Smith, 1979: 117) Male informants, the argument goes, are more relaxed or more inclined to accommodate (Giles, 1973) in a same-sex situation than are female informants with a male interviewer, and thus produce more casual speech. This is in fact simply not the case, since studies employing female field-workers (see Romaine, 1978; Milroy, 1980; Cheshire, 1982) produce exactly the same results.

3   A further attempt to find an explanation lies in an appeal to the notion of 'appropriateness'. In Trudgill (1974b) I wrote that:

geographical, ethnic group, and social-class varieties are, at least partly, the result of social *distance*, while sex varieties are the result of social *difference*. Different social attributes, and different behaviour, is expected from men and women, and sex varieties are a symbol of this fact. Using a female linguistic variety is as much a case of identifying oneself as female, and of behaving 'as a woman should', as is, say, wearing a skirt. What would happen to a man who, in our society, wore a skirt? His fate would be the same as that of Carib men who attempted to use women's language: 'The women have words and phrases which the men never use, *or they would be laughed to scorn'*.

It is interesting to observe how analogies of this type are reacted to. For example, Spender (1980) takes the skirt analogy to imply that

if a man wore a skirt ... he would be identifying himself with all that is negative and undesirable in our society and would be open to ridicule or abuse. To Trudgill, linguistic variety helps to maintain the demarcation lines between the sexes, to prevent contamination – for men – and, implicitly then, is to be upheld.

There are a number of comments that can be made here. It will be apparent, I hope, that Spender's version is actually a caricature of what I wrote, and it is certainly a travesty of my actual feelings about this phenomenon. To describe a particular state of affairs does not, obviously, mean that one, implicitly or otherwise, wishes this state of affairs 'to be upheld'. A description is simply a description, and to report that men who wore skirts would be 'open to ridicule and abuse' is to report the truth. It does not, moreover, seem to be that this situation is a matter of 'contamination' or of men identifying themselves 'with all that is ... undesirable in our society'. Rather, it is a matter of appropriateness. It is widely, and strongly, held in our society that it is inappropriate for men to wear skirts – and use certain vocabulary items – just as it is felt to be inappropriate, by many, for women to swear or wear a three-piece pin-stripe suit. A woman wearing such a suit would seem incongruous, not because she was contaminating herself or identifying herself with 'all that is undesirable', but simply because what she was doing was inappropriate and unusual.

The skirt analogy, it is true, may not be without its deficiencies, but the parallel with language is clear, and it is actually encouraging, for many people, to note that notions about appropriateness can change. A hundred years ago the wearing of trousers by women was highly inappropriate. This is no longer so. Similarly, the use of taboo vocabulary is now much more evenly distributed between the sexes than formerly.

A criticism of the appropriateness explanation that Spender ought to have made, but did not, is that it still begs the very large question of *why* different forms of linguistic behaviour are widely, if usually subconsciously, held to be appropriate for men and women. Explanations in terms of appropriateness, that is, are not really explanations at all.

4   A further set of discussions of sex differences in language rest on what I would argue is a mistaken attempt to equate the findings produced by sociolinguistic surveys of the kind discussed above with the results of other studies of a different type. The sociolinguistic surveys found evidence of sex differentiation in phonetics, phonology and morphology. The evidence, as we saw above, is very clear, but it concerns no more than the fact that, on average, women say, for example, the less prestigious form [pæʔ] rather than the more prestigious form [pæt] *pat* less often than men; and that they also say, for example, the less 'correct' *I done it* rather than the more 'correct' *I did it* less often than men. These features, we can say, are matters of *dialect and accent*. Other types of work have found linguistic sex differences of other – and, I would suggest, not necessarily comparable – kinds. These include linguistic phenomena such as the use of particular hesitation phenomena, particular syntactic devices (such as ellipsis and tag-questions), and particular communicative and conversational strategies. These we can perhaps label collectively as *language use* differences.

As an example of work which attempts to make this equation, we can cite Brown (1980). In a highly insightful paper on language use in a Mayan community, Brown attempts to interpret the *dialect and accent* findings of sociolinguists as an indication that women demonstrate greater linguistic *politeness* than men, and relates this 'politeness' to deference and subservience. (Spender (1980) also equates more prestigious speech with 'politeness or subservience'.) However, it can very readily be argued that to equate the usage of more standard, 'correct' linguistic variants with 'politeness' is to confuse the issue. In some cases, it is true, to speak in a more standard, formal or prestigious manner may be to indicate politeness. But in other cases it can certainly indicate the reverse. In English the desire to convey an impression of politeness may well often lead to a greater usage of standard linguistic features, but the reverse is not true: the usage of more 'correct' language does not *necessarily* indicate politeness. It is perfectly possible to employ high-status pronunciations and standard grammatical forms together with impolite lexis and other signals of distance and dominance. (Indeed, Giles' (1973) notion of 'accent divergence' suggests precisely this kind of phenomenon: in order to be impolite to an interlocutor who speaks a less standard variety, a speaker can employ more standard linguistic forms than normally.)

In fact, Brown's 'politeness' interpretation works mainly with *language use* sex differences, and it is for the most part these to which she devotes her paper. (Features she cites include: emphatic particles, intonation, negative questions, repetition, rhetorical questions, and diminutives.) These differences can indeed be used to signal greater or lesser politeness and/or deference and/or subservience. Preisler, for example, has indicated (see Laver and Trudgill, 1979) that speakers playing a dominant role in a conversation make more suggestions, use more imperatives, and employ fewer interrogatives than people taking a subordinate role – and dominant speakers are more often male than female. *Dialect and accent* differences, on the other hand, are not, I would maintain, so widely employed in this way, and are not to be explained entirely in the same terms.

Brown (1980) also makes the interesting point that, when we are attempting to explain linguistic sex differences, we should consider the possibility that one reason for these differences may lie in the fact that women and men may be trying to achieve different things through language. If this is so, then clearly it will be the *language use* level that will be a reflection of these differences, since *dialect and accent* variants must be held to be socially different (but linguistically equivalent) ways of doing the *same* thing (cf. the discussion in the literature on the nature of linguistic variables – see Lavandera, 1978; Labov, 1978; Romaine, 1981).

This distinction between the two types of linguistic sex differentiation is reinforced by Togeby (1978). He points to the finding (see Jörgensen, 1970) of the Lund project on spoken Swedish that women use fewer syntactic markers of prestige style (such as longer or more complete sentences) than men. Togeby in fact argues, with reference to discussions such as Trudgill (1974b), that 'all claims that women are more sensitive to prestige than men collapse in the fact of counterevidence of this type' (my

translation). He subsequently, however, gives a very clear explanation for these findings, and makes it plain that he is actually
comparing two rather different types of phenomena – *language use*
data from the Lund study, and the *dialect and accent* data discussed in Trudgill (1974b). Prestigious or stigmatized phonological and morphological variants, Togeby says, are readily perceived as such by speakers involved in conversational interaction,
whereas syntactic features and devices typical of less or more
formal styles are not directly perceived as low status or prestigious
at all. One does not, for example, normally notice the fact that
one's interlocutor is using more words per sentence than oneself.
And even if one does, we can add, differences of this type are not
generally perceived as being a matter of greater or lesser 'correctness'. It is therefore no surprise that women do not employ these
devices as they do 'correct' pronunciations and standard morphological forms.

Language use differences, then, may indeed be due to differential
expressions of politeness etc., which may in turn be due to subservience and deference – but we still remain without an entirely
satisfactory explanation for the *dialect and accent* differences that
have been so fully documented and with which this chapter is
chiefly concerned.

5   Interestingly, both Brown and Togeby also attempt to provide explanations for linguistic sex differentiation in terms of
social networks. This is obviously a very promising avenue for
research, since Milroy (1980) has shown that the type of social
network in which speakers participate, and the strength of their
participation, can have a significant effect on their linguistic
behaviour. If men and women in particular communities participate in different types of network, then they will demonstrate
different types of linguistic behaviour, as Milroy has shown for
Belfast.

Brown's discussion of the role of social networks applies most
pertinently in her own research to *language use* differences. She
writes:

Positive politeness prevails if and when social networks involve multiplex relationships, that is, members have many-sided relationships with each person
they interact with regularly .... Where men dominate the public sphere of life
and women stick largely to the domestic sphere, it seems likely that female
relationships will be relatively multi-stranded, male ones relatively single-
stranded, and where these conditions prevail, positive politeness should be
strongly elaborated in women's speech.

It seems perfectly plausible, however, that networks can be appealed to also in explanations for *dialect and accent* sex differences. Togeby, for instance, attempts to relate both types of sex differentiation to differential responses by men and women to the 'authority norm' and the 'ambition norm'. These in turn stem from the fact that the two sexes are differentially involved with the 'intimate, family sphere' and the 'social and economic sphere' of social life. The family sphere, Togeby argues, is the only area in which the 'authority norm' can predominate (though he does not give a satisfactory explanation of why this is so). Since women are more closely connected with this sphere than men, they are more responsive to the 'authority norm', i.e. they are more susceptible to the linguistic influence of those members of society who wield the power – and therefore employ more prestigious pronunciations. (Men, correspondingly, are more involved with 'ambition', and therefore use more competitive, attacking conversational strategies.)

6   A further explanation, or series of explanations, that is frequently advanced is one that depends on the findings of sociologists (see Martin, 1954) that women in our society are, generally speaking, more status-conscious than men, and are therefore more aware of the social significance of linguistic variables. There are three reasons which are, in turn, advanced for this greater linguistic/social awareness:

(a)   Women are more closely involved with child-rearing and the transmission of culture, and are therefore more aware of the importance, for their children, of the acquisition of (prestige) norms.

(b)   The social position of women in our society has traditionally been less secure than that of men. It may be, therefore, that it has been more necessary for women to secure and signal their social status linguistically and in other ways, and they may for this reason be more aware of the importance of this type of signal.

(c)   Men in our society have traditionally been rated socially by their occupation, their earning power, and perhaps by their other abilities – in other words, by what they *do*. Until recently, however, this has been much more difficult for women, and indeed women continue to suffer discrimination against them in many occupations. It may be, therefore, that they have had to be rated instead, to a greater extent than men, on how they *appear*. Since they have not been rated, to the same extent that men have, by their occupation or by their occupational success, other signals of status, including speech, have been correspondingly more important. (The fact that I have written the above should, once again, be taken to be a straightforward reportage of what I take to be the facts concerning our society's traditional evaluation and provision of occupations for women. It does not mean that I approve of occupational discrimination against women, and it most certainly does not mean 'that Trudgill does not take women's work into account and does not value it' (Spender, 1980). One should not, as Spender does, blame the messenger for bringing bad news, however much one dislikes the news.)

7   A final, though not necessarily unrelated, explanation, lies in the claim that working-class speech appears in our society to have connotations of masculinity. We examine this explanation in more detail in the following chapter.

CHAPTER 10

Sex and Covert Prestige

Linguistic Change in the Urban Dialect of Norwich

In the previous chapter we discussed the phenomenon of sex differentiation in language, and explanations that have been advanced for this differentiation. In this chapter we present some data which illustrate quite clearly the nature of this type of differentiation in one variety of British English. We then examine an explanation for this differentiation, and consider what role it plays in the propagation of linguistic change.

The results from which the following figures are taken are based on an urban dialect survey of the city of Norwich carried out in the summer of 1968 with a random sample, 60 in number, of the population of the city, and reported in detail in Trudgill (1974a). This sociolinguistic research was concerned mainly with correlating phonetic and phonological variables with social class, age, and stylistic context. Some work was also done, however, in studying the relationships that obtain between linguistic phenomena and sex.

In order to relate the phonological material to the social class of informants and the other parameters, a number of phonetic and phonological variables were developed, and index scores calculated for individuals and groups in the manner of Labov (1966a – and see also chapter 3). The first of these variables that I wish to discuss is the variable (ng). This is the pronunciation of the suffix *-ing* in *walking*, *laughing*, etc., and is a well-known variable in many types of English. In the case of Norwich English there are two possible pronunciations of this variable: [ɪŋ], which also occurs in the prestige accent, RP, and [ən ~ n̩]. The former is labelled (ng)-1 and the latter (ng)-2.

Index scores were developed for this variable by initially awarding 1 for each instance of (ng)-1 and 2 for each instance of (ng)-2. These scores were then summed and divided by the total number of instances, to give the mean score. Indices were finally calculated by subtracting 1 from the mean score and multiplying the result by 100. In this case, this gives an index score of 000 for consistent use of RP (ng)-1, and 100 for consistent use of (ng)-2, and the scores are equivalent to the simple percentage of non-RP forms used. (For variables with more than two variants this simple relationship, of course, does not apply.) Indices were calculated in the first instance for individual informants in each contextual style and subsequently for each group of informants. The four contextual styles:

word list style: WLS
reading passage style: RPS
formal speech: FS
casual speech: CS

are equivalent to the styles discussed by Labov (1966a) and were elicited in a similar manner. Indices for other variables were calculated in the same way.

Table 10·1 shows the average (ng) index scores for informants in the five social class groups obtained in the survey, in the four contextual styles. The social class divisions are based on an index that was developed using income, education, dwelling type, location of dwelling, occupation, and occupation of father as parameters. The five classes have been labelled:

TABLE 10·1   (ng) Index scores by class and style

| | Style | | | | |
Class	WLS	RPS	FS	CS	N
MMC	000	000	003	028	6
LMC	000	010	015	042	8
UWC	005	015	074	087	16
MWC	023	044	088	095	22
LWC	029	066	098	100	8

middle middle class: MMC
lower middle class: LMC
upper working class: UWC
middle working class: MWC
lower working class: LWC

The table shows very clearly that (ng) is a linguistic variable in Norwich English. Scores range from a high of 100 per cent non-RP forms by the LWC in CS to a low of 0 per cent by the MMC in RPS and by the MMC and LMC in WLS. The pattern of differentiation is also structured in a very clear manner. For each of the social classes, scores rise consistently from WLS to CS; and for each style scores rise consistently from MMC to LWC.

In his study of this same variable in American English, Fischer (1958) found that males used a higher percentage of non-standard [n] forms than females. Since we have shown that (ng) is a variable in Norwich English, we would expect, if sex differentiation of the type we have been discussing also occurs here, that the same sort of pattern would emerge. Table 10·2 shows that this is in fact very largely the case. In 17 cases out of 20, *male* scores are greater than or equal to corresponding *female* scores. We can therefore state that a high (ng) index is typical not only of WC speakers in

TABLE 10·2   (ng) Index scores by class, style and sex

Class	Sex	WLS	RPS	FS	CS
MMC	M	000	000	004	031
	F	000	000	000	000
LMC	M	000	020	027	017
	F	000	000	003	067
UWC	M	000	018	081	095
	F	011	013	068	077
MWC	M	024	043	091	097
	F	020	046	081	088
LWC	M	060	100	100	100
	F	017	054	097	100

Norwich but also of *male* speakers. This pattern, moreover, is repeated for the vast majority of the other nineteen variables studied in Norwich.

In the previous chapter we examined a number of different explanations for this phenomenon. In this chapter we seek an explanation in terms of the fact that WC speech, like other aspects of WC culture, appears, at least in some western societies, to have connotations of masculinity (see Labov, 1966a: 495), probably because it is associated with the roughness and toughness supposedly characteristic of WC life which are, stereotypically and to a certain extent, often considered to be desirable masculine attributes. They are not, on the other hand, widely considered to be desirable feminine characteristics. On the contrary, features such as 'refinement' and 'sophistication' are much preferred in some western societies.

As it stands, this argument is largely speculative. What it requires is some concrete evidence. This need for evidence was discussed by Labov (1966b: 108) who wrote that in New York

the socio-economic structure confers prestige on the middle-class pattern associated with the more formal styles. [But] one can't avoid the implication that in New York City we must have an equal and opposing prestige for informal, working-class speech – a covert prestige enforcing this speech pattern. We must assume that people in New York City want to talk as they do, yet this fact is not at all obvious in any overt response that you can draw from interview subjects.

It is suspected, in other words, that there are hidden values associated with non-standard speech, and that, as far as our present argument is concerned, they are particularly important in explaining the sex differentiation of linguistic variables. Labov, however, has not been able to uncover them or prove that they exist. We can guess that these values are there, but they are values which are not usually overtly expressed. They are not values which speakers readily admit to having, and for that reason they are difficult to study. Happily, the urban dialect survey carried out in Norwich provided some evidence which argues very strongly in favour of our hypothesis, and which managed, as it were, to remove the outer layer of overtly expressed values and penetrate to the hidden values beneath. That is, we now have some objective data which actually demonstrates that for male speakers WC non-standard speech is in a very real sense highly valued and prestigious.

Labov has produced evidence to show that almost all speakers in New York City share a common set of linguistic norms, whatever their actual linguistic performance, and that they hear and report themselves as using these prestigious linguistic forms, rather than the forms they actually do use. This 'dishonesty' in reporting what they say is of course not deliberate, but it does suggest that informants, at least so far as their conscious awareness is concerned, are dissatisfied with the way they speak, and would prefer to be able to use more standard forms. This was in fact confirmed by comments New York City informants actually made about their own speech.

Overt comments made by the Norwich informants on their own speech were also of this type. Comments such as 'I talk horrible' were typical. It also began to appear, however, that, as suggested above, there were other, deeper motivations for their actual linguistic behaviour than these overtly expressed notions of their own 'bad speech'. For example, many informants who initially stated that they did not speak properly, and would like to do so, admitted, if pressed, that they perhaps would not *really* like to, and that they would almost certainly be considered foolish, arrogant or disloyal by their friends and family if they did. This is our first piece of evidence.

Far more important, however, is the evidence that was obtained by means of the Self-Evaluation Test, in which half of the Norwich informants took part. This is particularly the case when the results of this test are compared to those obtained by a similar test conducted by Labov in New York. In the Norwich Self-Evaluation Test, 12 lexical items were read aloud, to informants, with two or more different pronunciations. For example:

tune   1. [tjʉːn]   2. [tʉːn]

Informants were then asked to indicate, by marking a number on a chart, which of these pronunciations most closely resembled the way in which they normally said this word.

The corresponding Self-Evaluation Test in New York for the variable (r) – presence or absence of post-vocalic /r/ (a prestige feature) – produced the following results. Informants who in FS used over 30 per cent /r/ were, very generously, considered to be (post-vocalic) /r/-users. Seventy per cent of those who, in this sense, were /r/-users reported that they normally used /r/. But 62 per cent of those who were *not* /r/-users *also* reported that they normally used /r/. As Labov says (1966a: 455): 'In the conscious report of their own usage. . . . New York respondents are very inaccurate'. The accuracy, moreover, is overwhelmingly in the direction of reporting themselves as using a form which is *more* statusful than the one they actually use. Labov (1966a: 455) claims that 'no conscious deceit plays a part in this process' and that 'most of the respondents seemed to perceive their own speech in terms of the norms at which they were aiming rather than the sound actually produced'.

The full results of this test are shown in table 10·3. It shows that 62 per cent of non-/r/-users 'over-reported' themselves as using /r/, and 21 per cent of /r/-users 'under-reported', although in view of Labov's 30 per cent dividing line, the latter were very probably simply being accurate.

TABLE 10·3   Self-evaluating of (r) – New York

	Percentage reported		
Used	/r/	ø	
/r/	79	21	= 100
ø	62	38	= 100

In the Norwich test, the criteria used were much more rigorous. In comparing the results obtained in the Self-Evaluation Test to forms actually used in Norwich, *casual speech* was used rather than *formal speech*, since CS more closely approximates everyday speech – to how informants normally pronounce words, which is what they were asked to report on. Moreover, informants were allowed *no* latitude in their self-evaluation. It was considered that the form informants used in everyday speech was the variant indicated by the appropriate CS index for that individual informant. For example, an (ng) index of between 050 and 100 was taken as indicating an (ng)-2 user rather than (ng)-1 user. In other words, the dividing line is 50 per cent rather than Labov's more lenient 30 per cent. If, therefore, the characteristics of the Norwich sample were identical to those of the New York sample, we would expect a significantly *higher* degree of *over-reporting* from the Norwich informants.

TABLE 10·4   Self-evaluation of (yu)

Used	(yu) Percentage reported		
	1	2	
1	60	40	= 100
2	16	84	= 100

The results, in fact, show the exact reverse of this, as can be seen from table 10·4.

This table gives the results of the Self-Evaluation Test for the variable (yu), which is the pronunciation of the vowel in items such as *tune, music, queue, huge.* In Norwich English items such as these have two possible pronunciations: (yu)-1 has [j] as in RP-like [kjuː ~ kjʉː]; (yu)-2 omits [j] as in [kʉː ~ kɜʉ], *queue.*

Table 10·4 provides a very striking contrast to the New York results shown in table 10·3 in that only 16 per cent of (yu)-2 users, as compared to the equivalent figure of 62 per cent in New York, over-reported themselves as using the more statusful RP-like variant (yu)-1 when they did not in fact do so. Even more significant, however, is the fact that as many as 40 per cent of (yu)-1 users actually *under*-reported – and the under-reporting is in this case quite genuine.

A further breakdown of the scores given in table 10·4 is also very revealing. Of the 16 per cent (yu)-2 users who over-reported, *all* were women. Of the (yu)-1 users who under-reported, half were men and half women. Here we see, for the first time, the emergence of the hidden values that underlie the sex differentiation described earlier in this chapter. If we take the sample as a whole, we have the percentages of speakers under- and over-reporting shown in table 10·5. Male informants, it will be noted, are strik-

TABLE 10·5   Percentage of informants over- and under-reporting (yu)

	Total	Male	Female
Over-r	13	0	29
Under-r	7	6	7
Accurate	80	94	64

ingly more accurate in their self-assessment than are female informants.

The hidden values, however, emerge much more clearly from a study of the other variables tested in this way, (er), (ō) and (ā), illustrated in tables 10·6, 10·7, and 10·8, respectively. The variable (er) is the vowel in *ear, here, idea*, which in Norwich English ranges from [ɪə] to [ɛː]; (ō) is the vowel in *road, nose, moan* (but not in *rowed, knows, mown*, which are distinct) and ranges from [ɵu] through [uː] to [ʊ]; and (ā) is the vowel in the lexical set of *gate, face, name*, which ranges from [eɪ] to [æi].

For each of these variables, it will be seen, there are more male speakers who claim to use a *less* prestigious variant than they actually do than there are who over-report, and for one of the

TABLE 10·6 Percentage of informants over- and under-reporting (er)

	Total	Male	Female
Over-r	43	22	68
Under-r	33	50	14
Accurate	23	28	18

TABLE 10·7 Percentage of informants over- and under-reporting (ō)

	Total	Male	Female
Over-r	18	12	25
Under-r	36	54	18
Accurate	45	34	57

TABLE 10·8 Percentage of informants over- and under-reporting (ā)

	Total	Male	Female
Over-r	32	22	43
Under-r	15	28	0
Accurate	53	50	57

variables (ō), the difference is very striking: 54 per cent to 12 per cent. In two of the cases, moreover, there are more male speakers who under-report than there are who are accurate.

Although there are some notable differences between the four variables illustrated here,[1] it is clear that Norwich informants are much more prone to under-report than New York informants, and that – this is central to our argument – *male* informants in Norwich are much more likely to *under*-report, *female* informants to *over*-report.

This, then, is the objective evidence which demonstrates that male speakers, at least in Norwich, are at a subconscious or perhaps simply private level very favourably disposed towards non-standard speech forms. This is so much the case that as many as 54 per cent of them, in one case, claim to use these forms or hear themselves as using them *even when they do not do so*. If it is true that informants 'perceive their own speech in terms of the norms at which they are aiming rather than the sound actually produced' then the norm at which a large number of Norwich males are aiming is *non-standard WC speech*. This favourable attitude is never overtly expressed, but the responses to these tests show that statements about 'bad speech' are for public consumption only. Privately and subconsciously, a large number of male speakers are more concerned with acquiring prestige of the covert sort and with signalling group solidarity than with obtaining social status, as this is more usually defined. (This does not, of course, mean, as Spender (1980) would have it, that the male linguistic 'variety' is 'the norm'. Nor does it mean that 'females have no identity and cannot develop solidarity'. It would be nonsensical to maintain anything like this, and no sociolinguist has ever maintained anything of the kind. Spender's account of sociolinguistic research is at this point simply a caricature.) By means of these figures, therefore, we have been able to demonstrate both that it is possible to obtain evidence of the 'covert prestige' associated with non-standard varieties, and that, for Norwich men, working-class speech is statusful and prestigious. The clear contrast with scores obtained by female informants, with as many as 68 per cent of the

---

[1] These differences may be due to a skewing effect resulting from the necessity of using only a small number of individual lexical items to stand for each variable in the tests. (Informants' reports of their pronunciation of *tune*, for example, do not *necessarily* mean that they would pronounce or report *Tuesday* or *tube* in the same way.)

women over-reporting, in one case, underlines this point and indicates that women are much more favourably disposed towards MC standard forms. This in turn explains why the sex-differentiation pattern of table 10·2 takes the form it does.

Why it should have been possible to obtain this sort of evidence of covert prestige from Norwich speakers but not from New York speakers it is difficult to say. This may be due to the fact that WC speakers in Britain have not accepted MC values so readily or completely as WC speakers in America. If this is the case, it could be explained by 'the conspicuous lack of corporate or militant class consciousness [in America], which is one of the most important contrasts between American and European systems of stratification' (Mayer, 1955: 67) and by the related lack of 'embourgoisement' of the British WC (cf. Goldthorpe and Lockwood, 1963).

On the other hand, tables 10·9 and 10·10 show that this cannot be the whole story. These tables illustrate the amount of over- and under-reporting of (er) and (ō) respectively by male speakers as a whole, and then by MC as opposed to WC male speakers. It can be seen that there is no significant difference in the behaviour of the two classes. The MC, it is true, shows a slightly greater tendency to over-report than the WC, but this is very small. The significant parameter controlling presence or absence of this 'covert prestige'

TABLE 10·9   Percentage male informants over- and under-reporting (er)

	Total	MC	WC
Over-r	22	25	21
Under-r	50	50	50
Accurate	28	25	29

TABLE 10·10   Percentage male informants over- and under-reporting (ō)

	Total	MC	WC
Over-r	12	15	11
Under-r	54	54	54
Accurate	34	30	35

is therefore sex rather than social class. Recognition of these hidden values is something that is common to a majority of Norwich males of whatever social class (and something that they do not share with WC female informants). Many MC males appear to share with WC males the characteristic that they have not so completely absorbed the dominant mainstream societal values as have their American counterparts.

Having established that covert prestige does in fact exist, and can be shown to exist, we are now in a position to move on to a discussion of one of the problems that arises from the Norwich data. It was shown in table 10·2 that for the variable (ng) men had higher index scores than women. We also stated that the same pattern occurred for the vast majority of other Norwich variables, and we have since been able to offer at least a partial explanation of why this pattern occurs. There is one Norwich variable, however, which does not conform to this pattern of sex differentiation. This is the variable (o), the pronunciation of the vowel in the lexical set of *top, dog. box*. There are two main variants in Norwich English: (o)-1, a rounded RP-like vowel [ɒ]; and (o)-2, an unrounded vowel [ɑ ∼ a]. Table 10·11 gives index scores for this variable by social class, contextual style and sex, and shows a pattern of differentiation markedly different from that shown for (ng) in table 10·2.

TABLE 10·11   (o) Indices by class, style and sex

Class	Sex	Style			
		WLS	*RPS*	*FS*	*CS*
MMC	M	000	000	001	003
	F	000	000	000	000
LMC	M	004	014	011	055
	F	000	002	001	008
UWC	M	011	019	044	060
	F	023	027	068	077
MWC	M	029	026	064	078
	F	025	045	071	066
LWC	M	014	050	080	069
	F	037	062	083	090

As far as the two MC groups are concerned in all eight cases men again have scores that are higher than or equal to those of women. The striking fact to emerge from this table, however, is that for the three WC groups the normal pattern of sex differentiation is almost completely *reversed*. In ten cases out of twelve, women have higher scores than men. If it is true that for Norwich men WC non-standard speech forms have high covert prestige, then this would appear to be a counter-example which we have to explain. (This is the only Norwich variable for which a reversal of the pattern of sex differentiation was found.)

In order to be able to handle this problem we must first turn our attention to the examination of another variable, the variable (e). This is the pronunciation of the vowel in *tell*, *bell*, *hell*, for which there are three main variants: (e)-1 = [ɛ]; (e)-2 = [ɜ]; (e)-3 = [ʌ]. Table 10·12 shows index scores for this variable by class and style.

TABLE 10·12   (e) Indices by class and style

Class	Style			
	WLS	RPS	FS	CS
MMC	003	000	001	002
LMC	007	012	023	042
UWC	027	039	089	127
MWC	030	044	091	087
LWC	009	026	077	077

The figures given in this table illustrate quite clearly that the pattern of class differentiation for (e) differs rather strikingly from the normal pattern of differentiation illustrated for (ng) in table 10·1. The difference lies in the fact that the bottom group, the LWC, consistently has scores that are *lower* (more nearly standard) than those of both the UWC and MWC. A regular pattern of differentiation could only be obtained by placing the LWC scores between those for the LMC and UWC. It should also be noted that the MWC has a *lower* score than the UWC in CS. In CS, in fact, the class differentiation pattern for the WC is completely the reverse of the normal pattern.

The answer to the problem of why this should be the case lies in some research that was carried out into linguistic change in Norwich English. It was noted several times in the course of this research that the LWC, as a relatively underprivileged group, appeared to be isolated from certain innovating tendencies. Since we have found in the case of (e) that the LWC is differentiated from the UWC and the MWC in an unusual way, we can guess that high scores for this variable (that is, a large amount of non-standard centralization) represent an *innovation* in Norwich English: the variable (e) is involved in linguistic change, in that centralization of this vowel is increasing. We can further hypothesize that in the vanguard of this linguistic change, which would appear to be leading Norwich English in a direction away from the RP standard, are the *upper* members of the WC. The LWC and LMC are also participating in this change, but at a lower level, and the MMC are not participating at all, or very little.

This hypothesis is in fact confirmed by the pattern of age differentiation illustrated in table 10·13. This illustrates that younger people in Norwich, those aged under 30 and in particular those aged under 20, have much higher (e) scores than the rest of the population. This is particularly true of the crucial CS scores. Only the youngest two age groups achieve scores of 100 or over. This large amount of age differentiation confirms that a linguistic change is in fact taking place in Norwich.

TABLE 10·13   (e) Indices by age and style

Age	Style			
	WLS	RPS	FS	CS
10–19	059	070	139	173
20–29	021	034	071	100
30–39	025	031	059	067
40–49	015	026	055	088
50–59	006	013	035	046
60–69	005	018	055	058
70+	005	031	050	081

It is therefore possible to suggest that linguistic changes in a direction away from the standard norm are led in the community by members of the UWC and MWC. In particular, because of the covert prestige non-standard forms have for them, we would expect changes of this type to be spear-headed by MWC and UWC *men*. (Correspondingly, standard forms will tend to be introduced by MC women.) This point is confirmed in the case of (e), since the highest (e) index score of all was obtained in CS by *male* MWC 10–19-year-olds, who had a mean index of 200, i.e. they all consistently used (e)-3 in CS.

It is interesting to relate this change in a non-standard direction to the concept of covert prestige. We have already seen that for Norwich men this kind of prestige is associated with non-standard forms. But it also appears to be the case that very high covert prestige is associated with WC speech forms by the young *of both sexes*. Tables 10·14 and 10·15 illustrate this point. They compare the figures obtained in the Self-Evaluation Test for (er) and (ō) respectively by male WC speakers as a whole with those obtained by male WC speakers aged under 30. In the case of female speakers, because of the size of the sample at this point, it was not possible to remove class bias from the data, and the figures for female speakers also shown in tables 10·14 and 10·15 simply com-

TABLE 10·14   Percentage of informants over- and under-reporting (er) by age

	Male		Female	
Percentage	*Total WC*	*WC 10–29*	*Total female*	*10–29*
Over-r	21	8	68	40
Under-r	50	58	14	20
Accurate	29	33	18	40

TABLE 10·15   Percentage of informants over- and under-reporting (ō) by age

	Male		Female	
Percentage	*Total WC*	*WC 10–29*	*Total female*	*10–29*
Over-r	8	8	25	0
Under-r	50	58	18	50
Accurate	42	33	57	50

pare scores obtained by female speakers as a whole with those of the female under-30 group.

In the case of (er) it is clear that younger informants are rather more accurate in their self-evaluation than are older informants. With the female informants this is particularly striking: 40 per cent accuracy as compared to only 18 per cent accuracy from the female sample as a whole. In the case of (ō), the differences are rather more striking. The younger informants are slightly less accurate than the sample as a whole, but this is due to a greater tendency – and in the case of the female informants a *much* greater tendency – to under-report. It is therefore not only male speakers who attach covert prestige to WC speech forms, but also the younger female informants. (This point has been consistently overlooked by other writers on this topic – see especially Spender, 1980: 38.) Whether this is a feature which is repeated in every generation of female speakers, or whether it reflects a genuine and recent change in ideology it is not possible at this stage to say. What is clear, however, is that the linguistic change associated with (e) is being caused, at least in part, by the covert prestige which the WC form [ʌ] has for certain Norwich speakers. Group-identification of a kind considered desirable by these speakers is signalled by the usage of the non-standard form, and this leads to its increase and exaggeration. Covert prestige, therefore, leads not only to the differentiation of the linguistic behaviour of the sexes, but also to the exaggeration of certain non-standard features, particularly by UWC and MWC men and by the young, which in turn leads to linguistic change.

If we now return once again to the unusual pattern associated with (o) illustrated in table 10·1, we might again hypothesize that the deviant configuration of scores obtained for this variable is due, as in the case of (e), to a linguistic change in progress. However, this does not at first sight appear possible, since, if the RP form [ɒ] were being introduced into Norwich English, we would clearly expect this process to be spear-headed by MC women. The answer would appear to lie in the fact that [ɒ] is not *only* an RP form. It is *also* the form that occurs in the speech of the Home Counties and, perhaps more importantly, in Suffolk. Field records made in the 1930s by Lowman,[2] some of which are published in

---

[2] I am very grateful to R. I. McDavid who went to a great deal of trouble to enable me to consult these records – and see also chapter 4.

Kurath and McDavid (1961), give the pronunciation of the vowel in items such as *bog* as [ɒ] in Suffolk and this pronunciation is also recorded for the Suffolk localities in Orton and Tilling (1969).

It would therefore seem to be the case that the unusual pattern of sex differentiation of (o) is due to the following processes. The form [ɒ] in items such as *top, dog* is being introduced as a linguistic innovation into Norwich English. This is demonstrated by the scores shown for different age groups in table 10·16. The introduc-

TABLE 10·16   (o) Indices by age and style

Age	Style			
	WLS	*RPS*	*FS*	*CS*
10–29	017	017	045	055
30–49	020	030	039	063
50–69	021	037	058	067
70+	043	043	091	093

tion of this innovation, moreover, is taking place in two ways. First, [ɒ] is being introduced into Norwich English from RP by MC women, who are not only oriented towards RP, as the Self-Evaluation Tests show, but also have access to RP forms, in a way that WC women do not, because of their social class position. Secondly, this form is being introduced, as a result of geographical diffusion processes, from the non-standard WC speech forms of the Home Counties and particularly Suffolk by WC men, who not only are favourably disposed towards non-standard forms just as MC men are, but also, because of their social class position, have access to these forms as a result of occupational and other forms of social contact with speakers of [ɒ]-type accents. The variable (o) therefore represents a relatively rare example of two different types of linguistic change (change 'from below' and 'from above' in the terms of Labov, 1966a: 328) both leading in the same direction, with the result that it is now only WC women who, to any great extent, preserve the unrounded vowel.

We have therefore been able to argue that 'covert prestige' can be associated with certain linguistic forms, and that it is possible in some cases to provide evidence to show that this is in fact the case. This covert prestige reflects the value system of our society and of the different sub-cultures within this society, and takes the following form: for male speakers, and for female speakers under 30, non-standard WC speech forms are highly valued, although these values are not usually overtly expressed. These covert values lead to sex-differentiation of linguistic variables of a particular type that appears to be common to at least many varieties of language in urban societies. Covert prestige also appears to lead to linguistic changes 'from below', with the result, for example, that in Norwich English non-standard variants of (e) are currently on the increase. A study of the actual form the sex differentiation of a particular linguistic variable takes, moreover, can also usefully be employed in an examination of whether or not the variable is involved in linguistic change. Levine and Crockett (1966) have demonstrated that in one American locality 'the community's march toward the national norm' is spear-headed in particular by middle-aged MC women (and by the young). In Norwich, at least, there appears to be a considerable number of young WC men marching resolutely in the other direction.

CHAPTER 11

Standard and Non-Standard Dialects of English in the United Kingdom

Attitudes and policies

In Great Britain and Northern Ireland, as in many other countries, the relationship between social and regional language varieties is such that the greatest degree of regional differentiation is found among lower working-class speakers and the smallest degree at the other end of the social scale, among speakers from the upper middle class.

Speakers who would generally be regarded as 'educated' typically speak the dialect that is widely known as Standard English. This is the dialect that is normally used in the writing of English throughout the English-speaking world. It is possible to regard this form of English as a single dialect even though it is subject to a certain amount of regional differentiation. It is well-known that there are a number of grammatical and, in particular, lexical differences between American and British Standard English. Within the United Kingdom there are similar differences. To take a single example, speakers of Standard English from the south of England tend to use forms such as:

I won't do it
I haven't done it

while speakers from elsewhere in the country are more likely to say:

I'll not do it
I've not done it

Generally speaking, however, these differences are few in number and linguistically rather slight.

Standard English is also unusual in that it is spoken with a large number of different accents. Accent and dialect normally go together, to the extent that we have usually to consider an accent as an integral part of a particular dialect. Most speakers of the (more or less regionless) Standard English dialect, however, speak it with a (usually not too localized) regional accent, so that most educated people betray their geographical origins much more in their pronunciation than in their grammar or lexis.

There are also a number of Standard English speakers who employ the highest status British English accent, RP (Received Pronunciation), which is, at least within England, genuinely regionless. These speakers tend to have been educated at the large Public Schools or to have acquired the accent as the result of conscious effort or training. RP speakers form a very small percentage of the British population. A random sample of the population of the city of Norwich in southern England (Trudgill, 1974a), produced one RP speaker out of a total of sixty informants. (Figures for northern England, Scotland and Northern Ireland would be likely to be much smaller even than this.) The accent is nevertheless very familiar to most people as a result of its use by radio and television announcers and other public figures.

A much larger number of educated speakers have what might be termed near-RP accents: accents which have many of the features of RP but incorporate also a number of non-RP features, such as northern /a/ rather than /ɑː/ in items such as *bath, dance*, or southern /iː/ rather than /ɪ/ in items such as *money, ready*.

The further one goes 'down' the social scale, the larger become the grammatical and lexical differences from Standard English, and the phonetic and phonological differences from RP. The largest degree of regional variation is found at the level of rural dialects, particularly as spoken by elderly people of little education. I have attempted (Trudgill, 1974b) to represent this situation by means of the diagram shown here as figure 11.1. This emphasizes the continuum-like nature of linguistic variation in Britain: it is usually even less possible to talk of discrete social dialects than it is of discrete regional dialects, since varieties merge into one another and are often simply a matter of the frequency of occurrence of particular forms rather than of their presence or ab-

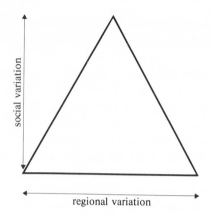

FIGURE 11.1   Dialect variation in the UK

sence. (An exception is the Standard English dialect. Since this dialect is to a considerable extent codified, it requires only one deviation from this norm for a stretch of speech or writing to be perceived as non-standard.)

The diagram presented in figure 11.1, however, is in some ways a distortion of the facts. The degree of linguistic distance between the standard dialect and regional varieties in fact varies quite considerably in different parts of the country. Standard English – to simplify somewhat – is descended from dialects of English originally spoken in the south-east of England (Strang, 1970). One result of this is that differences between Standard English and non-standard dialects in the south of England, while socially very significant, are linguistically rather trivial, and few in number. It is possible in most cases to list more or less exhaustively, and at not very great length, the differences involved. The following list, for instance, cites most of the forms which distinguish the working-class dialect of the town of Reading[1] from Standard English (from Cheshire, 1982). Most of the forms listed occur variably.

1   Present tense verb forms: *I wants it*
2   Irregular preterites: *He give it me yesterday*
3   Preterite auxiliary and main verb *do* distinct: *You done it, did you?*

---

[1] Reading is a town of some 160,000 inhabitants about 40 miles west of London.

4   Preterite of *be: We was playing. I weren't.*
5   Negative present of *be: It ain't that big*
6   Negative of *have: We ain't got one*
7   Negative preterite *never: She did yesterday, but she never today*
8   Multiple negation: *I don't eat none of that*
9   Reflexive pronouns: *He done it hisself*
10 Plural *that: Over by them bus stops*
11 Relative pronouns: *Are you the one what said it?*
12 Comparatives: *She gets more rougher*
13 Post-numeral plurality: *Thirteen mile*
14 Adverbs: *He done it nice*
15 Prepositions of place: *It was at London*

There are also a small number of lexical features such as:

> *They don't learn you nothing*
> *Can I lend your bike?*

It can be seen that the differences involved are not very numerous, or especially great.

In the south of England, generally speaking, social accent differentiation is much more noticeable than grammatical or lexical variation. Even so, the differences between, say, a working-class London accent and the high-status RP accent are nearly all phonetic rather than phonological. And most of the phonological differences are either variable, such as the merger of /f/ and /θ/, and the loss of /h/, or are found fairly high up the social scale, such as the merger of the vowels of *cot* and *coat* before /l/, as in *doll* and *dole*.

The further one travels away from the south-east of England, the greater become the differences between Standard English and RP, on the one hand, and broad regional dialects, on the other. These differences are greatest in the more isolated parts of rural northern England and, in particular, in the Lowlands of Scotland and those areas of Northern Ireland where the local dialects are Scottish in origin (Gregg, 1972). (In the Highlands of Scotland and in most of Wales English was originally, and still is in many cases, learned as a second language in schools. For this reason, the English dialects of these areas are not so radically different from Standard English.)

It is difficult to illustrate the nature of these differences except at length, but the following brief (and mainly phonological and phonetic) examples may give some impression:

(a) *goose* [gɪəs]
    loaf [lɪəf]
    coal [kʊəl]
    ground [gɹʊnd]
    blind [blɪnd]
    wrong [ɹaŋ]

(Conservative rural dialect forms from northermost England; from Wakelin, 1972)

(b) [ðə tičɛr wɪz afa gwid tʌlz]
    The teacher was awful good till's
    = *The teacher was very good to me*

(Rural Aberdeenshire dialect, Scotland; from Mather, 1975)

(c)			
die	[diː]	*open*	[ɑːpən]
high	[hiç]	*any*	[ɔːne]
haven't	[hɪne]	*where*	[ʍɔːr]
above	[əbɨn]	*pound*	[pʌn]
shoes	[šɨn]	*not*	[noː]
blind	[blæn]	*cow*	[kʉː]
bridge	[bræg]	*suck*	[sʉk]
move	[meːv]	*nothing*	[nɪθən]
grass	[grɛːs]	*with*	[weː]
dinner	[dɛːnər]	*make*	[mɑːk]

(Glenoe, rural Northern Ireland dialect; from Gregg, 1964)

One consequence of this differentiation is illustrated in figure 11.2. This is an attempt to illustrate the fact that, while social dialect continua ranging from local dialect to Standard English are found in much of England, in lowland Scotland and in parts of the rural north of England there is discontinuity because of the greater linguistic differences involved. Southern English speakers will often command a range of the social dialect continuum and, as it were, slide up and down it according to social context. Many Lowland Scots, on the other hand, will indulge in genuine dialect switching: they will jump rather than slide. The difference is also

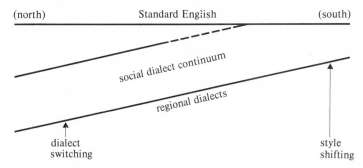

FIGURE 11.2   Contextual variation in UK English

apparent in schools. Children in the south of England will not normally adapt their spoken language very greatly between home, play and school. Much of the adaptation, moreover, will be subconscious and go unrecognized. Many Scottish children, on the other hand, are well aware that they have one dialect for school and another for other situations.

Conservative rural dialects of the type illustrated above (see further Orton and Wright, 1975) are almost certainly gradually dying out. (The vast majority of the population of the UK, it is safe to say, have never heard most of the forms cited in (a), (b) and (c) above.) They survive for the most part only in rural districts, and England, in particular, is a very heavily urbanized country. Increasing geographical mobility, education, centralization and urbanization are undoubtedly factors in this decline, as is the fact that Britain has very few areas that are remote or difficult of access. The decline has been noted by a number of writers (Orton, 1933) and seems bound to continue. For example, work recently carried out with small-town junior-school children in Cumbria, north-eastern England, suggests that they are now much more ignorant of regional vocabulary items such as *yat* (*gate*); *lake* (*play*); *loup* (*jump*) than 10 or 15 years ago.[2]

Much of the regional variation in language currently to be found in the country is, then, being lost. On the other hand, it is probably also the case that urban dialects are still undergoing

[2] Work carried out by Alison White, student in the Linguistics Department of Reading University, in Brampton, Cumberland.

developments of a divergent type (Wells, 1970; Trudgill, 1974a, 1978a) and that phonological differences between urban varieties in particular may be on the increase (Labov *et al.*, 1972).

Movements for the preservation of conservative rural dialects are not particularly strong, and the amount of regional dialect literature produced in England is very limited. There are, however, a number of dialect societies, in particular the Yorkshire Dialect Society, the Lakeland Dialect Society and the Lancashire Dialect Society. In Scotland, where Scots was used as the normal written language until the eighteenth century, the tradition of writing in Scottish varieties (either regional dialects or generalized varieties – somewhat artificially – descended from earlier literary Scots, such as Lallans) has survived much more strongly. It is currently, moreover, undergoing a revival (McClure, 1975) and beginning to find its way back into schools.

There is also another important group of English speakers in Britain: those members of the population who are West Indian in origin. We are currently reasonably well supplied with descriptions of West Indian English-based creoles as they are spoken in the Caribbean (for example, Bailey, 1966), and we know that in their most localized forms they are so radically different from other forms of English as to warrant, from a purely linguistic point of view, classification as a separate language. (There are, of course, numerous cultural, social and political motives for not actually doing this in practice.)

We have, though, very little information on the varieties spoken by West Indians in Britain (but see Wells, 1973; Sutcliffe, 1976, 1982). It is certain, however, that a whole range of varieties is spoken by the West Indian community, stretching from broad creole to West Indian or British Standard English. Many speakers, too, are bidialectal in creole and some form of British English, and many younger people speak non-standard British dialects with varying degrees of creole admixture, depending on background and situation (see Sutcliffe, forthcoming).

This social and regional dialect and accent variation in the United Kingdom, although obviously slight when compared to that found in many other countries, brings with it a number of problems. The most salient of these is educational. It has often been noted that working-class children do not perform so well educationally as might be expected, and it has been suggested that language may play an important role in this under-achievement (for example, Barnes *et al.*, 1969). One component of this language problem is widely felt to be connected with dialect (Trudgill, 1975). Standard English is the dialect of education: it is spoken by most teachers; it is the dialect normally employed in writing; and it is rewarded in examinations. A majority of children, on the other hand, are not native speakers of this particular dialect. (The survey of the – not very industrial – city of Norwich showed that only about 12 per cent of the population used no non-standard grammatical forms.) Most children, then, and in particular those from the working-class and lower middle class, have to learn to handle a new dialect on entering school.

In educational circles this contrast between Standard English and the non-standard dialects is currently the focus of some considerable debate. To what extent, the question has been asked, are we justified in continuing to encourage and reward the use of Standard English in British schools? Many arguments have been put forward – in colleges of education, by teachers, in the press and in writings by educationists and linguists – both for and against the continuation of this practice.

One argument that is frequently heard is that Standard English needs to be taught in schools because children need to be able to understand it when they hear it. Now it is of course true that it is necessary for British children to be able to understand Standard English, but this is not in fact a skill that needs to be taught. All the inhabitants of the country are now very familiar indeed with this dialect, as a result of hearing it over the radio and television and from Standard English speakers in their own community. The linguistic differences involved are also, as we have seen, very small indeed in most areas and are simply not great enough to cause comprehension difficulties. Hearing and understanding, too, is a relatively passive skill, and all speakers are able to understand many more varieties than they are able to use.

This argument, then, appears to be invalid – with one possible exception. This is provided by the case of some children of West Indian origin. The linguistic differences between 'deep' West Indian creoles and Standard English may be, as we have already noted, very large indeed, and many children newly arrived in the UK from the West Indies may not have had so much exposure to Standard English as indigenous children. Even long-term exposure, moreover, may not be too effective in the case of profound grammatical differences.

It would not be too surprising then if some West Indian children did experience difficulties of this type, and indeed the *prima facie* case for examining comprehension difficulties among West Indians is good. West Indian children perform, on average, less well in school than might be expected. And British people find it extremely difficult, especially initially, to understand West Indian English-based creoles in their most localized forms.

Edwards (1976) has in fact demonstrated that some children of West Indian origin do have comprehension difficulties. By administering a standard test of reading and comprehension to groups of West Indian and English children, she has shown that, matching groups for reading ability, West Indians score on average significantly lower on the comprehension tasks. Edwards was also able to show, by means of a test of 'creole interference', that there was a significant relationship between the influence of creole in individual children and low comprehension scores. Edwards points out that West Indian subjects divide into those whose comprehension scores remain low, although they have acquired the mechanical skills of reading, and those who conform to the English pattern, which 'would be consistent with a picture where some but not all West Indians become completely bidialectal'.

Even this evidence, however, does not really argue for the teaching of Standard English in schools. The West Indians that have this type of difficulty have problems not simply with Standard English but with British English as a whole. And, except perhaps in the case of any new arrivals who might be favourably disposed to such an exercise, there would clearly be resistance to attempts to withdraw some West Indians from classes for special attention. Much more helpful would be a recognition, especially by teachers, that some West Indian children in British schools may be faced with what is perhaps best described as a semi-foreign language problem. (It is probably also true to say that the main problem is the belief, widely held by West Indians and British people alike, that native West Indian dialects are 'bad' or 'broken'.)

A further argument that is often encountered is that Standard English has to be taught in schools because children have to learn to read in this dialect. It is certainly true that all reading materials are written in Standard English and that many children learning to read have also to cope with a new and different dialect. However, once again we have to say that the extent of the linguistic differences, especially in the south of England and in urban areas generally, is not sufficient to cause great difficulties, and most children appear to become skilled at 'translating' as they go along at a very early stage. Probably the most important factor here is a sympathetic understanding, on the part of teachers, of the problems involved.

In the teaching of reading, accent differences, which are generally larger than grammatical differences, might be thought to be more likely than dialect to produce difficulties. Most teachers report, however, that this is generally not the case. (English spelling is probably sufficiently distant from pronunciation not to favour one accent over any other: all speakers are at an equal disadvantage.) And even in cases where accents, as in the case of rural southern Scotland, diverge markedly from the orthography, difficulties do not appear to be too severe. Many Scottish children, for example, will have to learn that /ben/, /hem/ are also pronounced /bon/, /hom/, before they can make sense of the spellings *bone*, *home*. But most of them are sufficiently bidialectal to know this already. And – crucially – *all* the children in a rural Scottish school will have exactly the same difficulty and, usually, a teacher who is sufficiently local to be aware of the phonological differences involved. West Indian children in England, on the other hand, may experience much greater difficulties. They will probably be part of a class where English children are experiencing difficulties much less severe, and with a teacher whose knowledge of West Indian phonology is very limited. Again, perhaps the most important solution to this problem is simply an awareness of the existence and nature of the problem.

A further argument for the teaching of Standard English in schools is that children need to be able to speak it. As can be imagined, this argument is often couched in terms of 'correctness', although the efforts of linguists and educationists to bring a more informed point of view to notions of this type appear to be bearing fruit among teachers, if not with the general public. (Most popular ideas about 'correctness' in English are tied to the relationship between dialect and social class, since it is in most cases grammatical forms associated with working-class dialects that are held to be 'wrong' – see chapter 12).

A particular problem with dialect and 'correctness' is an inadequate, if unsurprising, appreciation of the nature of dialectal forms. The rubric to an important British examination in oral English states that children will not be penalised for the use of local dialect forms. A recent examiners' report, however, criticizes the use by London examinees of forms such as *I done it* and *I ain't got none*, which are an integral part of working-class London dialect, as 'mistakes'. There is, in fact, a widespread tendency to regard rural dialect forms as acceptable (if somewhat quaint) but to treat urban dialect forms simply as 'errors'.

A further problem is the failure of many to distinguish between dialect, on the one hand, and style and use of language, on the other. A recent correspondent to the Scottish Times Educational Supplement wrote: 'There are, we are told, no correct forms in language: the child who tells a teacher to f... off [*sic*] is not being incorrect or impertinent, he is merely using the language of his sub-culture and should not be asked ... to use the dialect of his teacher'. Swearing at the teacher, of course, has no connection whatsoever with dialect and, although sub-cultural differences in the use of and attitudes to language are a subject of considerable importance, confusions of this type are not at all helpful.

A more important argument in favour of the teaching of spoken Standard English is one that is based on comprehension. It is often said that if children do not modify their speech at least in the direction of Standard English (and RP) they will be at a serious disadvantage, since people in other parts of the country will be unable to understand them.

This kind of argument is obviously of some potency in some countries, although it has to be noted that claims for lack of mutual intelligibility are often exaggerated, are usually unsupported by research data and fail to acknowledge that it is normally much simpler and quicker to learn to understand a new variety than to learn to speak one. In the UK, although again we do not have any data to support this, this argument is almost certainly not worthy of attention. The fact is that linguistic differences between at least a majority of English dialects are not serious enough to cause permanent comprehension problems. Some difficulties do occur, it is true, but they are normally temporary and fairly readily overcome. Individuals moving from one area to another may initially have some difficulties in making themselves understood, but they generally adjust their speech fairly rapidly and automatically. This again, it seems, is not a skill that has to be taught. Certainly difficulties of this type are not serious enough to warrant wholesale educational programmes to change children's dialects and accents. Claims about comprehension difficulties, in fact, are probably most often rationalizations for unfavourable attitudes to low-status varieties.

(Another interesting argument which is sometimes heard, and even acted on, is that some accents are aesthetically much more pleasing than others. This is discussed in chapter 12.)

Arguments in favour of the teaching of Standard English in written work are probably stronger than those involving the spoken language. Standard English is accepted as the dialect appropriate for writing throughout the English-speaking world, and pressures for its written use are therefore very strong.

Some of the arguments along these lines, however, are not particularly persuasive. It is often claimed, for instance, that Standard English is much more logical and/or expressive and/or adequate for the treatment of many topics than any other dialect. The point about logic has already been very convincingly argued against (Labov, 1972d), and the adequacy argument, while not entirely straightforward (Hymes, 1975), is not one that linguists would feel is especially convincing (Labov, unpublished) – see chapter 12. It is, in fact, extremely difficult to see how minimal grammatical differences, of the type cited above between Reading dialect and Standard English (for further examples see Hughes and Trudgill, 1979), could possibly cause any differences in expressive power. It is true, of course, that particular lexical items are necessary for the adequate discussion of particular topics. But, while regional lexical equivalents certainly are characteristic of individual dialects, it has to be recognized that there is no necessary connection between dialect and lexis. Vocabularies are open-ended, and it is possible to combine academic and scientific vocabulary with non-standard grammatical forms. This is, of course, not usual in English, but there are language communities, notably Norway (Haugen, 1966), where something of the sort does occur.

There is probably, in fact, only one legitimate reason for the teaching of Standard English to British children who do not normally use it. This is that in many circumstances it is socially, and economically, advantageous to be able to employ this variety.

Attitudes towards non-standard dialects (and low-prestige accents) are very unfavourable in many sections of the community, and speakers of these varieties may often be discriminated against in employment and other situations.

As far as accent is concerned, there is now research that shows that teachers may evaluate children with RP accents as having more academic potential than others. Perhaps more importantly, since presumably it is at least a relatively simple task to point out this danger to teachers, the general public are much more favourably disposed to the RP accent than to others, in a number of ways. RP speakers, for example, are generally evaluated as more intelligent and reliable than regionally accented speakers, although they may also be seen as less friendly and sociable (Giles and Powesland, 1975 – and see chapter 12.)

Most of the attitudes tapped in this research are of the subconscious type. At the level of more overtly expressed attitudes, accent tolerance seems to be somewhat on the increase (Macaulay and Trevelyan, 1973), and the BBC now permits a wider range of regional accents from its announcers than was previously the case. There is still, however, some considerable way to go in the area of accent tolerance.

Dialect tolerance, moreover, is still minimal. In fact attitudes towards non-standard dialects in some quarters are very unfavourable indeed. The strength of these attitudes can be gauged from reaction to press reports (and misreports) of Trudgill (1975) (which is a book containing arguments very much along the line of those presented here). The following are among some of the more coherent comments to appear in the press:

Bad grammar is incomplete and lazy. It is wrong and therefore inferior. (Peter Black, *The Guardian*, 6 Dec. 1975)

Some poor children already suffer from progressive teachers who think it wrong to make them read. They are now threatened with a rash of Trudgills who won't correct their grammar. Yet nothing could penalise the working class more than to be denied the right to knowledge. (*Sunday Telegraph*, 28 Nov. 1975)

Dr. Peter Trudgill says that Grammar is unimportant.[3] There is no reason, he says, to ask that children should use standard English in creative writing or in personal letters since no advantages are likely to result from this. He appeared looking sloppy and unattractive on television. He implied – fairly inarticulately – that if a child wanted to say 'I don't want none of that', it would be acceptable

---

[3] It will, I hope, be clear to linguists that I said nothing of the kind!

because, crikey, we know what he means, don't we. (Lynda Lee-Potter, *Daily Mail*, 3 Dec. 1975)

Dr. Peter Trudgill says children should be allowed to write as they like without regard to the rules of spelling or grammar.[4] Teachers who stand by the rules are, he says. 'unfairly penalising the working class'. What an insult to most of us! It presumes that there is a 'working class' and that it is unable to understand how to write properly. (*Reading Evening Post*, 28 Nov. 1975)

It seems to me a matter of observable fact that some young children growing up with, for example, an East London dialect offshoot pronouncing 'station' as 'stition' and 'shouldn't have' as 'shoodenov' are lacking entire sounds and words in their vocal repertoire. (John Ezard, *The Guardian* (Education Section), 12 Aug. 1975)

Strong and often personal attacks of this nature reveal the strength of feeling that non-standard dialects produce and demonstrate the type of uninformed and unsympathetic attitude that non-standard dialect speakers are likely to encounter.

A further interesting example of dialect intolerance is provided by a much-publicized case of a well-qualified postgraduate student who applied for a post as lecturer in a College of Further Education (Rosen, 1974). The following is an extract from a letter written to him, after his application had been rejected, by the Chairman of the interviewing panel:

I am writing to give you some personal advice which I hope you will accept in the spirit it is given, to help a young man whom most of us felt had much to offer if one failing can be eradicated. We were generally impressed by your written statement and you interviewed well except that we were all very worried by grammatical and other faults in your spoken English. It is not a question of accent[5] but of grammar and aspirates, looseness of which could be felt to be harmful for pupils and inhibit full cooperation with colleagues.

Sentiments such as these reveal that the greatest dialect-related problem in the UK are the attitudes and prejudices many people hold towards non-standard dialects. In the long term, it will probably be simpler to ease this problem by changing attitudes (as has already happened to some extent with accents) than by changing the linguistic habits of the majority of the population.

In the short run, however, we have to acknowledge the existence of these attitudes and attempt to help children to overcome

---

[4] Again not the case.
[5] The disclaimer about accent is interesting. It suggests, as do certain comments in Macaulay and Trevelyan (1973), that attitudes about accents have now, as suggested above, changed sufficiently for many people to feel that discrimination on grounds of accent is no longer respectable. As the subsequent reference to 'aspirates' shows, however, this writer clearly *was* reacting to features of accent.

them. Clearly many jobs and opportunities for upward social mobility will be denied to those who are not able to use Standard English. To act on these motives in school with some degree of success, however, it is important to recognize that the teaching of higher-status accents and of spoken Standard English in school is almost certain to fail. Standard English is a dialect which is associated with a particular social group in British society and is therefore symbolic of it. Children will in most cases learn to speak this dialect only if they wish to become associated with this group and feel that they have a reasonable expectation of being able to do so. And if they are so motivated, they will almost certainly learn to speak Standard English anyway, regardless of what is done in school: 'What the ... teacher does in the classroom with regard to spoken standard English is irrelevant' (Fasold, 1971 – see also Edwards and Giles, forthcoming).

Writing, on the other hand, is a different matter. It is much easier to learn to write a new dialect than to learn to speak it, and in writing there is time for planning and checking back. Standard English, moreover, can be regarded as a dialect apart which is used in writing and whose use in written work does not necessarily commit one to allegiance to any particular social group. Teachers using the bidialectalism approach to the teaching of written Standard English are therefore likely to achieve a fair degree of success.

It is probably also the case, though, that if, in the long term, greater dialect tolerance could be achieved even in written English, children would become more articulate and enthusiastic writers. Schemes such as the Initial Teaching Alphabet and Breakthrough to Literacy, which permit children to write using forms which occur in their native dialects, are reported on favourably by teachers as achieving just that. This degree of dialect tolerance is perhaps more likely to be achieved in Scotland, where there is (see above) still a tradition of writing in Scots, but generally speaking the achievement of a certain amount of flexibility as to the grammatical forms permitted in written English is still only a distant possibility.

CHAPTER 12

Sociolinguistics and Linguistic Value Judgements

Correctness, adequacy and aesthetics

It is well known that linguistics is a descriptive rather than pre-scriptive science, and that linguists are concerned with describing and accounting for what speakers actually say rather than with what various 'authorities' believe they ought to say.[1] This means that linguists are not normally prepared to say that some forms of language are 'good' or 'correct' and that other forms are 'bad' or 'wrong'. Some linguists (for example, Hall, 1950) have taken a much stronger and more proselytizing stand on this issue than have others, but it is safe to say that the vast majority of linguists are agreed that notions of 'correctness' have no part to play in objective discussions of language, at least as it is used by native speakers (see also chapter 11).

In this chapter we want to argue that, at any rate in the English-speaking world, it is important, for educational reasons, for some linguists at least to make their views more widely known on the 'correctness' issue. We also want to suggest that linguists should, in addition, resist value judgements about language on other counts, notably that of the 'inadequacy' of certain language varieties, and that of the inferior 'aesthetic' quality of certain types of speech, since judgements of this type are also important in the educational field. More particularly, we want to suggest that em-pirical sociolinguistic research that has been carried out both under experimental conditions and in the speech community itself

[1] The co-author of this chapter is Howard Giles. We are very grateful to Paul Fletcher and Nick Gadfield, who commented on an earlier version, and to those who helped with the experiment re-ported in section 6: Ralph Fasold, Gae Fasold, Dick Hudson, John McClure, Fred Genesee, John Edwards, and Knud Larsen.

can now be employed to demonstrate that value judgements of all three types are equally unsound. Section 1 will deal with 'correctness' judgements; section 2 with notions of 'adequacy'; and the rest of the chapter will be concerned with various arguments connected with the 'aesthetic' merits of different types of language.

1   CORRECTNESS IN LANGUAGE

On the correctness issue, of course, linguists are set apart from most of the rest of the community, who are generally still persuaded that some grammatical forms and pronunciations are 'wrong' and that it is possible for native speakers to make 'mistakes' in this way. There are signs, it is true, that several decades of arguments from linguistics, together with other influences, are beginning to have some small effect. Many people involved in issues connected with language and education, for example, are starting to suggest – as most linguists have long believed – that what has traditionally been conceived of as a matter of 'right' and 'wrong' is in fact simply a question of dialect differences, and considerable discussion of topics of this sort is now taking place. This is especially true in the United States, where there is now heightened consciousness of dialect-related problems as a result, largely, of educational difficulties connected with the racial situation. (See, amongst many others, Burling, 1973.) There is still a long way to go, however, and many linguists addressing audiences of teachers and others have been very surprised to discover the depth of feeling that any attack on the notion of correctness produces.

This argument is an important one from an educational and social point of view. Many children, in many different language communities, are still discriminated against, both consciously and unconsciously, for using non-standard dialects and low-status accents. This is particularly true in schools, but it also occurs in certain areas of employment, for example. Language, we can say, functions as a social disadvantage for these children – for no good linguistic reason.

It is therefore necessary for those linguists who are concerned with this problem to bring pressure to bear at appropriate points, and to marshal as many arguments as can be found to support their case. Simple assertions that no one dialect is any more 'correct' than any other, such as are often found in introductory linguistics texts, are not adequate to persuade intelligent and educated laymen, who have long believed the opposite, of the justice of the linguist's case. It is therefore fortunate that a body of data has now emerged from empirical sociolinguistic studies, particularly those into urban dialects, which can be used to demonstrate the true nature of value judgements based on correctness.

The best strategy for linguists to adopt would appear to be to point to the clear relationship between language and social class that emerges from these studies, and to suggest that judgements about 'right' and 'wrong' in language are not linguistic judgements at all, but social judgements. Most people, of course, are already aware of the correlation between social class and language, but they are most often conscious of it only in a rather unreflecting way. The advantage of the linguistic research that we are discussing is that it can illustrate the nature of this relationship in a clear, accurate and often somewhat dramatic way, the implications of which cannot be ignored. It is now possible, that is, to show very clearly that notions of 'correctness', when applied to pronunciations and grammatical constructions used by native speakers, are based on social factors, and do not make linguistic sense.

A good example of the way in which this can be done is provided by an English grammatical construction which is universally considered to be 'wrong'. This is the feature which is known to the English-speaking layman as 'the double negative', and to linguists as *multiple negation* or *negative concord*. Most dialects of English permit constructions of the type:

> *I don't want none*
> *He hadn't got no shoes*
> *I can't find none nowhere*

where indefinites in the sentence can be negated as well as the verb. The Standard English dialect, on the other hand, permits negation of only one or the other, but not both. Dialects vary, too, in the extent to which they permit multiple negation in different constructions (see Labov, 1972a). Forms such as the following can be found in some dialects, but not in others:

She hadn't got hardly any
They stood there without no shoes on
We haven't got only one
It ain't no cat can't get in no coop

In one of the earliest urban dialect surveys, that carried out in Detroit (Shuy *et al.*, 1967; Wolfram, 1969), multiple negation of the type illustrated in the first set of examples above was investigated, and the extent of its usage was correlated with social class membership. It emerged, in fact, that there was a very close relationship between the number of multiple negative forms used and the speaker's social class background. The average scores obtained by the different social class groups were:

upper middle-class	2%
lower middle-class	11%
upper working-class	38%
lower working-class	70%

It is certain that comparable scores would be obtained from most other parts of the English-speaking world.

Another feature investigated in the Detroit survey was the usage of the -*s* marker on third-person singular present-tense verb forms. The same feature was also investigated in Norwich, England (Trudgill, 1974a), where forms such as

He like it
and *It taste good*

are also found. The percentage of third-person -*s* used by members of different social-class groups in the two areas was:

Detroit	*Norwich*
UMC 98	UMC 100
LMC 64	LMC 71
UWC 23	UWC 25
LWC 12	MWC 19
	LWC 3

In another British study, in Reading, an opposite tendency has been investigated (Cheshire, 1982): the occurrence of the -*s* marker on other persons of the verb, as in *I likes it, They goes every day*. It has been noted that, whereas middle-class adults use 0 per cent -*s* on persons other than third-singular, lower working-class children employ a very much higher percentage.

The implications of figures of this sort are clear, especially if they are allied to scores for other similar grammatical features studied in Detroit, New York (Labov *et al.*, 1968), Washington (Fasold, 1972); Montreal (Sankoff and Cedergren, 1971); and elsewhere. Multiple negation, absence of third-person singular -*s*, and presence of -*s* on other persons are all widely considered to be 'wrong'. The above figures show that they are most typical of working- or lower-class speech. We can interpret this to mean the following: grammatical forms which are most typical of working-class dialects have low status, because of their association with groups who have low prestige in our society. This low status leads to the belief that these forms are 'bad' and they are therefore judged to be 'wrong'. Evaluations of this type are therefore clearly social judgements about the status of speakers who use particular forms, rather than objective linguistic judgements about the correctness of the forms themselves. (We cannot account for all 'wrong' forms in this way. Many innovations, introduced as the result of linguistic change, may be considered 'wrong' in a similar sort of way, regardless of which social class uses them. Social class dialect features, however, remain the principal source for 'correctness' judgements.)

With accurate information of this sort at their disposal it should be possible for those linguists who are concerned to do so to begin to persuade the rest of the community that 'correction' of 'mistakes' is in reality the imposition of an alien dialect. This view is in fact gaining ground in some educational circles, where it is now recognized by many that attempts to eliminate non-standard dialects in school can have very harmful effects. (On the other hand, some colleges of education have now begun to argue that although, say, Standard English is no more 'correct' than other varieties, it is nevertheless 'appropriate' to certain situations and should be taught for that reason. 'Appropriateness' can easily become simply 'correctness' under another name, and our view is that this approach should be treated with caution.) Generally speaking, however, the debate seems to be moving in the direction of a discussion as to whether it is desirable to teach Standard

English to children in addition to their native dialects, for what are ultimately social reasons to do with employment prospects, and so on; or whether we should try to achieve greater 'dialect tolerance', and recognize that if children suffer because of attitudes to non-standard dialects, it is the attitudes that should be changed and not the dialects (see Fasold and Shuy, 1970 – and cf. chapter 11).

In any case, we can say that linguists are generally agreed on the 'correctness' issue, and that there are some signs that others, including, importantly, many in the world of education, are following their lead in attempting to avoid making value judgements of this kind about language. Results from empirical linguistic research can perhaps help to speed this process.

2 ADEQUACY IN LANGUAGE

The second area where value judgements are frequently made about language concerns the 'adequacy' of particular types of language. The 'correctness' issue is confined, for the most part, to intra-linguistic comparisons (although of course the notion that Latin grammar was more 'correct' than that of other languages has had an effect on a number of modern European languages – an example of this is the tendency to avoid sentence-final prepositions in formal styles of English).

On the adequacy issue, however, we have to take note both of inter- and intra-linguistic comparisons. As far as inter-linguistic comparisons are concerned, the majority of linguists appear to subscribe to the view that one language is as good and adequate as any other. As Halliday says: 'all languages are equally capable of being developed for all purposes,' (Halliday et al., 1964: 100).

Many laymen, on the other hand, are convinced that English, for example, is *inherently* more adequate for certain (often academic) topics than, say, some indigenous African languages. This view, although it is often held by the speakers of the indigenous languages themselves, is surely without foundation, and there are educational and language-planning situations where it is important for linguists to say so.

There is also some discussion centring around the adequacy of pidgin and creole languages (see Labov, unpublished). It is generally agreed that pidgins are *not* adequate for a number of purposes. When creolization takes place, however, there is evidence indicating that a number of developments occur which render the former pidgin entirely adequate for all the needs of its speakers in all its functions – although there are some who might be prepared to dispute this (see Craig, 1971). For a very interesting account of on-going creolization processes, with evidence and examples of some of the devices employed to make a pidgin language fully adequate, see Mühlhäusler (1977) – and see also chapter 6.

From an educational point of view, however, the most serious issue would appear to be the intra-linguistic comparison of some varieties as more adequate than others. There are in fact two separate but related theories that can be interpreted as suggesting that some varieties of a language are less 'adequate' than others. The first is Bernstein's theory of 'elaborated' and 'restricted codes'. Bernstein (1962) writes, for example: 'The net effect of the constraint of a restricted code will be to depress potential linguistic ability.' And his earlier writings generally – which have been extremely influential amongst educationists – have been interpreted by many as indicating that 'elaborated code' is in some ways a superior form of language. In his later writings, however, Bernstein (see the later papers in Bernstein, 1971) has stated that the one 'code' is *not* superior to the other, although this is somewhat paradoxical in view of statements of the educational advantages of 'elaborated code'. (Bernstein says that 'elaborated code' gives access to 'universalistic orders of meaning' and that school 'is necessarily concerned with the transmission and development of universalistic orders of meaning'.) But it also becomes clear that Bernstein is now more concerned with the way in which speakers *use* language, rather than with the inherent adequacy of the 'codes' themselves. We can therefore omit his work from this discussion.

The second theory, which is based in part on Bernstein's writings as well as on misunderstandings of them, is the so-called 'verbal deprivation hypothesis'. This view holds – as it has been advanced by mainly American educationists and psychologists – that the language of some children is inadequate for certain purposes, such as handling abstract concepts and logical operations. Some writers on this topic make it plain that they regard some dialects (for example, American Black English Vernacular) as inherently inferior in this way (Bereiter, 1966). Others relate the 'inadequacy' less to specific features of dialect, and more to features of verbal interaction in working-class homes.

There is no space here to discuss the 'verbal deprivation' or 'language deficit' hypothesis in full. (This is done at greater length in Trudgill, 1975). But we should note here that linguists, once again, are for the most part strongly opposed to these ideas. Indeed, Labov (unpublished) has written, in connection with the claim that some children are 'verbally deprived': 'The evidence put forward for this claim is transparently wrong, as linguists unanimously agree.' And, again, empirical linguistic research can be employed to support the linguist's argument. In the first place, any linguist who has actually worked with working-class speakers and language knows from first-hand experience that working-class children are not 'verbally deprived'. But more importantly, data from linguistic studies can be used actually to demonstrate the strength of the linguist's case, as in Labov (1972d).

It is, however, difficult to argue that there is no such thing as 'verbal deprivation' except by cataloguing and illustrating at length and in detail the language resources and verbal skills of precisely those groups that are said to suffer from 'language deficit'. It is therefore fortunate that, to back up the convictions and the tape-recorded evidence of linguists who have carried out research in different speech communities, we have available at least one such carefully documented study, that of Labov and his colleagues carried out in Harlem, New York City (Labov et al., 1968).

Once again, then, we can say that linguists reject the invidious comparison of linguistic varieties on the grounds of adequacy, and that, although in this case it is much more difficult to do so, we can provide data from sociolinguistic studies that can be used to argue this case. It is important that this case should be argued, since the educational implications of labelling some varieties of language as inherently inferior are very serious indeed. In particular, the setting up of 'compensatory' educational programmes to 'give' language to children who, of course, already have it, is both economically wasteful and psychologically and educationally dangerous. We can as linguists recognize that children can be helped to develop expressive ability and verbal skills, but we cannot agree that some varieties of language are inherently more 'adequate' than others.

3   AESTHETIC VALUE AND LANGUAGE

There is also a third area in which value judgements about language tend to be made: that of apparently aesthetic judgements about different languages, dialects and accents. This area appears to have received less attention from linguists than the other two, although in some respects it is equally important from an educational and social point of view. In fact, it appears, although there is little documentary evidence for this, that this is an area where many linguists are prepared, at least informally, to make as many value judgements as laymen. It seems to us that some linguists, at least, are just as prone as other people to say that, for example, Italian is more beautiful than Danish – or vice versa. At the level of informal discussion, of course, views of this type have no particularly serious consequences. On the other hand, though, inter-linguistic comparisons may be harmful if, in multilingual situations, educational and other policy decisions are based on them.

At the intra-linguistic level, however, the discussion of the 'aesthetic' merits of different varieties can be of some considerable importance – again particularly in the field of education. The fact is that, even if teachers are persuaded that all varieties of English or other languages are equally 'correct' (and of course many of them are not persuaded of this) there is still a widespread feeling that some dialects and, in particular, some accents are much 'nicer', 'more pleasant' or 'more beautiful' than others. It may appear at first sight that views of this sort are harmless and not worth the linguist's concern. However, the 'aesthetic' argument is often used by teachers and others who attempt to change children's accents: there may be nothing 'wrong' about the accent, the argument runs, and it may be perfectly comprehensible – but it is very 'ugly'; it is therefore only fair to the children to give them the chance to speak in a more aesthetically satisfying manner. The grave danger here is that, whether views of this sort are accompanied by ridicule or by kindness, they lead speakers to disparage their own language, and children in particular to develop feelings of linguistic insecurity and even of what has been called 'linguistic self-hatred'. The result is, often, individuals who become, in certain circumstances, inarticulate and reluctant to express themselves. It would therefore be very useful if, by means of research data, we could demonstrate that aesthetic judgements, just like judgements concerned with correctness and adequacy, have no place in the objective evaluation of spoken language. (We are not, of course, concerned with literature.) If this could be done, then perhaps something could be achieved towards persuading all speakers that their language is pleasant with, one would hope, a resultant increase in fluency and articulateness.

4   INHERENT VALUE OF LINGUISTIC VARIETIES

It may be that speakers of British English are unusual in the extent to which they are prepared to make value judgements on the aesthetic merits of linguistic varieties, but similar judgements are certainly made in other communities. Views of this sort were noted, for example, in research carried out in Norway (some of it reported in chapter 3) as well as in work on Greek varieties of Albanian (see chapters 6 and 7). Similar evaluations have been noted with American English (Tucker and Lambert, 1969), Canadian French (d'Anglejan and Tucker, 1973) and Arabic (Ferguson, 1959).

There are two opposing explanations one can adopt for this widespread phenomenon. The first is a view that has been labelled by Giles et al. (1974a) the 'inherent value' hypothesis. This view maintains that some linguistic varieties are inherently more attractive and pleasant than others, and that these varieties have become accepted as standards or have acquired prestige simply because they are the most attractive. According to this view, for example, British RP is the most prestigious British accent because it has, as it were, risen to the top – or, according to Giles et al., been elevated to this position by a socially powerful group – as a result of its inherent outstanding attractiveness.

It is certain that this hypothesis would find favour with a majority of laymen, including, crucially, many teachers. Terms such as 'nicely spoken' and 'with a pleasant voice', as used by the general public in England, are normally equivalent to 'with an RP accent', and it is obvious that very many people simply take this hypothesis for granted. Some linguists, too, have accepted this position (see Wyld, 1934). There is also a certain amount of research evidence that could be interpreted as providing support for this hypothesis which we have to examine carefully before we can reject it altogether – as we would wish to be able to do in order to encourage linguistic self-confidence.

First, we have to note that a number of experiments carried out into listeners' subjective reactions to different linguistic varieties (Buck, 1968; Cheyne, 1970; Strongman and Woosley, 1967) have all succeeded in obtaining a pronounced uniformity of response. For example, Giles (1971a) has demonstrated that speakers with RP accents are more favourably evaluated on a number of different parameters than speakers with regional accents. They are almost universally evaluated as more intelligent, more reliable and more educated (Giles, 1971b) than other speakers. And there is also considerable evidence to show that most British people find RP the most aesthetically pleasing of all English accents (Giles, 1970). These experiments have all been carried out using the matched-guise technique where, although subjects believe they are evaluating different speakers, they are in fact reacting to the same speaker using different accents. In other words, different responses are entirely due to linguistic differences. The crucial point here is the high level of agreement that is obtained in the experimental results. Not only do subjects react to a change in accent, they all react in a very similar way. Supporters of the 'inherent value' hypothesis could therefore point to these facts and suggest that the majority response indicates that, for example, RP really is more beautiful than other accents.

In arguing against these views, however, we can suggest that the undoubted high uniformity of response is not due to any inherent aesthetic or other qualities. Rather it is the result of the fact that these reactions are due to certain cultural norms which are strong and pervasive, and which affect most listeners in a similar way. We could suggest, perhaps, that the subjects in these experiments have been 'brain-washed' to an extent that renders objective responses on their part very unlikely. We shall discuss this point in section 5 below.

The second piece of evidence that we have to consider is rather similar. This consists of a series of overt statements made by informants, in a number of sociolinguistic studies, about different linguistic varieties. These statements, too, show a significant degree of agreement that could be interpreted as lending support to the 'inherent value' hypothesis. It has emerged from a number of urban dialect studies, for instance, that even where speakers within a community themselves use very varied varieties of language, they nevertheless often appear to share, as a community as a whole, a common set of norms as to what is 'good' and 'bad' in the language. For example, Labov (1966a) writes that 'most New Yorkers think or feel that particular variants are better, or more correct, or are endowed with superior status' (p. 405). More importantly for our purposes, it appears that this level of agreement extends also to the apparently aesthetic. In the survey of Norwich reported in Trudgill (1974a), for example, overt statements such as the following were recorded, showing the high regard in which the aesthetic qualities of BBC RP are held:

I talk horrible, I think. But BBC announcers and that, they really sound nice when they talk. (house-wife, 45)

I think the Norwich accent is awful – but people you hear on the wireless, some of them have got really nice voices. (night-watchman, 57)

Similarly, Macaulay and Trevelyan (1973) report comparable agreement from Glasgow as to the superior aesthetic qualities of 'English' accents (the informants most probably had RP in mind):

If you were an employer and somebody came in to see you in a broad Glasgow accent and then another man came in with an English accent, you'd be more inclined to give the English man the job because he had a nicer way of speaking. (schoolboy, 15)

There's no doubt the English ... have us beaten there. Their speech is much preferable to ours. (commercial artist)

(Many other similar instances of agreement could be cited. American and British urban dialect studies, for instance, have shown that most speakers are prepared to praise prestige varieties as 'pleasant', as well as, often, to denigrate their own speech as 'ugly'.) Again we could consider this uniformity to be significant. If a majority of informants are willing to go on record as saying that, say, RP is beautiful and their own accents are less so, can they all be wrong?

Against this argument we can cite, first, the cultural norms point we have already made above – if everyone has been subjected to the same cultural pressures, it is hardly surprising that they all produce the same sort of overt statement. Secondly, we must also reckon with less overt feelings which speakers must also have: evidence for the existence of covert prestige is provided in chapter 10. *Overt* statements of the type we have cited, we can say, are by no means the whole story, since they are for public consumption only and take no account of more private or subconscious feelings.

The third point that we have to consider arises out of some work produced by Brown *et al.* (1975). Their research has shown that French Canadian listeners can correctly allot French Canadian speakers to their social background on the basis of tape-recordings the speakers made of a passage of prose. There is nothing particularly surprising about this, of course. What was more interesting was that American listeners with no knowledge of French were able to do the same thing with a fair degree of success. This does not necessarily tell us anything about inherent *aesthetic* value, of course, but it does suggest that there may be *something* inherent in, say, working-class accents which led the Americans to react in this way. In other words, we have to ask if this evidence can be used in any way to support the 'inherent value' hypothesis.

We cannot argue conclusively against this, but we can at least shed serious doubts on the matter. One possibility that has to be considered, for instance, is that, since the matched-guise technique was not employed in Brown's work, listeners were reacting to social-class-linked differences in reading and recitation skills. A second possibility is that there were perceptible differences of voice quality between the middle- and working-class speakers – something that is in fact suggested by comments made by the French Canadian listeners. It may well be that there is, as elsewhere (see Trudgill, 1974a: 185; Sachs, 1973), a relationship in Canadian French between sociological parameters and articulatory setting – long-term adjustments of the vocal tract which are acquired through social imitation, and are unconsciously and habitually maintained (Laver, 1968). If so, the American listeners may have been reacting to this. This does not, however, necessarily support the inherent value hypothesis, since it is not impossible (in fact linguistic area studies such as Emeneau, 1956, suggest that it is quite likely) that a similar relationship between the same paralinguistic features and social class exists in some varieties of American English. If that were the case, it would provide an explanation for why the Americans reacted as they did.

We cannot assume, in other words, that certain types of setting are universally perceived as pleasant or unpleasant, regardless of culture or language. Indeed, there is some evidence to the contrary. Nasalization, for example, is a component of setting commonly associated with many 'unpleasant' Australian accents of English, but it is also a feature of many 'nice' RP speakers (Laver, 1968). Similarly, pharyngealization is a component of working-class Norwich voice quality which middle-class Norwich people are almost entirely agreed is very unpleasant (Trudgill, 1974b), but it is also a feature of some high-status Arabic and German accents (see Honikman, 1964).

5   IMPOSED NORMS AND LINGUISTIC VARIETIES

We are not, then, in a position as yet to reject the 'inherent value' hypothesis out of hand, but we have attempted to demonstrate that three types of evidence that could be cited in its favour also have other, perhaps more probable, explanations.

Now we can attempt to argue more forcibly against the 'inherent value' hypothesis by presenting some research data in favour of another, opposing hypothesis. Giles *et al.* (1974a) have labelled this competing view the 'imposed norm' hypothesis. According to this view, different varieties of the same language are objectively as pleasant as each other, but are perceived positively or negatively because of particular cultural pressures operating in each language community. Standard dialects and prestige accents acquire their high status directly from the high-status social groups that happen to speak them, and it is because of their high status that they are perceived as 'good' and therefore as 'pleasant'. Social pressures, Giles *et al.* argue, are placed on speakers to emulate these varieties, and because of these pressures the varieties in question come to be regarded as desirable and superior on many counts, including the aesthetic. (I am aware that this might appear to be somewhat paradoxical, in that aesthetic judgements are possibly never entirely objective or culture-free. The argument here, however, is that evaluations of language varieties, unlike those of, say, music, which are similarly culture-bound, are the *direct* result of cultural pressures. It is true that we tend only to like and be in a position to judge music that is part of our own culture, but, although there is some broad degree of agreement as to what is good and bad in music, there is nothing at all like the striking total uniformity of response in relative evaluations of music that we find in evaluations of language.)

This view, in some form or other, is one that would probably find favour with many linguists (see Spencer, 1958), even in the absence of research data. In this section, however, we present some research evidence which permits us actually to demonstrate, rather than simply assert, the at least partial validity of the 'imposed norm' hypothesis.

In two empirical studies, of the experimental type, evidence has now been gathered which strongly suggests that the 'imposed norm' hypothesis is worthy of acceptance in many respects. The first study, reported in Giles et al. (1974a), aimed to evaluate the merits of the two competing hypotheses. This it did by investigating the extent to which British adults with no knowledge of French were able to differentiate between varieties of French on aesthetic grounds, in a matched-guise experiment. The value of this test was that, if speakers are evaluating varieties of a language which they are not familiar with and do not understand, they are unable to use their knowledge of cultural norms in order to formulate an aesthetic response, and they are similarly not subject to pressure from those cultural norms. We can be certain that they are reacting to the sounds of the accent, and to nothing else.

It is known (cf. d'Anglejan and Tucker, 1973) that, of the three varieties used in the experiment, French Canadians agree in evaluating educated European French as more pleasant than educated Canadian French, which in turn is rated as more pleasant than working-class Canadian French. The results of this experiment showed that the British listeners did not react in the same way. They were in fact in total disagreement with the French listeners as to the relative aesthetic merits of the three varieties. On average, all three were rated at approximately the same level of pleasantness. No significant differences at all in aesthetic evaluation emerged.

Because of the rather restricted nature of this data, it is fortunate that we also have results for another similar experiment that was carried out with a different group of subjects. In this case, the accents to be evaluated were matched-guise recordings of Cretan and educated Athenian Greek (details of the experiment are given in Giles et al., 1974b). Greek informants had previously indicated that the Athenian variety was a prestige form of the language 'possessing over the other varieties considerable advantages within that language community in terms of perceived pleasantness'. In the experiment, however, 46 British subjects with no knowledge of Greek showed no signs at all of any agreement on the relative aesthetic (and other) merits of the two types of Greek. In fact, the results show that the Cretan variety was rated slightly more pleasant than the Athenian, although not significantly so. The results are given in table 12.1. These results, although restricted to two languages and two experiments, do lend considerable support to the 'imposed norm' hypothesis. They suggest that the uniformity of response obtained in the research discussed in section 4 is indeed the result of strong and pervasive cultural norms: remove these cultural norms, as with British listeners reacting to French and Greek, and the 'aesthetic' response disappears too. So while French Canadians do not hesitate to evaluate French aesthetically, and in a uniform manner, British listeners do not concur with these evaluations, and react in a way that suggests that for them all varieties of French are equally pleasant.

TABLE 12·1   Mean ratings and *t* values for differences between Greek accents

	Prestige	Aesthetic	Intelligent	Sophisticated
Athenian	4.70	5.39	4.22	4.89
Cretan	4.61	4.96	4.20	4.74
t values (d.f. = 45)	0.28	1.45	0.08	0.87

The lower the mean rating, the more prestigious and aesthetic the accent, and so on.

6 SOCIAL CONNOTATIONS OF LINGUISTIC VARIETIES

In the rest of this chapter we want to argue that the 'imposed norm' hypothesis is sound, as the experiments just reported suggest, but that it needs to be broadened and extended. The experiments demonstrated that aesthetic judgements about language varieties are culture-bound to a far greater extent than other types of aesthetic judgement. Apparently aesthetic responses to language, it seems, are in fact reactions to cultural norms. From the educational point of view, however, an important factor is that it can still be argued, by those hostile to the 'imposed norm' hypothesis, that these judgements are worth acting on. It can be said, for instance, that just as Europeans are not trained to discriminate between good and bad Asian music, so British listeners cannot distinguish between beautiful and ugly French or Greek simply because they do not have sufficient experience of these languages. They are not part of the culture in question and are not therefore qualified judges. The results of our experiments can therefore be disregarded.

We therefore want to oppose this objection by suggesting that, while aesthetic norms in language certainly are imposed to an extent, aesthetic evaluations are not simply a matter of cultural norms. Rather, aesthetic judgements of linguistic varieties are the result of a complex of *social connotations* that these varieties have for particular listeners. (We use the term *social* here in its general sense. We do not intend to refer only to social class and status.) Connotations of this type are by no means only a question of prestige or lack of it, and, crucially, they can and do vary within cultures. This means, first, that the 'imposed norm' hypothesis is not entirely adequate; and, secondly, that we cannot argue that cultural outsiders are not qualified judges of aesthetic merit. Indeed, they are in a better position to make aesthetic judgements than most. They are unaware of the social connotations of the varieties involved, and are therefore reacting only to the sounds that they hear. The British listeners in the experiments reported in section 5 reacted as they did because they did not know what the social connotations of the different varieties were. The fact that they rated all the varieties as approximately equal on aesthetic grounds, moreover, strongly suggests that there are good reasons for arguing that all dialects and accents are equally pleasant.

This hypothesis, which we can call the 'social connotations' hypothesis, has already been argued for briefly by other linguists. Halliday (Halliday *et al.*, 1964: 105) writes, for example: 'The chief factor in one's evaluation of varieties of a language is social conditioning'. It suggests that it is not possible to obtain uniform responses from listeners on the aesthetic merits of different accents unless their social connotations are the same for all concerned; that these social connotations will not always be identical for all the members of a culture; and that if the social connotations of a variety are not known to a listener, he will not be capable of ranking it aesthetically relative to other varieties. Aesthetic judgements about language, that is, are just as much social judgements as those concerned with correctness.

(Note that we do not mean to imply that a listener is unable to make aesthetic judgements about an accent which he has never heard before. People clearly do this. We would suggest, however, that he must be familiar with the social connotations of at least one phonetic feature or combination of features of the accent. The English glottal stop realization of /t/ would be a good example.)

If we can show that this hypothesis is valid, we shall then be in a position to suggest that all varieties of a language are objectively equally pleasant. This would be helpful in many educational situations. What evidence then is there in favour of this 'social connotations' hypothesis?

We can consider, first, an area where the 'imposed norm' hypothesis is clearly inadequate. If we examine the aesthetic evaluations that are normally made in Britain of non-prestige accents, it is clear that, by and large, rural accents are regarded as aesthetically much more pleasing than urban accents by the vast majority of British people. As one Glaswegian said (Macaulay and Trevelyan, 1973): 'it's the slovenly speech in the industrial areas I don't care for – these industrial cities, I don't like the accents they have'. Those accents which are most frequently singled out for opprobrium are the working-class accents of large cities such as Birmingham, Glasgow, Liverpool and London. On the other hand, rural accents such as those of the West Country and the Scottish Highlands are widely accepted as 'beautiful', 'nice' or at worst 'charming' or 'quaint'. (One college of education 'speech' teacher distinguishes between 'proper' accents such as 'Yorkshire' and 'Devon', and 'unfortuante bastardized monstrosities' such as 'Cockney' and 'Birmingham'.)

We cannot attribute this phenomenon to the 'imposed norm' hypothesis. No non-RP accent can be regarded as a 'norm' in England, since they all have depressed status relative to RP. The fact remains, however, that low-status accents are evaluated differently, and that this differential evaluation has often no connection with any objective linguistic distance from the RP 'norm'. Very often it is the urban accents which are objectively most like RP.

We can therefore claim instead that this phenomenon is the result of the different social connotations rural and urban accents have for most British people. The vast majority of British people now live in towns, and many townspeople (particularly the middle class who are probably instrumental in the formulation of mainstream public attitudes of this sort) have a romanticized nostalgic view of the countryside and the country way of life. They are much more realistic, on the other hand, in their assessment of the stresses and disadvantages of town life – particularly that of the urban working class whose accents are most disliked. These views are transferred to the linguistic varieties associated with the different areas, which are therefore subject to different aesthetic evaluations. If, say, French listeners do not react in the same way, it is not because they know nothing about the English language as such. It is because they do not know a Birmingham accent when they hear one, and are not aware of its social connotations.

Secondly, it is possible to take this point somewhat further. The fact is that the social connotations of accents are not limited to a contrast between rural and urban. They are subject to much finer gradations. The 'social connotations' hypothesis is in fact particularly strongly supported by the way in which accents associated with even large urban areas which lack heavy industry and are widely regarded as pleasant are much more favourably evaluated than others. This is true, for instance, of the city of Bristol and the Bristol accent. Similarly, rural accents from less well known or attractive areas such as parts of Lincolnshire or East Anglia are generally not rated as so attractive as accents from more strikingly beautiful parts of the country.

Perhaps, though, the most striking evidence in favour of this aspect of the social connotations hypothesis comes from the work of geographers. Although we have no figures for this, it is probable that there would be widespread agreement in England that the most unattractive accents in the country are those of the West Midlands in general and Birmingham in particular. In work reported in Gould and White (1974), research has been carried out into 'mental maps' that people have of different areas. Studies of 'environmental perception' have investigated subjects' images of Britain by asking them to plot on a map their preferences for where they would like to live if they had a free choice. By combining responses from different parts of the country, a 'national perception surface' was constructed. This shows that the Midlands, and the West Midlands in particular, is perceived as much less desirable than the surrounding areas in the country. We can suggest that it is not an accident that accents from this area are regarded in the same way.

Thirdly, we can present evidence which shows that when social connotations vary, or information about them is lacking, then aesthetic responses to linguistic varieties also vary or disappear. In the Norwich survey, for instance, it emerged that working-class Norwich speech was consistently both distinguished from that of rural Norfolk (the area surrounding Norwich) *and* considered aesthetically inferior to it by local people. 'Outsiders', however – unless they had been in the city for some considerable time – did not rate Norwich speech as more unpleasant than that of Norfolk and were in fact surprised to learn that local people felt that they were different. They had less access to information about differences between the two varieties, and did not know what the social connotations were.

Similarly, one can observe that while British people often readily favour, say, a rural Shropshire accent over one from the nearby urban West Midlands, visiting English speakers such as Americans do not react in the same way, and most probably do not even notice any linguistic difference.

Observations of this sort have led us to develop a further experiment. This involves obtaining aesthetic responses to English English accents from American, Canadian, Scottish, Irish and English listeners. The motivation for this experiment is as follows. If we can show that, even from within what can be considered to be the same culture, there are differences in listeners' aesthetic evaluations of linguistic varieties, depending on how much and what sort of information is available to the listener on the social connotations of the varieties, then the social connotations hypothesis will receive considerable support. If we can show too that, say, American and British listeners vary in their aesthetic evaluations, we shall also be able to dismiss arguments of the 'incompetent-to-judge' type that we discussed above. While it is possible to claim that British listeners had not had sufficient experience of Greek or French to be able to distinguish between 'ugly' and 'beautiful' in those languages, it is not possible to argue in the same way that Americans have not had sufficient experience of English. We shall also be in a strong position to suggest that aesthetic responses to dialects and accents are entirely based on social connotations and that therefore all varieties, objectively speaking, are equally attractive.

The experiment itself consisted of playing a tape of ten different speakers, each with a different United Kingdom accent and each reading the same passage of prose, to two groups of Americans (one eastern, one western), and to one group each of eastern Canadian, southern English, Southern Irish, and Scottish listeners. (In most cases the groups were composed of students.) The subjects were asked to rate the voices they heard on a number of different parameters. We present results here only for the aesthetic parameter. They are based on ratings made on a seven-point scale ranging from 'very pleasant' to 'very unpleasant'. Subjects were also asked to state as accurately as they could where they thought each speaker came from.

Since this was not a matched-guise experiment, subjects would clearly react to each speaker's voice quality and to his reading style. We would expect this to bias the results towards a greater uniformity of response. They would also, however, respond to the often very markedly different accents, and it was of course this component of the reaction we were concerned with.

English and Scottish subjects were generally rather successful at placing the readers regionally, showing that they knew what the accents were and that information on the social connotations of the different varieties was therefore available to them. It also emerged, however, that in many of those cases where mistakes were made, reactions were probably to the social connotations of the supposed rather than of the actual accent. For example, subjects who correctly identified the Bradford accent as 'Yorkshire' generally found it much more pleasant than a number who incorrectly identified it as from the West Midlands. Similarly, American listeners generally found the Gloucestershire and Northern Irish accents more pleasant if they incorrectly identified them as American than if they did not.

Americans and Canadians were for the most part very much worse than the British listeners at identifying the accents, with the exception of RP and, to a certain extent, the London accent. Indeed, a number of Americans gave responses such as 'Spanish', 'Mexican' or 'Norwegian' in a number of cases. We can therefore be certain that these listeners had very little information about these accents, and that any social connotations the accents had for them would be very different from those they had for British listeners.

The results of the experiment show that the English listeners had the following order of preference for the different accents on the pleasant–unpleasant scale. (Informal impressionistic characterizations of the accents and readings are given in parentheses.)

1   RP (not advanced or conservative, measured delivery)
2   South Wales (mild, distinctive intonation)
3   Bradford (fairly broad, lively reading)
4   Northern Ireland (mild, soft and slow – not Belfast, very like Southern Irish)
5   Tyneside (fairly broad, confident reading)
6   Gloucestershire (fairly broad, plain delivery)
7   Glasgow (mixed – mild but a few glottal stops)
8   Liverpool (quite broad, rather hesitant)
9   West Midlands (broad, lively delivery)
10   London (quite broad, slow reading)

Allowing for the influence of reading style and voice quality, these results are very much as expected. The 'ugliest' accents are those of London and the West Midlands, closely followed by those of two other heavily industrial areas, Liverpool and Glasgow. The high-prestige RP accent and the 'charming' mild south Welsh variety, on the other hand, are very favourably rated. (RP in fact comes out top of the list for all the groups except the Scots, who preferred the Welsh accent. This, however, must be disregarded for the purposes of the present experiment, since all the subjects were familiar with the RP accent and its status, and therefore reacted accordingly. Even Americans labelled it 'upper-class British', 'Oxford', 'Sandhurst' or something similar.)

Now, if the 'inherent value' hypothesis has any validity – if, that is, these accents are inherently more or less attractive – we would expect there to be a high level of agreement between the English subjects' preferences and those given by the other groups. However, the results demonstrate that only the Scottish listeners show a significant degree of agreement with these rank orderings. No other group shares the aesthetic responses of the English listeners. The full results are given in table 12.2, which is a correlation matrix for the different rank orderings of preference produced by the different groups of subjects. Out of the fifteen pairings there are only three significant agreements as to aesthetic merit. The first, not surprisingly, involves the two British groups, which comprised the only listeners to be well-informed as to the location and social connotations of the British accents. The second significant agreement concerns the USA (E) and Canadian groups. This may be the result of the relative geographical proximity of these two groups (tests were carried out in Virginia and Montreal) but we are very far from being able to show that this is so. And, finally, there is a high level of agreement between the USA (E) and Irish groups. We have no specific explanation for this. The crucial point, however, is that none of these three groups agrees with the British ratings, and that there is no *overall* agreement.

TABLE 12·2   Correlation matrix – rank orderings on aesthetics parameter

(N)	England (S) (23)	Scotland (19)	Ireland (S) (28)	Canada (E) (28)	USA (E) (22)	USA (W) (47)
England (S)	—	0.82**	0.35	0.16	0.42	0.63
Scotland		—	0.35	0.04	0.06	0.59
Ireland (S)			—	0.59	0.87**	0.41
Canada (E)				—	0.70*	0.48
USA (E)					—	0.39
USA (W)						—

** = highly significant
* = significant

The results show, then, that there is very little correlation indeed between the results from the different areas – and it should be noted that agreement would be even lower if we excluded the results for RP, the social connotations of which were obviously known to all. British, American, Canadian and Irish listeners do not make the same aesthetic responses to British accents. Six different groups of listeners made very different aesthetic evaluations of the ten accents – and this in spite of the fact that this was not a matched-guise experiment and their responses were therefore undoubtedly influenced by voice quality and reading.

We therefore feel justified in claiming that these results lend strong support to the social connotations hypothesis. The results from the different areas vary, we suggest, because the social connotations of the different accents either vary for different listeners or are not known. The information available to the Scottish and English listeners was not shared by the other groups, and they therefore reacted differently. And even where accents were recognized, it is clear that their social connotations varied from place to place. The 'ugly' London accent, which was rated 10th by both the English and the Scots, was rated 3rd by the Canadians and eastern Americans, and 4th by the Irish. It is also worth noting that the major point of disagreement between the Scots and English groups – the fact that the Scots placed RP only second – is probably not unconnected with the different social connotations, involving nationalist sentiments, this accent has in the two countries.

The 'inherent value' hypothesis, too, seems again to be disproved. If some of these accents were genuinely inherently more attractive than others, we would have expected a far higher degree of agreement than that portrayed in table 12.2. It cannot be claimed, either, that the differential ratings are due to the fact that the judges were unqualified, since all were native speakers of English.

7   CONCLUSION

We can conclude that those linguists who are concerned with problems of this nature should attempt to persuade others that the belief that some varieties of language are wrong and/or inadequate is untenable. We cannot, on the other hand, tell people that their aesthetic responses are false. Rather, we should encourage teachers and others, not to abandon their aesthetic judgements, but to recognize them for what they are: the result of a complex of social, cultural, regional, political and personal associations and prejudices. Most listeners know of linguistic varieties that they do not like, but we should recognize that these feelings are very subjective and have no basis in objective linguistic fact. In particular, feelings of this sort should not be allowed to influence teachers' attitudes and policies towards children's language – the more so since they are likely to produce linguistic insecurity, and are in any case almost certainly not shared by all members of the wider culture. In the classroom there is a big and important difference between 'Birmingham speech is ugly', a statement of apparently objective fact, and 'I personally find Birmingham speech unattractive' which, even if better left unsaid, is nevertheless a recognition of the subjectivity of responses due to social connotations.

References

Afendras, E. (1969) Sociolinguistic history, sociolinguistic geography and bilingualism. In *Giornale internazionali di sociolinguistica*. Rome: Istituto Luigi Sturzo.

Afendras, E. (1970a) Spatial and social aspects of multilingual communication. *Pensiero e linguaggio in operazioni*, 1, 131–9.

Afendras, E. (1970b) *Diffusion Processes in Language: Prediction and Planning*. Quebec: Centre International de Recherches sur le Bilinguisme. Mimeo.

Bach, A. (1950) *Deutsche Mundartforschung*. Heidelberg: Winter.

Bailey, B. L. (1966) *Jamaican Creole Syntax*. London: Cambridge University Press.

Bailey, C.-J. N. (1971) Trying to talk in the new paradigm. *Papers in Linguistics*, 4, 312–38.

Bailey, C.-J. N. (1972) The integration of linguistic theory: internal reconstruction and the comparative method in descriptive analysis. In R. P. Stockwell and R. K. S. Macauley (eds) *Linguistic Change and Generative Theory*. Bloomington: Indiana University Press.

Bailey, C.-J. N. (1973) *Variation and Linguistic Theory*. Washington: Center for Applied Linguistics.

Bailey, C.-J. N. and Maroldt, K. (1977) The French lineage of English. In J. M. Meisel (ed.) *Langues en contact*. Tübingen: TBL-Verlag Narr.

Bailey, C.-J. N. and Shuy, R. W. (eds) (1973) *New Ways of Analyzing Variation in English*. Washington, DC: Georgetown University Press.

Barnes, D., Britton, J. and Rosen, H. (1969) *Language, the Learner and the School*. Harmondsworth: Penguin Books.

Becker, D. (1967) *Generative Phonology and Dialect Study: An Investigation of Three Modern German Dialects*. Ann Arbor: University Microfilms.

Berdan, R. (1977) Polylectal comprehension and the polylectal grammar. In R. W. Fasold and R. W. Shuy (eds) *Studies in Language Variation*. Washington, DC: Georgetown University Press.

226

Bereiter, C. (1966) An academically oriented pre-school for culturally deprived children. In F. Hechinger (ed.) *Pre-School Education Today*. New York: Doubleday.

Bernstein, B. (1962) Linguistic codes, hesitation phenomena and intelligence. *Language and Speech*, 5, 31–46.

Bernstein, B. (1971) *Class, Codes and Control*. Vol. 1. London: Routledge & Kegan Paul.

Bickerton, D. (1975) *Dynamics of a Creole System*. Cambridge: Cambridge University Press.

Biris, K. (1960), *Arvanites i Dorieis tu neoteru ellinismu*. Athens.

Brown, L. A. (1968) *Diffusion Processes and Location: A Conceptual Framework and Bibliography*. Philadelphia: Regional Science Research Institute.

Brown, L. A. and Moore, E. G. (1971) Diffusion research: a perspective. In C. Board, *et al.* (eds) *Progress in Geography*. London: Edward Arnold.

Brown, P. (1980) How and why women are more polite: some evidence from a Mayan community. In S. McConnell-Ginet *et al. Women and Language in Culture and Society*. New York: Praeger.

Brown, R., Strong, W. and Rencher, A. (1975) Acoustic determinants of the perceptions of personality from speech. *International Journal of the Sociology of Language*, 6, 11–33.

Buck, J. (1968) The effects of negro and white dialectal variations upon attitudes of college students. *Speech Monographs*, 35, 181–6.

Burling, R. (1973) *English in Black and White*. New York: Rinehart & Winston.

Butters, R. (1973) Acceptability judgments for double modals in Southern dialects. In C.-J. Bailey & R. W. Shuy (eds) (1973).

Chambers, J. K. and Trudgill, P. (1980) *Dialectology*. London: Cambridge University Press.

Chen, M. and Hsieh, H.-I. (1971) The time variable in phonological change. *Journal of Linguistics*, 7, 1–13.

Cheshire, J. (1982) *Variation in an English Dialect: A Sociolinguistic Study*. Cambridge: Cambridge University Press.

Cheyne, W. (1970) Stereotyped reactions to speakers with Scottish and English regional accents. *British Journal of Social and Clinical Psychology*, 9, 77–9.

Chomsky, N. and Halle, M. (1968) *The Sound Pattern of English*. New York: Harper & Row.

Christaller, W. (1950) Das Grundgerüst der räumlichen Ordnung in Europa: die Systeme der europäischen zentralen Orte. *Frankfurter Geographische Hefte*, 11.

Clyne, M. (1968) Zum Pidgin-Deutsch der Gastarbeiter. *Zeitschrift für Deutsche Mundartforschung*, 35, 130–9.

Cochrane, G. R. (1959) The Australian English vowels as a diasystem. *Word*, 15, 69–88.

Craig, D. (1971) Education and Creole English in the West Indies: some sociolinguistic factors. In D. Hymes (ed.) *Pidginisation and Creolisation of Languages*. London: Cambridge University Press.

Crystal, D. (1966) Specification and English tenses. *Journal of Linguistics*, 2, 1–34.

Crystal, D. (1971) Prosodic and paralinguistic correlates of social categories. In E. Ardener (ed.) *Social Anthropology and Language*. London: Tavistock.

Daan, J. (1971) Verschuiven van isoglossen. *Taal en Tongval*, 23, 77–9.

d'Anglejan, A. and Tucker, G. (1973) Sociolinguistic correlates of speech style in Quebec. In R. Shuy and R. Fasold (eds) *Language Attitudes: Current Trends and Prospects*. Washington: Georgetown University Press.

De Camp, D. (1971) Toward a generative analysis of a post-creole speech continuum. In D. H. Hymes (ed.) *Pidginisation and Creolisation of Languages*. London: Cambridge University Press.

De Camp, D. and Hancock, I. (eds) (1974) *Pidgins and Creoles: Current Trends and Prospects*. Washington D.C.: Georgetown University Press.

Dickinson, R. E. (1967) *The City Region in Western Europe*. London: Routledge Kegan Paul.

Dorian, N. C. (1973) Grammatical change in a dying dialect, *Language*, 49, 413–38.

Duncan, O. D. (1957) Population distribution and community structure. *Cold Harbor Springs Symposium in Quantitative Biology*. 22, 357–71.

Edwards, J. R. and Giles, H. (forthcoming) On the applications of the social psychology of language: sociolinguistics and education. In P. Trudgill (ed.) *Applied Sociolinguistics*. London: Academic Press.

Edwards, V. K. (1976) Effects of dialect on the comprehension of West Indian children, *Educational Research*, 18, 83–95.

Emeneau, M. (1956) India as a linguistic area, *Language*, 32, 3–16.

Ewert, A. (1963) *The French Language*, London: Faber.

Fasold, R. W. (1968) A sociolinguistic study of the pronunciation of three vowels in Detroit speech. Unpublished mimeo: Center for Applied Linguistics.

Fasold, R. W. (1971) What can an English teacher do about nonstandard dialect?, *English Record* (April), 82–93.

Fasold, R. (1972) *Tense Marking in Black English*. Washington: Center for Applied Linguistics.

Fasold, R. and Shuy, R. (eds) (1970) *Teaching Standard English in the Inner City*. Washington: Center for Applied Linguistics.

Ferguson, C. (1959) Diglossia. *Word*, 15, 325–40.

Fischer, J. L. (1958) Social influences on the choice of a linguistic variant. *Word*, 14, 47–56.

Fishman, J. A. (1968) Varieties of ethnicity and varieties of language consciousness. In J. Alatis (ed.) *In Georgetown University Round Table Selected Papers on Linguistics, 1961–1965*, pp. 69–79. Washington, D.C: Georgetown University Press.

Fretheim, T. (1970) Transformasjonell generativ grammatikk: en skisse. In E. Hanssen (ed.) *Studier i norsk språkstruktur*. Oslo: Universitetsforlaget.

Giles, H. (1970) Evaluative reactions to accents. *Educational Review*, 22, 211–27.

Giles, H. (1971a) Patterns of evaluation in reactions to R.P., South Welsh and Somerset accented speech. *British Journal of Social and Clinical Psychology*, 10, 280–1.

Giles, H. (1971b) Teachers' attitudes towards accent usage and change. *Educational Review*, 24, 11–25.

Giles, H. (1973) Accent mobility: a model and some data. *Anthropological Linguistics*, 15, 87–105.

Giles, H., Bourhis R. and Davies, A. (1974a) Prestige speech styles: The imposed norm and inherent value hypotheses. In W. McCormack and S. Wurm (eds) *Language in Anthropology. IV: Language in Many Ways*. The Hague: Mouton.

Giles, H., Bourhis, R., Trudgill, P. and Lewis, A. (1974b) The imposed norm hypothesis: a validation. *Quarterly Journal of Speech*, 60, 405–10.

Giles, H. and Powesland, P. F. (1975) *Speech Style and Social Evaluation*. London: Academic Press.

Giles, H. and Smith, P. (1979) Accommodation theory: optimal levels of convergence. In H. Giles and R. St Clair (eds) *Language and Social Psychology*. Oxford: Blackwell.

Goldthorpe, J. and Lockwood, D. (1963) Affluence and the British class structure. *Sociological Review*, 11, 133–63.

Gould, P. and White, R. (1974) *Mental Maps*. Harmondsworth: Penguin Books.

Gregg, R. J. (1964) Scotch–Irish urban speech in Ulster. In *Ulster Dialects: An Introductory Symposium*. Holywood: Ulster Folk Museum.

Gregg, R. J. (1972) The Scotch-Irish dialect boundaries in Ulster. In M. F. Wakelin (ed.) *Patterns in the Folk Speech of the British Isles*. London: Athlone Press.

Haas, M. (1944) Men's and women's speech in Koasati. *Language* 20, 142–9.

Hägerstrand, T. (1952) The propagation of innovation waves. *Lund studies in geography, series B, human geography 4*. Lund: Gleerup.

Hägerstrand, T. (1965a) A Monte Carlo approach to diffusion. *Archives Européennes de Sociologie*, 6, 43–56.

Hägerstrand, T. (1965b) Quantitative techniques for analysis of the spread of information and technology. In C. A. Anderson, and M. J. Bowman (eds) *Education and Economic Development*. Chicago: Aldine.

Hägerstrand, T. (1966) Aspects of the spatial structure of social communication and the diffusion of information. *Papers of the Regional Science Association*, 16, 27–42.

Hägerstrand, T. (1967a) On the Monte Carlo simulation of diffusion. In W. L. Garrison and D. F. Marble (eds) *Quantitative Geography*, pt. 1, Evanston, Ill: Northwestern University Department of Geography.

Hägerstrand, T. (1967b) *Innovation Diffusion as a Spatial Process*. Chicago: University of Chicago.

Haggett, P. (1965) *Locational Analysis in Human Geography*. London: Edward Arnold.

Hall, R. (1950). *Leave Your Language Alone*. New York: Anchor Press.

Halliday, M., McIntosh, A. and Strevens, P. (1964) *The Linguistic Sciences and Language Teaching*. London: Longman.

Hansegård N. E. (1968) *Tvåspråkighet eller halvspråkighet?* Stockholm: Aldus/Bonniers.

Haugen, E. (1966) *Language Conflict and Language Planning: The Case of Modern Norwegian.* Cambridge, Mass.: Harvard University Press.

Hertzler. J. (1954) *A Sociology of Language.* New York: Random House.

Hildebrand, B. (1965) Das deutsche R. *Linguistics, 5.*

Honikman, B. (1964) Articulatory setting. In D. Abercrombie *et al.* (eds) *In Honour of Daniel Jones.* London: Longman.

Hughes, G. A. and Trudgill, P. J. (1979) *English Accents and Dialects: an Introduction to Social and Regional Varieties of British English.* London: Edward Arnold.

Hymes, D. H. (ed.) (1971) *Pidginisation and Creolisation of Languages.* London: Cambridge University Press.

Hymes, D. H. (1974) *Foundations in Sociolinguistics.* Philadelphia: University of Pennsylvania Press.

Hymes, D. H. (1975) Speech and language: on the origins and foundations of inequality among speakers. In E. Haugen and M. Bloomfield (eds) *Language as a Human Problem.* London: Lutterworth Press.

Jernudd, B. (1968) Linguistic integration and national development: a case study of the Jebel Marra area, Sudan. In J. A. Fishman, *et al.* (eds) *Language Problems of Developing Nations.* New York: Wiley.

Jernudd, B. (1968) Chorology and linguistics (unpublished manuscript).

Jernudd, B. and Willingsson, T. (1968) A sociolectal study of the Stockholm region. *Svenska Landsmål och Svenskt Folkliv,* 141–7.

Jespersen, O. (1922) *Language: its Nature, Development and Origin.* London: Allen & Unwin.

Jörgensen, N. (1970) *Om makrosyntagmer i informell och formell stil.* Lund: Lund University.

Jørgensen, P. (1960) Zum Nordfriesischen r. In J. H. Brouwer (ed.) *Fryske Studzjes.* Assen: Gorcum.

Kay, P. and Sankoff, G. (1974) A language-universals approach to pidgins and creoles. In D. DeCamp and J. Hancock (eds) (1974).

Karlsson, C. (1958) *Social Mechanisms: Studies in Sociological Theory.* New York: Free Press.

Keller, R. E. (1961) *German Dialects: Phonology and Morphology.* Manchester: Manchester University Press.

Kett, J. (1975) *Tha's a Rum'un Tew!* Woodbridge: Baron.

King, R. (1969) *Historical Linguistics and Generative Grammar.* Englewood Cliffs: Prentice Hall.

King, R. (1975) Integrating linguistic change. In K. H. Dahlstedt (ed.) *The Nordic Languages and Modern Linguistics* 2. Stockholm: Almqvist & Wiksell.

Knowles, G. O. (1978) The nature of phonological variables in Scouse. In Trudgill (ed.) (1978a).

Kurath, H. (1964) *A Phonology and Prosody of Modern English.* Heidelberg; Winter.

Kurath, H. (1972) *Studies in Area Linguistics.* Bloomington: Indiana University Press.

Kurath, H. and McDavid, R. I. (1961) *The Pronunciation of English in the Atlantic States*. Ann Arbor: University of Michigan Press.

Labov, W. (1965) On the mechanism of linguistic change. In C. W. Kreidler (ed.) *Monograph Series on Languages and Linguistics*. Washington, DC: Georgetown University Press.

Labov, W. (1966a) *The Social Stratification of English in New York City*. Washington, DC: Center for Applied Linguistics.

Labov, W. (1966b) Hypercorrection by the lower middle class as a factor in linguistic change. In W. Bright (ed.), *Sociolinguistics*. The Hague: Mouton.

Labov, W. (1969) Contraction, deletion and inherent variability of the English copula. *Language*, 45, 715–62. Also in W. Labov (1972b).

Labov, W. (1972a) Negative attraction and negative concord in English grammar. *Language*, 48, 773–818.

Labov, W. (1972b) Rules for ritual insults. In *Language in the Inner City*. Philadelphia: University of Pennsylvania Press.

Labov, W. (1972c) Some principles of linguistic methodology. *Language in Society*, 1, 97–120.

Labov, W. (1972d) The logic of non-standard English. In *Language in the Inner City*.

Labov, W. (1973) Where do grammars stop? In R. W. Shuy (ed.) *Georgetown Monograph Series on Language and Linguistics*, 25. Washington: Georgetown University Press.

Labov, W. (1975) On the use of the present to explain the past. *Proceedings of the 11th International Congress of Linguists*. Bologna: Mulino.

Labov, W. (1978) Where does the sociolinguistic variable stop? A response to Beatriz Lavandera. *Working Papers in Sociolinguistics*, 44.

Labov, W. On the adequacy of natural language. Unpublished manuscript.

Labov, W., Cohen, P., Robins, C. and Lewis, J. (1968) *A Study of the Non-standard English of Negro and Puerto Rican Speakers in New York City*, Philadelphia: US Regional Survey.

Labov, W., Yaeger, M. and Steiner, R. (1972) *A Quantitative Study of Sound Change in Progress*. Philadelphia: US Regional Survey.

Lavandera, B. (1978) Where does the sociolinguistic variable stop? *Language in Society*, 7, 171–83.

Laver, J. (1968) Voice quality and indexical information, *British Journal of Disorders of Communication*, 3, 43–54.

Laver, J. and Hutcheson, S. (1973) *Communication in Face to Face Interaction*. Harmondsworth: Penguin Books.

Laver, J. and Trudgill, P. (1979) Phonetic and linguistic markers in speech. In K. Scherer and H. Giles (eds) *Social Markers in Speech*. London: Cambridge University Press.

Le Page, R. B. (1968) Problems of description in multilingual communities. *TPS 1968*, 189–212.

Le Page, R. B. (1975) Polarizing factors: political, social, economic, operating on the individual's choice of identity through language use in British Honduras.

In J. G. Savard and R. Vigneault (eds) *Les États Multilingues*. Quebec: Laval University Press.

Le Page, R. B. (1978) Projection, focussing, diffusion. *Society for Caribbean Linguistics Occasional Paper 9*.

Le Page, R. B., Christie, P., Jurdant, B., Weekes, A. and Tabouret-Keller, A. (1974) Further report on the sociolinguistic survey of multilingual communities. *Language in Society*, 3, 1–32.

Levine, L. and Crockett, H. J. (1966) Speech variation in a Piedmont community: postvocalic r. In S. Lieberson (ed.). *Explorations in sociolinguistics*. The Hague: Mouton.

Lowman, G. and Kurath, H. (1973) *The Dialectal Structure of Southern England*. American Dialect Society: Alabama UP.

Macaulay, R. K. S. and Trevelyan, G. D. (1973) *Language, Education and Employment in Glasgow*. Edinburgh: Scottish Council for Research in Education.

McClure, J. D. (1975) Modern Scots prose-writing. In J. D. McClure (ed.) *The Scots Language in Education*. Aberdeen: Aberdeen College of Education.

Martin, F. M. (1954) Some subjective aspects of social stratification. In Glass, D. V. (ed.), *Social Mobility in Britain*. London: Routledge & Kegan Paul.

Martinet, A. (1969) *Le français sans fard*. Paris: Presses Universitaires.

Mather, J. Y. (1975) Social variation in present-day Scots speech. In J. D. McClure (ed.) (1975).

Matthews, P. H. (1979) *Generative Grammar and Linguistic Competence*. London: Allen & Unwin.

Mayer, K. B. (1955) *Class and Society*. New York: Random House.

Milroy, J. and Milroy, L. (1978) Belfast: change and variation in an urban vernacular. In P. Trudgill (ed.) 1978a.

Milroy, L. (1980) *Language and Social Networks*. Oxford: Blackwell.

Milroy, L. (forthcoming) Sociolinguistics and communicative breakdown. In P. Trudgill (ed.) *Applied Sociolinguistics*. London: Academic Press.

Moser, H. (1954) Sprachgrenzen und ihre Ursachen. *Zeitschrift für Mundartforschung*, 22, 87–111.

Moulton, W. G. (1952) Jacob Böhme's uvular r. *Journal of English and Germanic Philology*, 51, 83–9.

Moulton, W. G. (1968) Structural dialectology, *Language 44*.

Mühlhäusler, P. (1974) *Pidginisation and Simplification of Language*. Canberra: Pacific Linguistics, pp. 13–26.

Mühlhäusler, P. (1977) Creolization in New Guinea Pidgin. In S. Wurm (ed.) *New Guinea Area Languages and Language Study*, 3. Canberra: Pacific Linguistics, pp. 567–57.

Newton, B. (1972) *The Generative Interpretation of Dialect*. London: Cambridge University Press.

Nunberg, G. (1975) A falsely reported merger in 18th century English. *Pennsylvania Working Papers in Linguistic Change and Variation 1, 2*.

Olsson, G. (1965) *Distance and Human Interaction*. Philadelphia: Regional Science Research Institute.

O'Neil, W. (1968). Paul Roberts' rules of order: the misuse of linguistics in the classroom. *The Urban Review*, 2, 12–17.

Orton, H. (1933) *The Phonology of a South Durham Dialect*. London: Kegan Paul, Trench, Trubner.

Orton, H. and Barry, M. V. (1969) *Survey of English Dialects*. Vol. II: *The West Midland Counties*. Leeds: E. J. Arnold.

Orton, H. and Halliday, W. J. (1962) *Survey of English Dialects*. Vol. I: *The Six Northern Counties and the Isle of Man*. Leeds: E. J. Arnold.

Orton, H. and Tilling, P. M. (1969) *Survey of English Dialects*. Vol. III: *The East Midland Counties and East Anglia*. Leeds: E. J. Arnold.

Orton, H. and Wakelin, M. F. (1967) *Survey of English Dialects*. Vol. IV: *The Southern Counties*. Leeds: E. J. Arnold.

Orton, H. and Wright, N. (1975) *A Word Geography of England*. London: Seminar Press.

Orton, H., Sanderson, S. and Widdowson, J. (1978) *Linguistic Atlas of England*. London: Croom Helm.

Panov, M. V. (ed.) (1968) *Russkij jazyk i sovetskoe obščestvo (sociologolingvističeskoe issledovanie)*, vol. 4, Moscow.

Payne, A. (1980) Factors controlling the acquisition of the Philadelphia dialect by out-of-state children. In W. Labov (ed.) *Locating Language in Time and Space*. London: Academic Press.

Phurikis, P. (1931) Pothen to ethnikon Arvanites. *Athena*, 43, 3–37.

Phurikis, P. (1932–3) I en Attiki ellinalvaniki dialektos. *Athena*, 44, 28–76; 45, 49–181.

Pickford, G. R. (1956) American linguistic geography: a sociological appraisal. *Word*, 12, 211–33.

Platt, J. T. and Platt, H. K. (1975) *The Social Significance of Speech*. Amsterdam: North Holland.

Popperwell, R. G. (1963) *The Pronunciation of Norwegian*. Cambridge: Cambridge University Press.

Postal, P. (1968) *Aspects of Phonological Theory*. Oxford: Blackwell.

Robinson, A. and Sale, R. (1969) *Elements of Cartography*. New York: Wiley.

Romaine, S. (1978) Post-vocalic /r/ in Scottish English: sound change in progress? In P. Trudgill (ed.) (1978a).

Romaine, S. (1981) On the problem of syntactic variation: a reply to Beatriz Lavandera and William Labov. *Working Papers in Sociolinguistics*, 82 (Southwest Educational Development Laboratory).

Rosen, H. (ed.) (1974) *Language and Class Workshop, 2*. L. and C. Workshop, 41A Muswell Avenue, London N10.

Sachs J. *et al*. (1973) Anatomical and cultural determinants of male and female speech. In R. Shuy and R. Fasold (eds.) *Language Attitudes: Current Trends and Prospects*. Washington, DC: Georgetown University Press.

Sankoff, G. and Brown, P. (1976) The origins of syntax in discourse. *Language*, 52, 631–66.

Sankoff, G. and Cedergren, H. (1971) Some results of a sociolinguistic study of

Montreal French. In R. Darnell (ed.), *Linguistic Diversity in Canadian Society*. Champaign, Ill.: Linguistics Research Inc.

Sankoff, G. and Laberge, S. (1974) On the acquisition of native speakers by a language. In D. De Camp and I. Hancock (eds) (1974).

Sapir, E. (1929) Male and female forms of speech in Yana. Reprinted in D. Mandelbaum (ed.) (1949) *Selected Writings of Edward Sapir in Language, Culture and Personality*. Berkeley and Los Angeles: University of California Press.

Scherer, K. and Giles, H. (eds) (1979) *Social Markers in Speech*. London: Cambridge University Press.

Schmidt, J. (1872) *Die Verwandtschaftsverhältnisse der indogermanischen Sprachen*. Weimar.

Scollon, R. and Scollon, S. (1979) Literacy as interethnic communication: an Athabaskan case. *Working Papers in Sociolinguistics*, 59 Austin: Southwest Educational Development Laboratory.

Shuy, R. W. (1969) Sociolinguistic research at the Center for Applied Linguistics: the correlation of language and sex. *Giornata internazionali di sociolinguistica*. Rome: Palazzo Baldassini.

Shuy, R. W., Wolfram, W. A. and Riley, W. K. (1967) *Linguistic Correlates of Social Stratification in Detroit Speech*. Cooperative Research Project 6-1347. East Lansing: US Office of Education.

Sjöstedt, C. G. (1936) *Studier over r-ljuden i sydskandinaviska màl*. Lund: University of Lund.

Skautrup, P. (1968) *Det danske sprogs historie*. Copenhagen: Gyldendal.

Smith, P. (1979) Sex markers in speech. In K. Scherer and H. Giles (eds) (1979).

Spencer, J. (1958) RP – some problems of interpretation. *Lingua*, 7, 7–29.

Spender, D. (1980) *Man Made Language*. London: Routledge & Kegan Paul.

Steinsholt, A. (1964) *Màlbryting i Hedrum*. Oslo: Universitetsforlaget.

Steinsholt, A. (1972) *Màlbryting i Hedrum 30 àr etter*. Oslo: Universitetsforlaget.

Strang, B. M. H. (1970) *A History of English*. London: Methuen.

Strongman, K. and Woosley, J. (1967) Stereotyped reactions to regional accents. *British Journal of Social and Clinical Psychology*, 6, 164–7.

Sutcliffe, D. (1976) The Speech of West Indian Adolescents in Bedford. M. Ed. dissertation, Leicester University.

Sutcliffe, D. (1982) *British Black English*. Oxford: Blackwell.

Sutcliffe, D. (forthcoming) British Black English and West Indian Creoles. In P. Trudgill (ed.) *Language in the British Isles*. London: Cambridge University Press.

Thorne, B. and Henley, N. (1975) *Language and Sex: Difference and Dominance*. Rowley, Mass.: Newbury House.

Togeby, O. (1978) Autoritets- og ambitionsnormer hos kvinder og mænd. In K. Gregersen (ed.) *Papers from the 4th Scandinavian Conference of Linguists*. Odense: Odense University Press.

Triandaphillidis, M. (1938) *Neoelliniki grammatiki*, vol. 1. Athens.

Trudgill, P. J. (1971) The social differentiation of English in Norwich. Edinburgh University. Unpublished Ph.D. thesis.

Trudgill, P. (1973) Phonological rules and sociolinguistic variation in Norwich English. In C.-J. Bailey and R. W. Shuy (eds.) (1973)

Trudgill, P. (1974a) *The Social Differentiation of English in Norwich*. London: Cambridge University Press.

Trudgill, P. (1974b) *Sociolinguistics: An Introduction*. Harmondsworth: Penguin Books.

Trudgill, P. (1975) *Accent, Dialect and the School*. London: Edward Arnold.

Trudgill, P. (1978a) (ed.) *Sociolinguistic Patterns in British English*. London: Edward Arnold.

Trudgill, P. (1978b) Sociolinguistics and sociolinguistics. In P. Trudgill (ed.) (1978a).

Trudgill, P. (forthcoming) *Dialects in Contact*. Oxford: Blackwell.

Trudgill, P. (n.d.) *A sociolinguistic study of linguistic change in urban East Anglia*. Report to the Social Science Research Council.

Trudgill, P. and Tzavaras, G. A. (1975) *A sociolinguistic study of Albanian dialects spoken in the Attica and Biotia areas of Greece*. Report to the Social Science Research Council.

Tucker, R. and Lambert, W. (1969) White and Negro listeners reactions to various American-English dialects, *Social Forces*, 47, 463–8.

Ullmann, S. (1962) *Semantics: an Introduction to the Study of Meaning*. Oxford: Blackwell.

Vakalopulos, A. (1973) *Istoria tu neu ellinismu*. Thessalonika: University Press.

Wagner, K. (1927) Deutsche Sprachlandschaften. *Deutsche Dialektgeographie*, 23.

Wakelin, M. F. (1972) *English Dialects: An Introduction*. London: Athlone Press.

Wang, W. S.-Y. (1969) Competing changes as a cause of residue. *Language*, 45, 9–25.

Weinreich, U. (1954) Is a structural dialectology possible? *Word*, 10, 388–400. Also in J. Fishman (ed.) (1968) *Readings in the Sociology of Language*. The Hague: Mouton.

Weinreich, U. (1974) *Languages in Contact*. The Hague: Mouton.

Wells, J. C. (1970) Local accents in England and Wales. *Journal of Linguistics*, 6, 231–52.

Wells, J. C. (1973) *Jamaican Pronunciation in London*. Oxford: Blackwell.

Wells, J. C. (1982) *Accents of English*. 3 vols. Cambridge: Cambridge University Press.

Whinnom, K. (1971) Linguistic hybridisation and the 'special case' of pidgins and creoles. In D. H. Hymes (ed.) (1971).

Wölck, W. (1965) *Phonematische Analyse der Sprache von Buchan*. Heidelberg: Groos.

Wolfram, W. A. (1969) *A Sociolinguistic Description of Detroit Negro Speech*. Washington, DC: Center for Applied Linguistics.

Wolfram, W. (1973) *Sociolinguistic Aspects of Assimilation: Puerto Rican English in East Harlem*. Washington, DC: Center for Applied Linguistics.

Wyld H. (1934) The best English – a claim for the superiority of Received Standard English, *S.P.E. Tract* 39.

Wyld, H. C. (1956) *A History of Modern Colloquial English*. Oxford: Blackwell.

Zwicky, A. (1976) Well, this rock and roll has got to stop. Junior's head is hard as a rock. In S. Mufwene *et al.* (eds) *Proceedings of the 12th Annual Meeting of the Chicago Linguistic Society*. Chicago: University of Chicago Press.

Index